A Course in GB Syntax

Current Studies in Linguistics
Samuel Jay Keyser, general editor

A Course in GB Syntax

Lectures on Binding and Empty Categories

Howard Lasnik and Juan Uriagereka

The MIT Press
Cambridge, Massachusetts
London, England

Third Printing, 1990

This book was set in Optima by Asco Trade Typesetting Ltd., Hong Kong, and printed and bound by Halliday Lithograph in the United States of America.

Library of Congress Cataloging-in-Publication Data

Lasnik, Howard.
  Lectures on binding and empty categories.

  Bibliography: p.
  Includes index.
  1. Government-binding theory (Linguistics) 2. Grammar, Comparative and general—Syntax. I. Uriagereka, Juan. II. Title.
  P158.2.L37   1988   415   87-24756
  ISBN 0-262-12130-1
  ISBN 0-262-62060-X (pbk.)

Contents

Preface 1

This book is intended as a reader's companion to several recent lines of work in the so-called Government-Binding approach to syntax. It began as a transcript (created from tapes) of the spring 1985 second-semester graduate course in syntax at the University of Connecticut, then proceeded through several rounds of editing, reorganizing, expanding, and deleting. The somewhat unconventional nature of the book is a result of its origin: it is less like a text for a course than like a course itself. One consequence of this is, I hope, that the book conveys the sense of a very active and lively field with a variety of approaches under investigation. The informal style, along with occasional dialogues with participants in the class, is intended to encourage the reader to challenge assumptions, seek alternatives, and generally participate in the exciting on-going intellectual activity of the field.

The book presupposes a certain amount of knowledge about generative grammar, that which would be obtained in an elementary syntax course or an intensive introduction to linguistics. The first few chapters of Andrew Radford's *Transformational Syntax* (1981) or Henk van Riemsdijk and Edwin Williams's *Introduction to the Theory of Grammar* (1986) should provide sufficient background. I take for granted familiarity with notions such as generative grammar, constituent structure, underlying versus superficial representation, syntactic transformation, constraint on transformations.

The center of the presentation is the material developed in Chomsky's very important *Lectures on Government and Binding* (1981b) and *Some Concepts and Consequences of the Theory of Government and Binding* (1982). A good mastery of those two books is fundamental to an understanding of all of the recent Government-Binding literature. But they are not always easy, and much is hidden between the lines. This book, in part, attempts to present a number of the concepts, issues, and assumptions of those two books in a clear, explicit, and unintimidating fashion. The goal is not to make it unnecessary to read Chomsky's books, however; it is to make it possible to read them with fuller understanding. In addition, I have presented analyses of further examples and potential and actual counterexamples, extensions of the theory, modifications, and, in some instances, alternatives. It must be kept in mind, however, that this book does not pretend to be a complete survey of the field. A great deal of important research has been ignored, either because it did not fit straightforwardly into the particular themes developed or because of limitations imposed by the too short (or so it often seems) school semester.

In the time since the lectures forming this book were presented, the theory has not been in a state of suspended animation. New analyses of novel phenomena in (often) previously unexamined languages have emerged in ever increasing numbers. However, the material in this book remains vital to an understanding of most of the more recent developments. To take two obvious examples, Chomsky's *Barriers* (1986b) is an extension of the framework discussed in chapter 4, and his presentation assumes familiarity with the concepts and analyses presented there. And Chomsky's *Knowledge of Language* (1986a) crucially builds on both the theory of Case (chapters 1 and 6) and the theory of Binding (chapter 2).

The book is organized into chapters as follows. Chapter 1 is an overview of the general approach to syntax assumed in the remainder of the book. Much of it is in the nature of review, for the reader who has already had some exposure to syntax. In some cases the discussion provides informal illustrations of concepts that will be explored in detail in later chapters. Chapter 2 begins with a review of the central concepts of Binding Theory (in its "classical" form in *Lectures on Government and Binding*) and then moves on to a number of conceptual and empirical questions that arise when proposals about this module are made precise. Analyses of empty categories are the focus of chapter 3. Of particular concern is the question whether empty categories have intrinsic features or whether their features are "functionally determined" by the contexts in which they appear. The analysis of parasitic gaps constitutes a detailed case study. The Empty Category Principle, which constrains the distribution of traces of movement, is explored in depth in chapter 4. Although the point of departure is *Lectures on Government and Binding*, the proposal goes well beyond what was presented there. Chapter 5 considers two extensions of (or alternatives to) classical Binding Theory. Section 5.1 discusses Aoun's "Generalized Binding Theory," which, among other things, extends Condition A to traces of *Wh*-Movement. Section 5.2 examines Higginbotham's "Linking Theory" of anaphora and in particular explores differences and similarities between Binding Theory and Linking Theory. Finally, chapter 6 presents a number of open questions, that is, questions that seem to me even more open than those specifically addressed in earlier chapters.

For their constant encouragement I would like to thank particularly Noam Chomsky, Harry Stanton, and Sylvain Bromberger. I am also deeply indebted to the participants in the course, both the advanced students and faculty members who sat in and, especially, the first-year students who were enrolled. Their important contribution is only dimly reflected in the questions presented in the book itself. Many other excellent questions, comments, and suggestions that they raised helped to shape the course and, ultimately, the book. The participants who are quoted are Lori Davis, Samuel D. Epstein, Paul Gorrell, Sungshim Hong, Michiya Kawai, Yinxia Long, Cecile McKee, Elaine McNulty, Mineharu

Nakayama, Juan Uriagereka, Marguerite Williams, Ewa Willim, and Su-In Yang.

Finally, I urge the reader to take my coauthor's overly modest preface with a grain of salt. He not only transcribed the tapes but also arranged the material into chapters, paragraphs, notes, and so forth, reconstructed and numbered the examples (a gesture toward a portion of the blackboard doesn't come across on audio tape), and constantly kept me honest ("Howard, doesn't this contradict what you said about example (XX)?"). Without his contribution, this project not only would have been impossible, it would have been unthinkable.

Howard Lasnik

Preface 2

A number of film directors say that cutting is more fun than shooting. They also say that when you cut, you are supposed to tell the story, create the characters, and cover up the flaws. However, they all admit that no matter how great you are at cutting, the whole business depends on how well you shoot. Put differently, cutting is a craft but shooting is an art. No wonder cutting is more fun—it's safer!

I've had the privilege of being the editor, more or less in the sense above, of Lasnik's lectures. His shooting took place in the spring of 1985, when I was one of his first-year students. Rumor had it that I was a good typist, so I was appointed transcriber of the 40 hours of tapes containing Lasnik's use and knowledge of language. The purpose of this project was simply to obtain a printout with the main ideas of that course, so that students could benefit from reading them. I volunteered to do the job mainly because I realized how much I myself would learn by going over all that material in detail. It soon became apparent to me that everyone would benefit much more from the printout if the lectures were somehow edited. In a class, there are always redundancies and digressions that (although surely of good use in their initial context) are out of place in a manuscript. I began to see that the material I had in my hands was very well shot. I tried my best at cutting it and took it to Lasnik with the suggestion that there was a book there. Various people liked the first draft, and Lasnik himself started believing there was a book coming. He carefully supervised the "final cut," and the manuscript started circulating. One day I saw it cited. To my surprise, I was mentioned as coauthor. I am grateful to Lasnik for this, but, for the record, I wish to make it clear that all I did was to put pieces together. It was fun, and it was safe.

There's one thing I should take the blame for. Listening to those tapes, one could not help but realize the Socratic environment in which the class had taken place. I have always been enchanted by Socrates's discussions with his friends. So the idea came to me that the manuscript should be edited in the form of dialogues. For this, I included the names of those who asked questions, both to credit them and to encourage those reading the book to ask questions. I think that some of Lasnik's most interesting points in the book are made in the course of answering questions. It is a pity that in modern scientific rhetoric one is not allowed to include such expressions as "Is it not true, Meno, that ...?" or "It most certainly is, Socrates." Those, together with the many jokes that took place in the class and are also beyond the scope of scientific prose, would have made this text look more like the long dialogue it is.

I want to take this opportunity to express my gratitude to all my colleagues in the Department of Linguistics of the University of Connecticut, for their encouragement and their several contributions to this project. Finally, Yasuo Ishii and Itziar Laka deserve my deepest appreciation for crucial last-minute help with the manuscript.

Juan Uriagereka

A Course in GB Syntax

Chapter 1   A Modular Model

In this course we will be exploring a theory of grammar that had its modern roots about thirty years ago and its more immediate antecedents in Chomsky and Lasnik 1977. Since then it has been developed in a number of articles and books—most especially Chomsky 1981b, 1982. Let us begin with a review of the basic ideas. The particular model of grammar looks like (1):

(1)

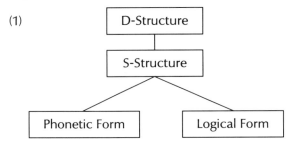

D-Structure is related to S-Structure by the transformational component. S-Structure is related to the interpretive components, Phonetic Form (PF) and Logical Form (LF), which provide the interface between formal grammar and something in the "real world": acoustic/articulatory properties on the one hand, and semantic properties on the other. PF includes perhaps low-level transformational processes (sometimes called stylistic rules), deletion rules, contraction rules, and ultimately, phonological rules. LF represents the contribution of the grammar to the meaning of particular sentences, and, in the model assumed here, it includes transformations very similar to those mapping D-Structure onto S-Structure—perhaps identical to those.[1]

1.1   The Base Component

1.1.1   Properties of D-Structure

Let us now consider (1) in more detail, beginning with D-Structure.[2] D-Structure is the level of representation that satisfies the requirements of X′ theory, in particular:

(2) a. Every category is a projection of a lexical head.
　　 b. X^n immediately dominates X^{n-1} (down to X^0).

It is also the level at which grammatical relations—the relations between arguments and heads, such as "subject of" and "object of"—

are defined. More specifically, it is the level of representation that crucially satisfies the θ-Criterion:[3]

(3) a. Every argument must be assigned a θ-role.

    b. Every θ-role must be assigned to an argument.

In Chomsky 1965 other properties were attributed to D-Structure (as an empirical claim). For instance, lexical insertion was supposed to take place at this level. This is now unclear, although nowadays the issue of whether all lexical insertion takes place at D-Structure or whether it can take place elsewhere between D-Structure and S-Structure engenders little discussion. Obviously, if lexical insertion took place at LF, one would never hear the results (but one could still imagine such a possibility, where, although the results are not heard, they are somehow understood; one might imagine a treatment of ellipsis along these lines). Another property of D-Structure in work of the late 1960s was base generability: D-Structure had to be generated by the base (phrase structure) rules. Later, when the Structure-Preserving constraint was introduced, (see Emonds 1970, 1976), base generability became less of an issue, because in the strongest version of that constraint S-Structure could essentially be base-generable too. This is so since the constraint ensured that movement took place only to base-generable positions, at least for cyclic transformations.

1.1.2 The Lexicon

Although base generability was considered at first to be a core property of D-Structure—in other words, it was considered that part of the syntactic description of a language is a set of phrase structure rules that generate phrase structure (PS) representations—it eventually became clear that such a theory contains a great many redundancies. What view of D-Structure emerges if we try to eliminate those redundancies?

Recall that D-Structure is the level of representation at which grammatical relations are determined. Grammatical relations are very closely linked to particular lexical items. So, for instance, it is well known that not any V can be the head of a VP that has a complement NP: only transitive verbs like *hit* can, whereas intransitive verbs like *sleep* cannot. This type of property somehow has to be specified in the lexicon and reflected at D-Structure. On one traditional view, part of the lexical entry for *sleep* or *hit* is a "subcategorization frame" specifying just what complements (if any) are allowed for a particular lexical item. Additionally, of course, a lexical entry contains information about how a lexical item is pronounced and what it means.

1.1.3 Are Phrase Structure Rules Necessary?

Traditionally, it was assumed that in addition to lexical subcategorization frames, a component consisting of PS rules like (4) is needed as well:

(4) a. VP → V
    b. VP → V NP

These rules allow us to generate (5a) and (5b), respectively:

(5) a. John slept
    b. John hit Bill

If we did not have a PS rule like (4a), then we could not have a sentence like (5a). But if we could not have a sentence like (5a), then we could not have a verb like *sleep*. Now, imagine a grammar containing a specification (in the lexicon) that it has a verb like *sleep*. Once the grammar contains this specification, it follows that the language must have a structure like (5a). But if the subcategorization frame of *sleep* implies that the structure in question exists, the PS rule does not tell us anything in addition. This is the redundancy we want to eliminate. We may ask, If redundancy is unwanted, why not eliminate subcategorization frames and keep PS rules? Well, when speakers know English, it is an entirely theory-internal question whether or not they know a PS rule like (4a). But it is not a theory-internal question whether or not they know what the properties of *sleep* are. To learn English, speakers minimally have to learn lexical properties of the sort in question. In fact, we can imagine a theory that says that to learn a language, this is almost all speakers do have to learn. So, since we cannot eliminate *sleep* from the lexicon, we ought to eliminate (4a) from the syntactic component.

Now, can we really completely eliminate PS rules of the type in (4)? That depends on how lexical properties are represented. Suppose all we say about *hit* is that it is transitive, in other words, that it has a complement. Notice that saying that and saying that *hit* occurs in a subcategorization frame like (6), as in Chomsky 1965, are not entirely equivalent:

(6) ⟨_____ NP⟩

Saying that *hit* occurs in (6) tells us more than saying that *hit* is transitive. In the latter case we know only that we have either a structure like (7a) or one like (7b):

(7) a.  b.

In fact, the way lexical entries were traditionally construed—namely, by specifying them in terms of subcategorization frames like (6)—it was possible to eliminate PS rules like those in (4) immediately: the lexical entry said not only that *hit* is transitive but also that the object follows the verb. But clearly that was a mistake. A lexical entry contains everything that is idiosyncratic about a particular word. That *hit* is transitive is idiosyncratic; that its object follows it is not. In fact, this is true of every transitive verb in the English language—exactly the kind of redundancy that isn't allowed in a principled lexicon. But then we seem to be arguing that there *should* be a PS rule, because such a rule captures exactly the overriding regularity that the object always follows the verb. However, this is part of a still wider regularity. That their objects follow them in English is true not just of verbs but of prepositions, nouns, and adjectives as well. Perhaps that is a universal phenomenon, which we should factor out of the grammar of English entirely. But then what about Japanese? There it is just the other way around: objects of verbs precede them; objects of prepositions precede them (that is, they are not prepositions at all, but postpositions); and so forth. Thus, we are dealing with a language-particular property, but one that is quite general within a given language. This is a reason for thinking that particular PS rules should not say anything about order. Rather, order should be factored out of the PS rules entirely. Using now commonplace terminology, we may say that X is the head of X′ and that in English X precedes its complements, whereas in Japanese X follows its complements (in other words, English is head-initial and Japanese is head-final).

1.1.4   Is Subcategorization Necessary?

What does the base component look like now? Just for these simple examples, there must be, first, a specification of the position of heads relative to complements (a value for the head parameter) and, second, a lexicon, to state in some form or another the idiosyncratic properties of lexical items (that *sleep* is intransitive, *hit* is transitive, and so on).

How idiosyncratic are those idiosyncratic properties? Could it be that the next language we look at will have a verb that means exactly what *sleep* means, but is transitive, and a verb that means exactly what *hit* means, but is intransitive? That seems implausible, and to the extent that it is implausible, we are missing a generalization. If we specify the relation (*sleep*, transitive), we are saying that this relation is arbitrary. Other relations we are specifying this way *are* arbitrary: we say *sleep* is pronounced exactly the way it is pronounced, and it happens to mean "sleep," and so on. It wouldn't surprise us at all if the next language we look at has a verb pronounced like *hit* that means "sleep." But the relationship between subcategorization and semantics does seem to be considerably tighter than that between phonology and semantics. The semantics of, say, a verb should, in general, determine its thematic properties. What will the thematic representation of *sleep* say about it? At least, that it has a thematic role (θ-role) to assign to a subject, something like *experiencer*, and no θ-role to assign to an object. The thematic representation of *hit* will say that it has a θ-role to assign to a subject, either *agent* or *instrument*, and a θ-role to assign to an object, call it a *theme* θ-role. If we tried to construct something like (8a) or (8b), it would violate the θ-Criterion:

(8)   a.   *John slept Bill
        b.   *John hit

Again, the subcategorization requirements of *sleep* and *hit* are violated, but apparently we do not need to say that: for instance, *hit* has an object θ-role to assign to a theme, but (8b) has no argument that can receive this θ-role. Thus, the θ-Criterion is violated. If this type of account can be made to work generally, we can eliminate subcategorization frames in favor of thematic entries, just as we eliminated PS rules in favor of subcategorization frames (modulo the residue of ordering in terms of the head parameter).[4] In no case has there been any extra cost: we did not add subcategorization frames to eliminate PS rules, or thematic entries as part of dictionary entries to eliminate subcategorization. This type of information is needed regardless. This program is basically suggested by some work of Pesetsky (1982a), developed further by Chomsky. It is not entirely unproblematic, but it seems quite plausible.

1.2 The Transformational Component

The general view of the transformational component has changed fairly radically from Chomsky 1965 to the present. Currently many syntacticians claim that there is only one transformation, "Move α," which means "Take anything and put it anywhere else, leaving behind a trace" (a trace being an empty category of the same syntactic type as the item that moved). What is "anything"? In all variants of the theory this must be at least a constituent (in some versions it must be a maximal projection; in other versions either a maximal projection or a head). And what does "move" mean? This hasn't changed from more traditional models: it means "substitute" or "adjoin." Substitution is assumed to obey a strong version of the Structure-Preserving Constraint: XP can only substitute for another XP (the clearest case being "Substitute NP for NP," as in Raising). Moving A to B in the sense of adjunction creates another instance of B from which A hangs as a sister to the original B, as in (9):

(9)
$$
\begin{array}{c}
A \\ | \\ a
\end{array}
\xrightarrow{\text{adjoin}}
\begin{array}{c}
B \\ | \\ b
\end{array}
=
\begin{array}{c}
B \\ \diagup\diagdown \\ A \quad B \\ | \quad\; | \\ a \quad\; b
\end{array}
\quad
\begin{array}{l}
\text{(Left adjunction} \\
\text{of A to B)}
\end{array}
$$

Note that this kind of operation, like substitution, does not lose any structural information. Before the adjunction in (9), *b* was of the category B. After the adjunction, this is still the case. Similarly, *a* was and is of the category A. Of course, (9) says as well that *ab* is also of the category B, after the adjunction. That is, after all, the function of the operation.

The theories of the 1950s and 1960s included a large variety of possible transformations composed of these types of elementary operations. If we view the theory of grammar as the center of an account of language acquisition, in the transformational model the child's task is to figure out which of these many possible transformation types actually occur in his or her language. I must say that the descriptions of, in particular, English that this list of rules gave us worked pretty well— better than any description of English that I know of now. But the theory had too many transformations that seemed to have nothing to do with each other. It was hard to see what the natural class of transformations was that allowed just those, and not any other sort of bizarre thing. That raised not a descriptive problem but an explanatory one: how could the child possibly have picked out exactly these transformations from all the ones available? This problem disappears once there is only one transformation. But then the descriptive problem reemerges: the general phenomena (*Wh*-Movement, Subject Raising, and so on) receive much better accounts; but for more specific rules (Particle Movement, Heavy NP Shift, even Subject-Auxiliary Inversion) it is not clear what the substitute is in current work. Hopefully, the interaction of Move α with various principles and parameters will eventually yield illuminating results here too.

Various constraints have been proposed on the application of Move α, the most familiar of which is the Subjacency Condition, which basically disallows moving something "too far" in one operation of movement. I will return to this constraint, as well as to some further specifics of Move α.

1.3 From S-Structure to LF

The output of the transformational component is the level of representation known as S-Structure. Does it have any properties? At least some of the so-called Binding Conditions (the conditions governing anaphoric relations; see chapter 2) must constrain S-Structure. This is somewhat curious: the Binding Conditions are about something eventually semantic (referential dependencies, coreference, and so on). We might expect, then—and it has been widely proposed in the literature— that these conditions constrain strictly the LF level of representation. To see that this is not the case, we must first look at the LF component itself.

1.3.1 *The LF Component*

May (1977) argues that the LF component is much like the transformational component, relating S-Structure to the LF level of representation in very much the way that transformations relate D-Structure and S-Structure. One rule he argues for in detail is Quantifier Raising (QR), which takes quantificational phrases and moves them in LF to a position where they receive their scope. Consider (10):

(10) a. Mary likes everyone
      b. For every x, x a person, Mary likes x

(10b) is basically the representation of (10a) in terms of standard logic. There are two ways of getting from (10a) to (10b). One is a direct transformation from S-Structure into (10b). But May argues that instead we should begin with the syntactic representation associated with (10a) and alter it syntactically into another syntactic representation (LF) that is more transparently translatable into (10b). One reason May offers for doing this is that there are constraints on the distribution of quantifiers that resemble the constraints on the distribution of positions from which movement has taken place. Huang (1982b) gives extensive arguments that this is in fact the case (see section 4.2–4.4). So from this point of view, (11) is produced as the LF representation associated with (10):

(11) [$_S$ Everyone$_1$ [$_S$ Mary loves t_1]]

The quantifier adjoins to S, leaving a trace in its S-Structure position. (11) is fairly transparent: the scope of *everyone* can be defined as its c-command domain (the original S).[5] In turn, *everyone* and t are coindexed, since movement took place, which can be directly translated into the relation between the quantifier and the variable it binds. May also shows how quantifier scope ambiguities can be captured in this way. Thus, consider (12a), with its associated interpretations (12b) and (12c); the LF representations proposed for these are (12d) and (12e), respectively:

(12) a. Someone likes everyone
      b. There is an x, such that, for every y, x,y persons, x likes y
      c. For every y, there is an x, x,y persons, such that x likes y
      d. [$_S$ Someone$_1$ [$_S$ everyone$_2$ [$_S$ t_1 likes t_2]]]
      e. [$_S$ Everyone$_2$ [$_S$ someone$_1$ [$_S$ t_1 likes t_2]]]

That is, there is only one S-Structure representation associated with two different LF representations: one with *someone* higher than *everyone*, and another with *everyone* higher than *someone*. This rather nicely predicts the scope ambiguity between (12b) and (12c).

Kawai: What makes QR an obligatory process? What would go wrong if the quantifier did not raise?

Lasnik: The general assumption is that movement is an optional transformation in all three components. (I will return to this point.) Yet the output of the LF component is constrained in a particular way: no vacuous quantification is allowed. This constraint, proposed by Chomsky (1982), means that if the sentence in question contains a quantifier, at the level of LF this quantifier must have a scope, and that scope must include a variable. This would demand the raising of, say, *everyone* in (12).

The prohibition against vacuous quantification also rules out sentences like (13):

(13) a. *Who does Mary like John
     b.   For which *x*, *x* a person, Mary likes John

Take *who* as an operator, as in (13b). Note that (13) is no more incoherent than (14):

(14) For all *x*, 2 + 2 = 4

In fact, standard logical notations allow (14) for two reasons: there is no particular reason to exclude it; and it would be a complication to do so. A priori, (13) could be interpreted, following the analogy of (14), as "Mary likes John," or perhaps as a yes-no question about this. But of course it cannot mean any of these things—so we do want to rule (13) out. Returning to the question about the apparently obligatory nature of QR, we could say then that QR is optional, but it must always apply. This is not a contradiction: formally speaking, the rule is optional; independent principles conspire to force it to apply. To say that the rule is obligatory would be to miss a generalization, needlessly complicating the theory.

1.3.2 S-Structure

To come back to the point of whether Binding Conditions apply at S-Structure, consider (15):

(15) a. [Who that John$_1$ knows]$_2$ does he$_1$ like t_2
     b.   *He$_1$ likes everyone that John$_1$ knows
     c.   [Everyone that John$_1$ knows]$_2$ [he$_1$ likes t_2]

(15b), unlike (15a), is unacceptable on the reading where *he* and *John* are coreferential. This is a standard violation of Binding Condition C: *he* binds *John*. But *John* is a name and hence must be free (see section 2.1.3.1). However, in (15a) we find a way of escaping this constraint—namely, by moving a phrase that contains the name out of the c-command domain of the pronoun. This indicates that the constraint under consideration does not constrain D-Structure, where we would have, roughly, (16):

(16) He$_1$ likes who that John$_1$ knows

But now the question is whether the constraint *only* constrains LF. (15a) does not tell us anything in this respect, because the S-Structure and LF representations of this example are identical for all relevant purposes. But this is not the case for (15b): its LF representation, (15c), is quite different from its S-Structure representation and is instead very similar to the S-Structure and LF representations of (15a). In particular, the quantifier phrase containing the name is outside of S, taking the latter as its scope domain. But the S-Structure representations are distinct. In (15b), but not (15a), the name is bound, and Condition C seems to attend to this fact. Thus, Condition C applies to S-Structure (perhaps in addition to LF—the present example provides no information in this regard). One can imagine a theory where S-Structure is purely the interface of D-Structure, LF, and PF and has no independent properties. But given what we've just seen, it appears that isn't so. In chapter 4 we will examine another important condition on S-Structure, Chomsky's (1981b) Empty Category Principle.

1.4 Case Theory

1.4.1 Configurations of Case Assignment

Requirements of Case arguably hold of S-Structure too. Chomsky and Lasnik (1977) observed a number of constraints on the distribution of NPs with phonetic content (so-called lexical NPs). Consider (17):

(17) John is likely [t to be here]

John is the understood subject not of is likely but of to be here. Therefore, John must have been in the position of the subject of to be here in D-Structure, because grammatical relations are defined at that level. There is a paraphrase of (17) that makes the relation of John to its predicate transparent:

(18) It is likely [that John is here]

The relevant issue is why John cannot stay put in its D-Structure position in (17), as opposed to (18). Suppose we wanted to construct a sentence identical to (17) except that John did not undergo movement:

(19) *It is likely [John to be here]

Chomsky and Lasnik (1977) described a variety of these cases and proposed a set of S-Structure constraints ("filters") to handle them. Jean-Roger Vergnaud (personal communication) observed that this solution missed a generalization: Suppose we take the traditional view that NPs are assigned Case. In a language like Latin or German, Case has a clear morphological realization. But suppose this is just a superficial property. Suppose all languages are abstractly like Latin or German, differing only in low-level realization properties. "What are the configurations in which Case is assigned?" Vergnaud asked. Traditionally, subjects of finite clauses are assigned nominative Case; direct objects of verbs are assigned accusative Case (though there are well-known idiosyncrasies in this regard, such as certain verbs in German that assign genitive Case); objects of prepositions are assigned oblique Case. Suppose for the moment we assume these are the only ways an NP can get Case. Finally, Vergnaud suggested adding the plausible requirement that every lexical NP *needs* Case. The basic idea is essentially to propose a morphological requirement: a lexical NP must be morphologically realized, but for this, the NP must have a particular Case slot in its morphological representation. If this slot is not filled, the NP cannot be morphologically realized, and the result is a violation of a morphological filter. Notice that as I have stated it, only NPs that are morphologically realized will need Case.

Consider (18) from this point of view. *John* is the subject of a finite clause, so it gets nominative Case. The expletive *it* is also the subject of a finite clause, so it gets nominative Case as well. No particular problem arises here with respect to this issue. Now consider (17). There, *John* is in a position where nominative Case can be assigned: subject of a finite clause. Notice that since *John* was not there at D-Structure, the requirement we are considering cannot hold of D-Structure. Since we are assuming that it is basically a morphological requirement, a priori we would not expect it to have anything to do with D-Structure. We might, then, state the condition as in (20):

(20) *Case Filter*
　　At S-Structure, every lexical NP needs Case.

What about the trace of *John* (the empty NP left behind by the movement)? It does not seem to be in a position where Case is assigned. On the other hand, a trace is not lexical: it is not something a speaker has to pronounce. So let us say that, for that reason, the trace does not need Case. (17) is then all right as well. But what about (19)? *It* is all right: it is lexical, and it is in a position to which nominative Case is assigned. However, *John* is clearly lexical, and it is not in any position to which Case is assigned. Therefore, (19) violates the Case Filter.

1.4.2　Exceptional Case Marking

Nothing I have said so far allows an example like (21):

(21) I am eager for John to be here

For is a complementizer here—that is, *for John* is not a PP. *John* is not the subject of a finite clause; nor is it the object of a verb; nor is it the object of a preposition. Surely, the presence of *for* is what makes (21) acceptable. This is clear from (22):

(22) *I am eager John to be here

Notice that if the complement clause did not have a lexical subject, *for* would not be required:

(23) I am eager *e* to be here

(*e* stands, in general, for an empty category.) We will talk later on (section 2.2) about how the grammatical relation "subject of *to be here*" is assigned—but the sentence must have some NP that will receive the subject role. Whatever that NP is, it clearly is not lexically realized, so it is perfectly all right for it to be in a position that cannot be assigned Case. Therefore, *for* does not have to be there.[6] It is as if *for* is treating *John* in (21) as its object, even though it is not. There is some relationship between *John* and *for* that is not the relation "object of" but is enough like that relation that *for* is allowed to assign Case to *John*. Following standard terminology, we may call this process *Exceptional Case Marking* (ECM). We will explore this further later on, when we will see that the exceptional Case marker must be "close enough" to the element to which it is assigning Case. This is so in two respects: in terms of linear order, and in terms of hierarchy.

Let us look at another example where the same basic process is at work:

(24) a. I believe John to be here
      b. I believe John is here

The grammatical relations in (24a) and (24b) are the same: *John* is the subject of the embedded construction in both cases and is not the object of *believe* in either. Thus, (24a) is another example with a lexical NP in a position that does not meet any of the paradigmatic requirements for Case assignment. We would like to reduce the process of Case assignment in (24a) to that in (21). There, *for* does not have *John* as its object, but it still is "close enough" to *John*. Let us use a traditional term to express this relation: *government*. In traditional terminology, a verb or a preposition *governs* its object. This is the paradigmatic situation, but let us suppose that there are more peripheral cases as well: if a preposition or a verb is "close enough" to an NP, government can hold, even if the NP is not the complement of the governor. Assuming that *for* in (21) is in Comp, evidently an S boundary does not count as too much intervening structure for the purposes of government. Similarly, in (24a) it is assumed that *believe* is capable of governing *John* because there is not too much intervening structure. In these circumstances *John* can receive accusative Case from *believe*.

Notice, however, that government is not the only requirement on Case assignment here. Consider (25):

(25) *I believe sincerely John to be here

The following claim is not established, but it is widely accepted: there is still a government relation between *believe* and *John* in (25) even if an adverb intervenes. To explain the ungrammaticality of (25) under that assumption, we can rely on a proposal by Stowell (1981). Stowell suggested that, at least in English, Case assignment requires not just government, but adjacency as well. In sum, the conditions for Case assignment are as follows:

(26) α assigns Case to β if
      a. α is a Case assigner;
      b. α governs β;
      c. α is adjacent to β.

With respect to (26a), verbs and prepositions are Case assigners but (crucially) adjectives are not; otherwise, the ungrammaticality of (19) cannot be explained.[7]

The core case for (26b) is where β is the complement of α, but we have also seen some extended instances of this. Basically, α governs β if there is not "too much structure" in between (for example, an S boundary may intervene, but not an S' boundary, where S' → Comp S, as first proposed by Bresnan (1970)). Chomsky (1981b) proposed a process for describing this. He said that in underlying structure all sentential complements are S'. Then, for some sentential complements (like the infinitival complement of *believe*), a process of S'-Deletion takes place, which reduces an S' complement to an S complement. An alternative approach is to claim that these complements are S all along. Then the issue is what kind of complement type a particular predicate selects. I will return to this momentarily.

Finally, (26c) states that α must be adjacent to β. This can be seen not only in ECM configurations but in simple sentences as well; hence the contrasts in (27):

(27) a. I sincerely believe John
     b. *I believe sincerely John

To summarize, we have seen evidence for a Case requirement that clearly cannot be a D-Structure requirement, for we can start with a structure that flatly violates it and change it to a perfectly grammatical structure. The requirement must therefore constrain some later level of representation. S-Structure is plausible, but so is PF, especially if we are dealing with a basically morphological requirement. Interestingly, Chomsky argues that it is neither an S-Structure nor a PF requirement: he argues that it holds at LF. So far we have seen no evidence bearing on this issue, one way or the other—but we will eventually return to it (in section 6.1). For the moment, let us assume an S-Structure condition: the Case Filter, a particular instantiation of (20):

(28) *Case Filter*

$$*\begin{bmatrix} \text{NP} \\ \text{lexical} \\ -\text{Case} \end{bmatrix}$$

1.5 Complementation

1.5.1 *Classes of Clausal Complements*

I have alluded to the possibly divergent selectional properties of different predicates with respect to sentential complements. I would like to take a brief look at classes of clausal complements that superficially look very similar but turn out to be quite different. Consider the pair in (29):

(29) a. I wanted John to leave
     b. I persuaded John to leave

These two are superficially identical. However, manipulating the material after the matrix verb produces striking differences:

(30) a. I wanted it to rain
     b. *I persuaded it to rain
     c. I wanted the bus to arrive on time
     d. *I persuaded the bus to arrive on time

What could account for these differences?

Let us look in some more detail at the plausible structures of these examples. To do this, we have the θ-Criterion at our disposal. The question is, what is it that I want when I want John to leave? I do not actually want John; that is, *John* is not the thematic object of *want*. Rather, I want a state of affairs, or event—in particular, John's leaving—to take place. This seems to be the sole θ-role that *want* assigns to a complement; in other words, the complement of *want* in this example is sentential. What about *persuade*? When I persuade John to leave, do I persuade a state of affairs? Obviously not; I persuade John. Thus, *John* is a complement of *persuade*. But then, what is *to leave*? That seems to be an independent complement. It seems, then, that *persuade* takes two complements. In fact, there are sentences with *persuade* where the grammatical relations are the same as those in (29b), and it is transparent that there are two complements. For instance:

(31) I persuaded John that he should leave

(Notice that a similar paraphrase is completely impossible for the complement of *want*.) If the thematic structure of (29b) is very much like that of (31), then we must ask, What portion of the structure in (29b) plays the role of *that he should leave*? It cannot be just *to leave*, because of the θ-Criterion: *leave* has the lexical thematic property of demanding a subject. Whatever this subject is in (29b), it is not pronounced. Thus, the representations of the examples in (29) and (30) should be roughly as follows:

(32) a. I wanted [John to leave]
     b. I persuaded John [e to leave]
     c. I wanted [it to rain]
     d. *I persuaded it [e to rain]
     e. I wanted [the bus to arrive on time]
     f. *I persuaded the bus [e to arrive on time]

Note that (32d) gives us an account for the ungrammaticality of (30b). Here, expletive *it* must be the complement of *persuaded*, in violation of the θ-Criterion, since an expletive, by definition, is not an argument and thus cannot receive the θ-role that *persuade* must assign. We also have an explanation for (30d) in terms of *the bus* must be the NP complement of *persuade*, but buses are not entities that can be persuaded. Put differently, *the bus* cannot receive the particular thematic role that *persuade* assigns. (In the terms of Chomsky 1965, this case violates selectional restrictions.)

Let us look at two more classes of verbs. First consider *try*:

(33) a. I tried to leave
    b. *I tried John to leave
    c. *I tried it to rain
    d. *I tried the bus to leave

Following the same reasoning we used with *want* and *persuade*, the complement of *try* needs a subject (that is, *leave* has the lexical property of needing a subject). But this subject does not seem morphologically realizable. In fact, we have a description of this type of example: the subject of an infinitival is not a position to which Case is assigned, so NPs in that position cannot be morphologically realized under normal circumstances. The reason why the infinitival complement of *want* can have a realized subject involves the Exceptional Case Marking process mentioned earlier.

Finally, consider again the *believe* class:

(34) a. I believe John to be here
    b. I believe that John is here
    c. I believe John to be a pathological liar

Again, the θ-Criterion tells us that the complement of *believe* is a clause, which is transparent in (34b), roughly a paraphrase of (34a). This is confirmed in (34c). *John* is presumably not the understood object of *believe*, because it is unlikely that I can believe John and believe him to be a pathological liar at the same time, unless I am some kind of schizophrenic. That is, there is no thematic relation between *believe* and *John* in the examples in (34). So the *believe* class is not like the *persuade* class, because the latter does have an NP object; nor is it like the *try* class, because the subject of the complement of *believe* can be overt. So far the class in question looks like the *want* class. (35) shows that this is not the case, however:

(35) a. I want to be clever
    b. *I believe to be clever

Using examples like (35), among others, Bresnan (1972) argued that there must be a basic difference between these two classes. First of all, though the subject of the complement of *want* is allowed to be overt, it *need not* be overt, as (35a) shows. Once again, there must be a subject, because of the thematic properties of *leave*, but this subject need not be overt. This is clearly not the case with *believe*, as (35b) shows. To allow (32a), we speculated that there is the possibility of assigning exceptional Case to the subject of the complement of *want*. But suppose we say that this is an *optional* property. On the other hand, *believe* has the property of assigning exceptional Case too. We might imagine, then, an extended version of the Case Filter: not only that every lexical NP needs Case, but also that every Case must be assigned. If *believe* is, then, *obligatorily* a Case assigner, (35b) would be ruled out because there would be no lexical NP to which *believe* could assign its exceptional Case. (See below for an alternative account.)

1.5.2 "Exceptional" Passivization

Another paradigm that distinguishes these classes of verbs is illustrated in (36). This paradigm involves passivization. Let us see how the verb classes we have considered behave with respect to it:

(36) a. John was persuaded to leave
    b. John was believed to be clever
    c. *John was wanted to leave

With *persuade* we certainly expect passivization to occur, as in (36a), since it is a core case of this process (as we will see momentarily): taking the direct object of a verb and fronting it to subject position. There are also noncore cases of passivization, which might be called *exceptional passives*, by analogy with cases of Exceptional Case Marking. This occurs when an NP that is not the direct object of a verb nonetheless moves into surface subject position of that verb. *Believe* is one such verb, as we see in (36b). Interestingly, as Bresnan also discussed, *want* diverges from *believe* with respect to passivization, as we see in (36c). This difference between *want* and *believe* is similar in some respects to the difference between *likely* and *illegal*:

(37) a. John is likely to park here
    b. *John is illegal to park here

In (37a) *John* is the understood subject not of *likely* but of *to park here*, so presumably movement takes place from the subject position of *to park here* to the subject position of *is likely*. This option is evidently unavailable in (37b). One major property that Bresnan pointed out (and related to other contrasting properties of these predicates) is the following. There is a way of expressing the content of the ill-formed (37b), as in (38b); that same construction is impossible with *likely*:

(38) a. *It is likely for John to park here
    b. It is illegal for John to park here

That is, *illegal* allows *for* and disallows movement, whereas *likely* allows movement and disallows *for*. This distinction carries over to the contrasts between *want* and *believe*:

(39) a. *I believe for John to be here
    b. John is believed to be here
    c. ?I want for John to be here
    d. *John is wanted to be here

Table 1.1
Some classes of infinitival complements

WANT hate like	___[$_{S'}$ (for) [$_S$]]	allow Exceptional Case Marking do not allow Exceptional Passive
PERSUADE convince tell	___[$_{NP}$] [$_{S'}$]	allow regular Passive
TRY attempt	___[$_{S'}$]	do not allow Exceptional Case Marking do not allow Exceptional Passive
BELIEVE consider prove	___[$_{S'}$[$_S$]] ↓ ___[$_S$]	must undergo Exceptional Case Marking allow Exceptional Passive

If we suppose that the underlying presence of *for* makes S'-Deletion impossible, and that S' blocks Exceptional Passive just as it blocks Exceptional Case Marking, this array of facts is correctly described.[8] Further, we correctly predict that where S'-Deletion is unavailable for whatever reason, Exceptional Passive will likewise be unavailable. Thus, with *try*, Case facts showed that there is no S'-Deletion (presumably as a lexical property of *try*). As predicted, Exceptional Passive is also impossible:

(40) *John was tried [*t* to win the race]

So far there is no real *explanation* for this S' constraint on passivization, but the correlation is surely significant. In chapter 4 we will look at a principle that explains this restriction.

Table 1.1 summarizes the cases we have considered.

One point worth reemphasizing is that the θ-Criterion can give us substantial information about the particular structure in which a particular verb appears. For example, it sharply distinguishes the *persuade* class from the others.

We have seen other cases in which the θ-Criterion helps us determine what a given structure is like.

(41) a. John is likely to win
     b. *e* is likely John to win
     c. It is likely that John will win
     d. *It is likely John to win

The θ-Criterion tells us that since *John* is the NP bearing the subject θ-role in the lower clause in (41a), (41b) should be the D-Structure representation of (41a). *Likely* does not have a subject θ-role to assign; hence, at D-Structure no argument will fill that subject position. *John* can therefore move into the empty subject position. In passing, recall that we can explain why this movement is forced, that is, why a sentence like (41d) is impossible. The ungrammaticality of (41d) has nothing to do with the θ-Criterion, since all θ-roles are correctly assigned, as in the well-formed (41c). But there is a more superficial requirement that differentiates these two: the Case Filter. *John* in (41c) is in a position to which Case (in particular, nominative Case) is assigned. However, *John* in (41d) is not in a position to which Case is assigned. By contrast, if this NP is moved to the subject position of the matrix clause, then nominative Case can be assigned, as desired.

1.5.3 Passive

With all this in mind, consider (42):

(42) John was arrested

What should the structure of (42) be? Notice, first, that there are no structures like (43):

(43) *They arrested

That is to say, *arrest* has a θ-role that it must be able to assign to an object. According to the θ-Criterion, then, there must be an argument in D-Structure in the object position of *arrested*. And in fact *John* in (42) is not the understood subject but the understood object of the verb. Let us then construct a D-Structure representation that is in accord with these properties, namely, (44a):

(44) a. *e* was arrested John
     b. John was arrested *t*

John moves from D-Structure object position to subject position. Abstractly, this is rather similar to what happened earlier with *likely*. The parallelism extends further. Suppose we elect not to perform the movement operation that changes (44a) to (44b). We then end up with something like (45):

(45) *It was arrested John

What could be wrong with (45)? Chomsky (1980, 1981b) proposed that the same thing is wrong with (45) that was wrong with (41d): *John* is in a position to which no Case is assigned. This in fact is trickier than it was in the earlier example: why is *arrested* in (45) not a Case assigner if *arrested* in (46) is?

(46) They arrested John

I will return to this momentarily.

Sentence (42) has another rather curious property: normally, *arrest* has a subject θ-role to assign, hence the ungrammaticality of (47) (where *it* is an expletive):

(47) *It arrested John

Is it then the case that *arrest* always has two arguments? Apparently not, given (42): there, only one θ-role is assigned. Thus, even though actives and passives are rather similar in some aspects of their θ-assignment properties, in other aspects they are quite different. In particular, passive verbs potentially have one θ-role fewer than their active counterparts. The subject θ-role may be missing.

We have now seen two important differences between active and passive verbs, one involving Case and the other involving θ-roles. A mechanism by which the first of these generalizations can be expressed was proposed by Chomsky and Lasnik (1977). When a verb is passivized, it is rather more like an adjective; more precisely, it is a neutralized verb-adjective. Under the standard assumption that an adjective is [+N, +V] and a verb is [−N, +V], a passivized verb, under this proposal, is simply [+V], with no value for [N]. This gave the correct results for the filters proposed by Chomsky and Lasnik. In current terms, lexical Case assigners can be characterized as the class of [−N] elements (V is [−N, +V] and P is [−N, −V]). Thus, a passivized verb is not a Case assigner. As for the second of the generalizations, the correct way to state it is that the subject role *need not* be assigned. That is, in addition to sentences like (42), in which no argument bears the subject role, we find sentences like (48), where the subject role is apparently assigned:

(48) John was arrested by the police

We do not have a principled explanation for why active and passive verbs differ in their thematic properties in this way. One standard *statement* of the fact is this: "Passive morphology absorbs the subject θ-role-assigning property of a verb." But this is just a fancy way of restating the problem. Note immediately that this stipulation may create a problem for (48), though, unless we say that *by* is what assigns a θ-role to *the police* (or at least *by* in conjunction—somehow—with *arrested*).

Importantly, not only do passive verbs lose their ability to assign Case to a complement; they in fact lose their Case-assigning ability altogether (as we would expect from the earlier discussion). Thus, consider ECM sites:

(49) a. I believe John to be intelligent
     b. *It was believed John to be intelligent
     c. John was believed *t* to be intelligent

Presumably, (49b) is ruled out for the same reason as (45): *John* is in a position where it cannot receive Case (either in the lower infinitival clause or, exceptionally, from the upper passive verb). (49c) is the grammatical counterpart of (49b), a case of Exceptional Passive of the sort considered earlier.

Returning to the θ-properties of (48), we may ask, Could *the police* there be in subject position in D-Structure?

(50) The police be arrested John by *e*

Under such a hypothesis, we would assume that the underlying subject, *the police*, ends up as the complement of *by* via NP-Movement. In turn, *John* could then move into the position vacated by *the police* after it moves. But if we assume (50), we clearly must assume that *be arrested* directly assigns a subject θ-role to *the police*; otherwise, an argument would lack a θ-role, in violation of one half of the θ-Criterion. But this means that the D-Structure representation for (44b)—namely, (44a)—contains a θ-Criterion violation, since there is no subject in (44b) to receive the hypothesized subject θ-role. This strongly suggests that we should reject (50) as the D-Structure representation for (48).

1.6   Toward "Move NP"

We have seen simple passives, as in (42), exceptional passives, as in (49c), and raising structures, as in (41a). The interesting question is whether we are dealing with three processes, all different, or one process, the differences following from independent properties. In fact, the null hypothesis in this model is that only one process is involved: Move NP. This kind of operation involves substitution: the NP must move to an empty NP position. Thus, there should be no significant difference with respect to the transformations applying in each of the cases we have considered. Furthermore, in all these constructions, for there to be an empty D-Structure subject position, no θ-role can be assigned to this position. Of course, the specific reasons why a θ-role is not assigned in each case may differ: *likely* does not have a subject θ-role to assign at all, whereas passive morphology takes away the property that *arrest* has of assigning a subject θ-role.

To further confirm this approach, consider the paradigm in (51):

(51) a. It is believed by everyone that John is intelligent
     b. That John is intelligent is believed by everyone

Here the complement of *believe* is *that John is intelligent*. This complement can be moved, as in (51b), but it need not be. It can be left in place, as in (51a). This option, as we have seen, is not available for complement NPs. The difference is that whereas a lexical NP needs Case (and hence cannot stay in the position of complement of a passive verb, where no Case is assigned), there is no reason to believe that a clause needs Case. (52) indicates that it does not:

(52) a. *I am proud John
     b. I am proud of John
     c. I am proud that John is here

Recall that adjectives are not Case assigners. Thus, (52a) is ruled out; its grammatical counterpart is (52b), where the "empty" preposition *of* is inserted to assign Case. Significantly, (52c) is perfect. If we compare

(52a) and (52c), we must conclude that a clause does not need Case. Therefore, when a clause is the complement of a passive verb, nothing forces this clause to move. Again, independent principles interact with Move NP—or, more generally, Move α—to yield the desired results.[9]

1.7 *Wh-*Movement and Subjacency

We have considered movement from a position that is potentially a recipient of a θ-role to another such position (for example, from object position to subject position, or from embedded subject position to higher subject position). Chomsky (1981b) calls such positions *A-positions* and such movement *A-movement.* The item that undergoes A-movement and its trace(s) constitute what is called an *A-chain.*

Let us now look at $\bar{\text{A}}$-movement, or movement to an $\bar{\text{A}}$-position (a position that is not an A-position). The paradigm case of movement of this sort is *Wh-*Movement—movement of a question phrase to Comp. This is illustrated in (53a), with its D-Structure form (53b):

(53) a. I wonder who [you will see *t*]
     b. I wonder [you will see who]

See has an object θ-role to assign, presumably assigned to *who* in D-Structure, as in (53b). *Who* then moves from its D-Structure position, not to an A-position, but rather to Comp. This movement can happen within a clause, as illustrated in (53), or it can happen long distance:

(54) I wonder who [you think [John said [you will see *t*]]]

This time *who* ends up two clauses away from where it started. Occasionally this type of movement is referred to as *unbounded movement.* In fact, this is an inaccurate term, because the movement is actually rather heavily bounded. The classical configurations where movement fails were originally termed *islands* (Ross 1967). (55) illustrates one island:

(55) a. Bill wonders who [*t* saw Mary]
     b. Bill wonders who [*t* saw what]
     c. ?*What does Bill wonder who [*t* saw *t*]

(55c) violates the *Wh-*Island Constraint. (Incidentally, this particular constraint is often attributed to Ross, but although Ross proposed a large number of island constraints, he specifically argued against a *Wh-*Island Constraint. The constraint is actually due to Chomsky.)[10] Another well-known island constraint, the *Complex NP Constraint,* which is indeed due to Ross, is illustrated in (56):

(56) a. ?*Who [did you mention [Bill's belief [that you saw *t*]]]
     b.   Who [did you mention [that Bill believes [that you saw *t*]]]

A complex NP is an NP containing a clause. The constraint disallows movement out of a clause within an NP (56a), while allowing movement out of a clause within a clause (56b). Note that *distance* is not at issue: *who* moves at least as far in (56b) as in (56a), by any rational measure.

Chomsky (1973) tried to unify these two constraints. First, he proposed that all movement is very local. This immediately subsumes the two island constraints, but of course it also rules out (54) and (56b). To deal with the latter problem, Chomsky proposed that movement is "successive cyclic." That is, instead of moving a *Wh*-phrase from its A-position all the way up to its S-Structure position in one fell swoop, we first move it to the lower Comp, and from that Comp to the next higher Comp, and so forth, as in (57):

(57) a. I wonder you think John said you will see who
      b. I wonder you think John said [who [you will see *t*]]
      c. I wonder you think [who [John said [*t* [you will see *t*]]]]
      d. I wonder [who [you think [*t* [John said [*t* [you will see *t*]]]]]]

Note that the movement from (57a) to (57b) is as local as that in (53); thus, no issue of distance arises here. Now, we must still make sure that the Comp-to-Comp movement (as in the mapping from (57b) to (57c)) is taken to be local enough not to be ruled out, whereas the movement in (55) or (56a) is excluded as too distant. Observe that in (55) *what* cannot be moved into the Comp of its own clause, since that Comp is already filled by *who*. (Let us stipulate for a moment that Comp has room for only one *Wh*-phrase.) That will force movement in that case to take place in one fell swoop. Moreover, this movement will be longer than any of the individual movements in (57). I will return to this immediately. Now consider (56a). There *who* can move into the lower Comp (just as in the well-formed (56b)); but where can it move next?[11] The next position it can move to is the ultimate landing site, since there are no Comps in between (there are no S's in between, and S' is the only element that contains Comp). So now, how local is "very local"? We know that *who* must move out of its VP. Let us therefore assume that VP is irrelevant. In (53), the good case, *who* is moving out of an S. In (57), the good longer case, *who* first moves out of an S and then out of an S' and an S. The good movements thus have the property of moving across just one S (and sometimes also an S'). In (55c), one of the bad cases, the movement crosses first one S' and one S (which should be all right, from what we saw in (57)). However, it then crosses *another S*, which must make the difference. File that information and return to (56a), the other bad case. The first movement crosses only one S (no problem there), and then it crosses one S, one S', and one NP. We have seen that crossing one S and one S' is all right, so it must be the NP that makes the difference. Chomsky's proposal, then, was as follows:

(58) A single instance of movement can cross at most one bounding node, where the bounding nodes are S and NP.

In (55c) *who* crosses two Ss, whereas in (56a) it crosses one S and one NP. Hence, in both cases the movement crosses two bounding nodes, violating (58). (58), the mechanism ensuring the locality of each instance of movement, is the *Subjacency Condition.*

One final point with respect to these cases. There is another derivation we must consider for (55c), namely, (59):

(59) a. Bill wonders [who saw what]
   b. Bill wonders [what [who saw *t*]]

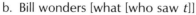

   c. What [does Bill wonder [*t* [who saw *t*]]]

   d. What [does Bill wonder [who [*t* saw *t*]]]

First we move *what* (not *who*) to Comp, as in (59b). That movement does not violate (58). Then we move *what* from the lower Comp up to the higher clause, as in (59c), again without violating (58). Finally, we move *who* into the intermediate Comp, as in (59d), again without violating (58). Each of these movements crosses only one bounding node. But if Subjacency does not rule out this derivation, how do we exclude the ungrammatical (55c)? There is one further plausible constraint on the mapping from D-Structure to S-Structure that is violated here, namely, the principle of *Strict Cyclicity* proposed by Chomsky (1973). The first step in the derivation involves the embedded S'. The second step involves the matrix S', moving from the lower Comp into the higher Comp. But the third step of the derivation involves solely positions within a lower cyclic domain. Strict Cyclicity was proposed to prevent just this kind of derivation.

1.8 *Wanna* Contraction: A Case Study

Given the perspective of the modular model we've been discussing, let's now look at the analysis of an old chestnut of a problem involving a very interesting paradigm that has been discussed for many years in the literature. The phenomenon, which is heard quite generally in colloquial English, is illustrated in (60a, b):

(60) a. I want to win the race
   b. I wanna win the race
   c. Who do you want to visit *t*
   d. Who do you wanna visit
   e. Who do you want *t* to visit Bill
   f. *Who do you wanna visit Bill

Want to in (60a) is usually contracted to *wanna*, as in (60b). This can be informally characterized as in (61) (from Chomsky and Lasnik 1977):

(61) want + to → wanna

This process can also be seen in the pair (60c, d). The crucial case is (60e) versus (60f), where contraction is unexpectedly bad. Descriptively, the position from which a *wh*-phrase moves blocks contraction. One way to say this is that the position from which a *wh*-phrase moves is a "real thing." "Trace theory" provides an account of that: when movement takes place, it really leaves something behind. The category that is left behind has no phonological realization, but it does have a whole set of syntactic features. We know this to be true because of agreement facts:

(62) a. Which man do you think *t* is here
     b. Which men do you think *t* are here

Now, if in (60c) something real intervenes between *want* and *to*, and if the contraction rule is stated as in (61), we will not be able to contract as in (60f). The paradigm is solved, isn't it? Well, not quite. Look at (60a). Nothing appears between *want* and *to*; but that is a trick. The θ-Criterion demands that *to win the race* have a subject. So what is that subject role assigned to? It looks as though it's not assigned to anything in (60a). Chomsky and Lasnik (1977) proposed a solution to this that worked rather well, though it quickly passed out of fashion. Specifically, we proposed that in D-Structure something like (63) corresponds to (60a):

(63) I want [myself to win the race]

To this, a rule of reflexive deletion applies. Unlike what happens in the case of movement, we argued that deletion does not leave a trace; rather, a category and its contents are entirely eliminated. This of course leaves nothing between *want* and *to*, allowing contraction to occur there. This approach probably passed out of favor because the idea of "identity deletion" rules of this sort in general passed out of favor.

So let us see how we can account for the same facts without deletion rules. What we need is a subject for *to win the race* that occupies this position all along, in which case this subject will have no phonetic realization. The standard notation for this item is PRO (see section 2.2), so (60a) has the following representation:

(64) I want [PRO to win the race]

Several current accounts of (60) make two assumptions—two stipulations, in effect. The first is that *wh*-trace needs Case. In fact, entirely independent of the paradigm under consideration, there is very strong evidence for a constraint with that effect. We have already seen a paradigmatic situation where a lexical NP is impossible:

(65) *It is likely John to be here

We decided that (65) is ruled out because *John* is in a position to which no Case is assigned. But (66) is equally bad:

(66) *Who is it likely *t* to be here

Apparently, *wh*-traces need Case as well as lexical NPs.[12] This is actually quite odd if the Case Filter is a morphological requirement (as seems plausible otherwise): *wh*-traces do not have morphological realization, and yet they need Case. For the moment we will simply adopt the stipulation. The second stipulation, for which there is no independent motivation, is the following: a category that is not Case-marked does not block contraction.

With these stipulations, the paradigm is accounted for. In (60e) *t* must be Case-marked; contraction is impossible there precisely because *t* is a Case-marked empty category. What about (60a)? We have evidence that PRO does not need Case; for instance:

(67) a. *It is important John to be here
  b. It is important PRO to be here

This is a minimal pair: (67a) is ruled out because *John* does not receive Case. (67b) is all right; therefore, PRO does not need Case. Then we can say that PRO does not block contraction in this example, precisely because PRO is a Caseless empty category.

This of course is a solution of rather little depth. Phenomenologically, the problem is that PRO does not block contraction, and *t* does. The answer is precisely the problem: PRO does not block contraction, and *t* does.

Pesetsky (1982a) suggested a more principled answer. I have assumed that the representation for (60a) is (64). However, suppose that it were (68) instead:

(68) I want [$_S$[$_{VP}$ to win the race][$_{NP}$ PRO]]

Can we in fact assume this? After all, it goes against the PS rules of English: there is no rule S → VP NP. But what PS rules? We have decided that we want to eliminate PS rules in favor of the head parameter and lexical properties of θ-role assigners. *Win* surely needs a subject (PRO in this case), but no particular property of *win* tells us that PRO must come before the VP. Does it then follow from the head parameter? The answer to this is apparently "no" as well. The head parameter states that the head must precede its complements in English, and PRO is not a complement of *win*; therefore, the parameter is irrelevant. Thus, there is no compelling reason why the subject of *to win the race* cannot follow the VP.

But now we have a terrible empirical problem: why can't we say (69)?

(69) *Won the race Mary

Incidentally, to avoid some confusion: Pesetsky did not propose that there is a transformation that can move a subject to a post-VP position. What he said is that nothing prevents a construction at D-Structure in which the subject appears postverbally. In other words, with Pesetsky's approach, the subject in the relevant cases is never in preverbal position. Now the question is why (69) cannot be a valid D-Structure form in English. To begin to answer this question, let us suppose that nominative Case assignment, like other instances of Case assignment, has an adjacency requirement. Suppose further that nominative Case is assigned under government from the agreement (Agr) morpheme in Aux (Infl). Let us take a closer look at the structure underlying (69):

(70)

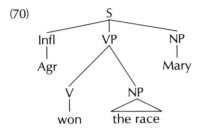

So far it is not clear precisely where Infl should go in (70), but we will return to this immediately. Suppose for now that Infl precedes VP. (70) presents a problem for Case assignment to *Mary* by Agr, if this operation is supposed to take place under adjacency, even if Agr governs *Mary*. Then why not hypothesize (71) as the relevant structure?

(71)

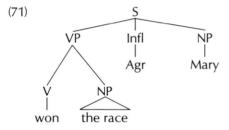

In (71) Agr *is* adjacent to *Mary*. However, the rule of Affix Hopping (which associates the bound morpheme, Agr, with its host verb) requires adjacency between V and the affix (see, for example, Lasnik 1981). This is crucial in ruling out sentences like (72a), derived from (72b):

(72) a. *John not left
    b. *John Agr not leave

(Note that without the adjacency requirement, Agr could incorrectly hop onto the verb in (72b).) But there is no way to satisfy *both* adjacency requirements (the one for Case assignment and the one for Affix Hopping in (72a)). Failure either to assign Case or to hop the affix onto the verb violates one or the other of two morphological requirements: the Case Filter, or the filter that demands that bound morphemes occur as syntactic dependents.

The obvious question is why (73) is still ruled out:

(73) *Left Agr Mary

To generate the ill-formed (73), we would rely on a particular structure, roughly like (71), where Infl is immediately dominated by S. However, in recent years another approach has begun to look more and more plausible. Notice that a structure like (71) is completely outside the X' system. There are two ways of incorporating clauses into this system. One is to say that S is a projection of V (as discussed, for instance, in Jackendoff 1977). The other is to say that S is a projection of Infl (following Pesetsky 1982a and Stowell 1981).[13] Let us see what the latter approach would tell us about (73). Clearly, the structure underlying (73) should be (74):

(74)

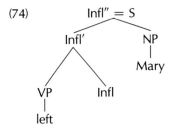

Here VP is the complement of Infl, and NP is the specifier of Infl' (in the usual X' terminology). But now the one parameter we have at our disposal is exactly relevant: English is head-initial; but Infl follows its complement, VP, in (74). So the only way Infl can come between VP and NP is if the structure is (75):

(75)

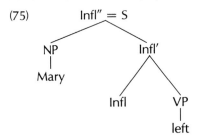

And this will not produce (73).

- *Uriagereka:* Adverbs seem to be able to intervene between NP and VP. How does that affect the adjacency requirement for Case assignment that we are assuming?

  Lasnik: Yes, that is a significant problem. Consider the contrasts in (76):

  (76) a. *John loves sincerely Mary
  b. John often arrives late

  For whatever reason (and this is extremely unclear) adverbs do not seem to prevent the needed adjacency for nominative Case assignment. It is rather tempting to say that adverbs have nothing to do with any of this but are built into their S-Structure position in a later component. Yet that won't work, because of examples like (76a), where the adverb is clearly present at exactly a level of representation relevant to Case assignment.

  •

How can this approach, modulo the technical difficulty just raised, account for the paradigm we started with? In (68) PRO is base-generated to the right of the VP, because there is no principle or parameter of English that prevents that representation. If the D-Structure form remains unchanged until S-Structure, *want* is left adjacent to *to*, and contraction can proceed. Now, why can't we do exactly the same in (77)?

(77) Who do you want [$_S$[$_{VP}$ to win the race] *t*]

If the subject is base-generated in post-VP position, the head parameter is not violated. But the additional stipulation that *wh*-trace needs Case *is* now violated (recall that PRO does not need Case). What is at issue here, incidentally, is exceptional Case, which (as earlier evidence showed) takes place under adjacency. The trace in (77), though, is clearly in a position where it cannot receive Case from anything: it is not adjacent to any Case assigner.

This analysis relies on the assumption that no principle of the grammar can say specifically where a subject must be in D-Structure. But at S-Structure there are certain Case requirements that do in general force the subject to be in a particular position. PRO is not subject to any of these, so it can occur in post-VP position. But a *wh*-trace is subject to Case requirements, as we have seen. Thus, in the first instance the nonovert category does not block contraction, but in the second it does. Hence, we do not have to stipulate that an empty category that is not Case-marked does not block contraction—this follows immediately from other assumptions.

- *Gorrell:* Are examples like (78) a problem for the analysis you proposed?

(78) *Book the

Lasnik: Yes, that is potentially a devastating problem. We've said that the only relevant structural parameter is the complement (head) parameter, but we've said nothing about the position of specifiers. Now if subjects are specifiers, as argued in Chomsky 1970, and if specifiers that are not NPs do not in general need Case, then why can't we say (78)? Pesetsky's elegant explanation for the contraction paradigm will remain questionable until we can come up with an independent way of ruling out such examples. •

1.9 The Extended Projection Principle

Another question arises with respect to (60e)—namely, why does a trace have to be there at all? Suppose we are dealing with a late phenomenon, and there is simply no trace at this level. Then *want* and *to* would be adjacent and would be predicted to contract, contrary to fact. What we need is some principle of grammar demanding that this trace be there. Two principles have been proposed that would have this effect. One I alluded to earlier: the principle preventing vacuous quantification. In particular, if we take a *wh*-phrase to be a question operator, this operator must bind a variable. The syntactic reflex of this variable is the trace. This, then, demands that the trace be there at least at LF. The second principle that would have a similar effect in this case is the *Extended Projection Principle* (Chomsky 1981b). To understand this principle, we should first consider the "unextended" Projection Principle.

D-Structure is a representation of θ-properties. The Projection Principle says, in effect, that what is true of D-Structure with respect to θ-properties must also be true of other syntactic levels, in the following sense. Take for instance an NP complement of a V in D-Structure. The Projection Principle demands that an NP be the complement of this V at S-Structure as well. Not necessarily the same NP, clearly, because otherwise movement would be ruled out altogether. That is, the Projection Principle does not say that D-Structure, S-Structure, and LF are all identical. In particular, suppose that a verb assigns a θ-role—say, theme—to its object, as in *solve the problem*. The Projection Principle demands that an NP to which the theme θ-role is assigned be left there, even if *the problem* moves, thus satisfying the lexical property of *solve* that it has a theme θ-role to assign. Now consider a D-Structure form like (79):

(79) Bill will solve which problem

According to the Projection Principle, if we move *which problem* as in (80), we still have an NP in the position of complement of *solve*, this time a null NP, a trace:

(80) Which problem will Bill solve *t*

There are other examples where the Projection Principle is relevant and where the principle prohibiting vacuous quantification has no obvious bearing on whether or not a trace is left. Consider (81):

(81) a. *e* was solved the problem
     b. The problem was solved *t*

The problem is in complement position in D-Structure, as in (81a), receiving the θ-role assigned by *solve*. In S-Structure, as in (81b), *the problem* has been moved to subject position, but, unlike the situation with *Wh*-Movement, quantification is not involved here. Still, the Projection Principle demands that a trace be left in the complement of *solve*. Later (section 2.1.4) we will see independent evidence for the existence of the trace of NP-Movement.

Returning to (60e), there is a sense in which the trace in subject position of *visit* is demanded by the Projection Principle if we take it as a lexical property of *visit* that it has a θ-role to assign to a subject. But this leaves open the question whether a subject trace to which no θ-role is assigned is demanded. Consider (82):

(82) a. It is raining
     b. It is likely ＿＿＿ to be raining
        ↑＿＿＿＿＿＿＿┘

Does the movement in (82) leave behind any empty category? It is not at all obvious that there is any lexical property that must be projected for *rain*. Actually, there is some controversy about this. In some respects, the subjects of weather predicates behave as though they were θ-marked. Chomsky, for that reason, calls them "quasi arguments," but for the moment let us assume they are genuine expletives. The real issue is that we do not have anything that demands a subject for *rain* altogether, even when movement is not involved. However, it seems that clauses must have subjects, as (83) shows:

(83) *Is raining

In Spanish and Italian (83) is perfect, but in these languages we can say that there *is* a subject for the equivalent of (83)—it just happens to be null, since these are null-subject languages. English is not such a language; hence, if a subject position is present in (83), the subject must be overt. But why do we need a subject position? This is what the Extended Projection Principle is supposed to ensure: that all VPs have a subject.

If we are not happy with the examples with weather predicates (because of their potential quasi-argument status), we can reproduce this phenomenon with uncontroversial cases of expletives:

(84) a.   It is likely that John is here
     b.   *Is likely that John is here

If we want to eliminate the stipulative nature of the extension of the Projection Principle, we might want to pursue a Case-theoretic solution to this problem. Earlier we looked at the Case Filter, which ensures that lexical NPs are assigned Case. That is reminiscent of one part of the θ-Criterion: arguments must be assigned θ-roles. The θ-Criterion has another part—namely, that every θ-role must be assigned. In passing, we briefly considered a second Case requirement of the sort "Every Case must be assigned," analogous to the other half of the θ-Criterion. Assuming this, if we tried to generate any of the subjectless structures above, in each case a nominative Case would not be assigned, which would violate this requirement. Similarly, an ECM configuration would have an unrealized accusative Case. Unfortunately, there are still examples that this account will not cover. Imagine a predicate that has no θ-role to assign. In addition, imagine a configuration such that the hypothesized subject position of that predicate could not receive Case. If the Extended Projection Principle followed entirely from θ and Case requirements, then in that configuration a subject would not be required. In fact, that is not the case:

(85) a.   *I tried to be raining
     b.   *I tried to be likely that John is here

Thus, the Extended Projection Principle is needed in addition to a number of other constraints with which it partially (in fact largely) overlaps. In what follows, we will therefore assume that clauses do in fact always need subjects.

Chapter 2   Binding

2.1   Essentials of Binding Theory

2.1.1   Antecedence and Binding

In this chapter we will explore the Binding Conditions, which govern necessary or possible anaphoric relations between different NPs in a sentence. The formulation we will examine is roughly that of Chomsky 1981b, which had its roots in Chomsky 1973. In the latter paper Chomsky examined in detail one paradigmatic binding phenomenon, and I will essentially adopt his account of it here. Consider (1):

(1) John likes him

In a sentence like (1) *John* and *him* cannot be coreferential; that is, informally speaking, those two NPs cannot be used to designate the same person. We will also look at a phenomenon complementary to this one: Consider (2):

(2) John likes himself

The obvious fact here is that *John* and *himself* must be coreferential, exactly the opposite of what happens in (1).

Following standard terminology, I will refer to NPs like *him* as pronominals, and NPs like *himself* as anaphors. In addition to reflexives, the latter category includes reciprocal NPs like *each other*. Anaphors are items that, in some sense, must pick up their reference from something else in the sentence. Pronouns, on the other hand, are very different in their behavior. In fact, the examples we've considered seem to indicate that pronouns are not allowed to pick up their reference from something else in the sentence. But this is an illusion based on limited data. Consider instead a more complicated example:

(3) John believes that Mary likes him

In (3) *John* and *him* can clearly refer to the same person. What appears to happen is that the element the pronoun picks up its reference from (its *antecedent*) is not allowed to be "too close" to the pronoun. Thus, in (1) the antecedent of *him* is too close, whereas in (3) it is far enough away. We should consider this issue of closeness for the anaphor as well. What can the anaphor pick up its reference from? Consider (4):

(4) *John believes that Mary likes himself

To characterize the unacceptability of (4), we must say two things: first, that *John* in (4) is not close enough to be the antecedent of *himself*, and second, that *himself must* pick up its reference from something (and it must "agree" with that something).

Just looking at these examples, we find a complementarity between anaphors and what we may call for now *bound pronouns* (pronouns that pick up their reference from something else in the sentence). Thus far it is exactly in the cases where bound pronouns can occur that anaphors cannot, and vice versa. (5) is an informal way of characterizing this complementarity:

(5) a. An anaphor must have an antecedent nearby.
   b. A pronominal must not have an antecedent nearby.

(Notice that (5b) does not say that a pronominal must not have an antecedent; rather, if a pronominal has an antecedent, this element is not allowed to be nearby.) Now let us try to make (5) more precise. So far we are not sure what "antecedent" and "nearby" mean. For the moment, based on the paradigms we have just discussed, we will take "nearby" to mean "within the same clause." This will have to be revised soon, though. Let us turn now to the notion "antecedent."

In fact, to properly characterize this notion, we will need to explore both syntactic and semantic issues. The latter I will discuss in section 2.1.5. For now let us pretend that we know the semantic import of "antecedent," and let us concentrate on its syntactic properties. Let it be the case that NPs are freely assigned any index from the set of natural numbers. And now suppose that an antecedent of an NP is another NP with the same index. Given the characterization of "nearby" as "within the same clause," we are predicting that (6a) (a more articulated version of (2) with indexed NPs) is all right with respect to (5), whereas (6b) (a more articulated version of (4) with indexed NPs) is ruled out, again with respect to (5):

(6) a. John$_1$ likes himself$_1$
   b. *John$_1$ believes that Mary likes himself$_1$

In turn, we are predicting exactly the opposite for (7a) and (7b) (articulated versions of (1) and (3) with indexed NPs). That is, (7a), where the pronoun has an antecedent nearby, is rejected, whereas (7b), where the pronoun does not have an antecedent nearby, is fine:

(7) a. *John$_1$ likes him$_1$
   b. John$_1$ believes that Mary likes him$_1$

But problems arise with this simplistic first approximation. Consider (8):

(8) *John$_1$'s mother likes himself$_1$

Nothing we have said rules out the ungrammatical (8). There are three NPs in (8): *John, John's mother,* and *himself.* We are free to assign *John* and *himself* the same index. We might speculate that a possessive-type NP is not capable of serving as the antecedent of an anaphor. That, however, is incorrect:

(9) John's picture of himself is nice

(9) is perfect. Earlier we decided that *himself* needs an antecedent, and the only one it could have here is *John's*. Thus, a possessive NP is fully capable of being the antecedent of an anaphor. We must therefore seek some relevant structural difference between (8) and (9). Observe that *himself* in (9) is included in the same NP as *John*. Such is not the case in (8). This can be easily seen in the diagrams in (10) and (11) (omitting irrelevant details):

(10)

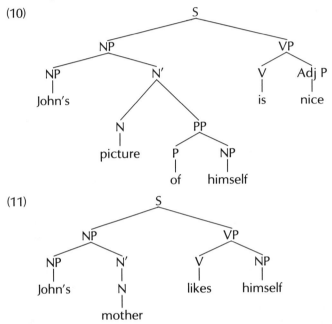

(11)

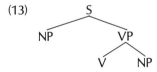

We will try now to capture the significance of this structural distinction.

Reinhart (1976) introduced the structural notion *c-command*.[1] This notion appears to play a central role in determining antecedence relations. C-command can be defined as follows:[2]

(12) For A, B nodes in a tree

A c-commands B iff every branching node dominating A dominates B and neither A nor B dominates the other.

Consider a tree like (13):

(13)

According to (12), the subject in (13) c-commands the object. The only branching node dominating the subject is S, and S dominates the object. The object, however, does not c-command the subject. There is a branching node dominating the object—namely, VP—which does not dominate the subject.

Let us now return to the trees in (10) and (11). In (11) the NP *John's mother* c-commands the object *himself*. However, *John* does not c-command *himself*. In particular, the first branching node dominating the NP *John*—namely, the NP *John's mother*—does not dominate *himself*. What we want to say, then, is that an NP A that does not c-command an NP B cannot be the antecedent of B (where B is an anaphor). This can be encoded as in the "Binding Condition" in (14):

(14) An anaphor must be bound within its clause.

"Binding" is defined as follows:

(15) A binds B iff
      (i) A c-commands B
   and (ii) A and B are coindexed.

It is easy to see that (14) correctly allows (9), while excluding (8). This is because, given the associated structural representations in (10) and (11), *John* in (10) does c-command *himself* and (since the two items are coindexed) therefore does bind *himself*. Thus, (9) satisfies (14). But in (11), *John* does not c-command *himself*, leaving the latter unbound, in violation of (14).

To capture the complementarity that we have observed between anaphors and pronominals—exactly where an anaphor must be bound, a pronominal must be free (= not bound)—we posit (14′) alongside (14):

(14′) A pronominal must be free within its clause.

Significantly, this complementarity carries over to the extension of the data we have now considered:

(16) a. *John$_1$'s mother likes himself$_1$
    b. John$_1$'s mother likes him$_1$

(17) a. John$_1$'s picture of himself$_1$ is nice
    b. *John$_1$'s picture of him$_1$ is nice

Condition (14) makes another prediction that is also confirmed. However, since there will be independent reasons why it is true, I will note the phenomenon here but will not present it as an argument for (14). Consider (18):

(18) *Himself$_1$ likes John$_1$

Himself and *John* have the same index in (18). If "antecedent" meant simply having the same index, given that both NPs in (18) are in the same clause, (18) should be fine. However, binding is stricter: in addition to coindexation binding requires c-command. *John* in (18) clearly does not c-command *himself*, and therefore does not bind *himself* either. We will see shortly, though, that there are other reasons to exclude (18) (having to do with the fact that *John* must also meet certain binding requirements).

The distribution of reciprocals (*each other, one another*) is essentially identical to that of reflexives:

(19) a. They like each other
     b. Their pictures of each other are nice

(20) a. *They believe Mary likes each other
     b. *Their mothers like each other
        (On the intended interpretation: "The mother of each child
        likes the other child")
     c. *Each other like them

It is thus natural to extend (14) to reciprocals, as is standardly done.

2.1.2 Toward the Characterization of Binding Domain

2.1.2.1 The Tensed Sentence Condition

Now that we have some reason to believe that we're at least on the
right track, let's consider some problems with (14) that will lead us to
a refinement. Consider the following paradigm:

(21) a. John believes himself to like Mary
     b. *John believes him to like Mary

The observed judgments are just the opposite of what (14) would predict,
since the minimal clause of the anaphor in (21a) and the pronominal in
(21b) is the embedded clause. We must revise (14) if we are to account
for these facts. It is already suggestive that the same complementarity
we have been seeing all along between anaphors and pronominals is
still present in (21). However, according to (14), the binding domain
(the domain in which the Binding Conditions are relevant) is the clause
of the bindee. We had good reasons for stating (14) that way—namely,
the ungrammaticality of (4) alongside the grammaticality of (3). So the
problem is how to distinguish (4) from (21a) and (3) from (21b).

Notice that alongside the grammatical (21a) and (22b) we have the
ungrammatical (22a):

(22) a. *John$_1$ believes that himself$_1$ likes Mary
     b. John$_1$ believes that he$_1$ likes Mary

(22a) is interesting because it contrasts minimally with (21a), suggesting
that an account of the difference between (22) and (21) in terms of
binding should rely on the fact that (22) is finite, whereas (21) is infinitival. This was, in essence, Chomsky's (1973) proposal. He characterized
the difference in question in terms of the *Tensed Sentence Condition*
(TSC). Given the current assumption that anaphors are base-generated
NPs (in other words, are not transformationally derived), this basically
amounts to requiring that the binder of an anaphor must be within the
same *finite* clause as the anaphor, and any binder of a pronominal must
be outside this domain.

Changing the binding domain from clauses to finite clauses gives the
correct results with respect to the paradigms we have considered. (21a)

is permitted because *himself* is bound within the same finite clause as *John*—namely, the matrix clause (the complement clause is not finite but infinitival). In turn, (21b) is ruled out because *him* is bound (hence, not free) within the same finite clause—again, the matrix clause. Where the embedded clause is finite, as in (3), (4), and (22), it will be the binding domain, exactly as before. Thus, there is good reason for somehow incorporating effects of the TSC into the Binding Conditions in (14). For now, let us try (23):

(23)   a.   An anaphor must be bound within the minimal finite clause containing it.
       b.   A pronominal must be free within the minimal finite clause containing it.

2.1.2.2   The Specified Subject Condition

One further refinement is needed. Consider (24):

(24)   a.   *John believes Mary to like himself
       b.   John believes Mary to like him

In (24) the only finite clause is the matrix sentence, and both *himself* and *him* are bound in that domain. (23) therefore predicts that (24a) should be acceptable, in satisfaction of (23a), whereas (24b) should not be, in violation of (23b). But exactly the reverse is true.

Chomsky (1973) proposed that the relevant difference between (24) and (21) is that in (24) a subject intervenes between the binder and the bindee, which is not the case in (21). That suggests a further condition, one stating that, as far as the Binding Conditions are concerned, a subject cannot intervene between the binder and the bindee. "Intervening" can be characterized as follows:

(25)   A intervenes between B and C if A c-commands C and does not c-command B.

This constraint, evidenced in (24), is independent of the TSC. Chomsky called it the *Specified Subject Condition* (SSC), and we will have to incorporate its effects into our characterization of binding domain. I will put off until section 2.3.2 the precise details of this incorporation.[3]

I want to add one more paradigm to the discussion, to demonstrate another effect of the SSC. Consider (26):

(26)   a.   John$_1$ likes Mary's pictures of him$_1$
       b.   *John$_1$ likes Mary's pictures of himself$_1$

Here, of course, the TSC cannot be at issue, since there is only one tensed sentence in the whole construction. Chomsky (1973) argued that sentences like (26) contain an intervening subject in the above sense. Following his (1970) account, Chomsky (1973) treated a genitive NP as the subject of an NP. That is, in the same way that the NP of S (the NP immediately attached to S) is the subject of that S, the NP of NP is the subject of that NP. In that case *Mary* in (26) is the subject of the NP headed by *pictures*. This subject intervenes between *John* and *him* or *himself*. (Note that *Mary* c-commands the object of *pictures*, *him* or *himself*, but does not c-command *John*.) So the SSC should be able to describe the facts in (26) in the same way as those in (24).

2.1.2.3 The Notion "Governing Category": Condition A and Condition B

Chomsky (1981b) proposed capturing the TSC and SSC effects with a new notion that has no immediately obvious connection with those two conditions. He presented a characterization of binding domain in terms of what he called a *governing category* (henceforth, GC). Thus, he stated the Binding Conditions as in (27):

(27) a. An anaphor must be bound in its governing category.

    b. A pronominal must be free in its governing category.

Binding Condition (27a) is generally called Condition A, and (27b) is generally called Condition B.

Let us turn now to the definition of GC. We are going to build this definition gradually. The first attempt will seem rather far removed from what we have been considering so far. Later on, though, we will be forced to revise this notion in a way that is quite reminiscent of older versions of what I called "binding domain."

We have seen both Ss and NPs serving as binding domains. Thus, we would expect that GC will be at least an NP or S. In addition, Chomsky proposed that for an NP or S to count as a relevant binding domain, it must also contain a *governor* for the bindee. That additional clause is crucial, as we will see:

(28) α is the GC for β iff α is the minimal NP or S containing β and a governor for β.

Now reconsider (21a) from the point of view of (28). We correctly allow (21a) because the embedded S is not the minimal S containing *himself* and a governor for *himself*. The governor for *himself* is *believe*, its exceptional Case marker. Thus, the minimal S containing both *himself* and its governor is the matrix clause; and in this binding domain the anaphor is bound by *John*. In the same way, we correctly rule out (21b). In that case *him* is bound within its GC (still the matrix S), in violation of (27b).

Further, we can account for the SSC effects in (24). The GC for *himself* in (24a) is the embedded clause, because *like*, the verb of that clause, governs the anaphor. This element is not bound inside that embedded S, and therefore the structure violates (27a). If *himself* is replaced by *him*, as in (24b), the sentence will be ruled in by (27b).

Now consider (22a). Here we want the lower S to be the GC for *himself*, so that this element will be free in that domain in violation of (27a)—thus predicting the ungrammaticality of the sentence. The question is whether the embedded S contains a governor for *himself*. However, if Case is assigned under government, the subject of a finite clause (*himself* in this instance) is governed within that clause. The usual assumption is that Agr in Infl assigns nominative Case, which makes a finite clause invariably a GC for the subject of this clause. In this way, we also rule in (22b), because this sentence contains the pronominal *he* instead of the anaphor *himself*. (27b) will be satisfied for the same reason that (27a) was not: the lower finite clause is the GC.

Finally, consider the NP examples in (26). *Himself* in (26b) receives Case inside the NP. Therefore, by hypothesis, this anaphor is governed within that NP, presumably by *of*. Thus, the NP is the GC for *himself*. But the binder of *himself* is outside the NP, and therefore (26b) violates (27a). Exactly the opposite happens in (26a), in accord with the general complementarity we have observed thus far.

- *Kawai:* But this incorrectly predicts that (29) is ungrammatical:

(29) John likes pictures of himself

Lasnik: You are absolutely right. And this is precisely the type of problem that will lead us to redefine (28). So hold on to your example for now (but note that what we are missing is a way of encoding the SSC into (28); that is, the relevance of the notion "subject" is not captured).   •

This is an appropriate time to point out some more general problems as well. The Binding Theory is designed to force anaphors and bound pronouns to be in complementary distribution. That the theory predicts this distribution is both a virtue and a defect: a virtue, because it is overwhelmingly true; a defect, because it is not always true. Consider (30) in this regard:

(30) a.   John$_1$ saw pictures of himself$_1$
     b. ?John$_1$ saw pictures of him$_1$

(30a) is perfect, as noted above. (30b) is somewhat deviant, but it seems substantially better than a Binding Theory violation of the sort we have been considering. The problem is this: regardless of our definition of GC, if this domain is the same for pronominals and anaphors, and if the conditions in (27) hold of the grammar, there is simply no way we can predict that both (30a) and (30b) are acceptable. With a "small" GC, the pronominal will be good and the reflexive bad. With a "large" GC, the pronominal will be bad and the reflexive good. At best we will be fifty percent right, whichever way we design the theory.

- *McKee:* Are "picture NPs" like the ones we've been discussing the only ones that give us that kind of problem?

Lasnik: Well, English has another construction that seems to present this same difficulty, namely, possessives:

(31) a. They read [their books]
    b. They read [each other's books]

Both examples in (31) are perfectly grammatical—the same paradoxical situation we saw in (30). Notice, however, that we can't have a reflexive there:

(32) *They read themselves' books

This is surprising, since a reciprocal *is* allowed. Anderson (1979) argues that in fact the position where possessives appear is one where only anaphors are possible, and not bound pronouns, contrary to appearances. That is, the GC for the possessive NPs in (31) is the sentence, rather than the immediately containing NP. (31b) is thus directly allowed. As for (31a), Anderson suggests that morphological suppletion is at work there, giving something (*their*) that looks like a pronoun but is potentially a reflexive. So essentially Anderson argues that the genitive form of *themselves* is pronounced *their* in English. Under this proposal, *their*, for example, is lexically ambiguous. It can be a pronoun or, by suppletion, a reflexive.   •

2.1.3   Condition C

2.1.3.1   R-Expressions

We have been examining a domain in which anaphors must be bound and pronominals must be free. But of course this does not exhaust the class of nominal expressions. At this point I would like to consider full referring-expressions (R-expressions), such as *John*, which also have a specific binding requirement. This requirement is different from that of anaphors, which we would expect because, in some pretheoretic sense, anaphors need antecedents and *John* doesn't. But the requirement in question is different from that of pronominals as well. The latter can be bound, as long as the binder lies outside the GC of the pronominal. R-expressions have a similar but even stricter requirement. Consider (33):

(33) *John₁ likes John₁

From (33) it is apparent that a name, like a pronoun, cannot be bound in its GC. However, (34) illustrates that a name cannot appear even in some contexts where a pronoun can:

(34) a. *John₁ thinks John₁ likes Mary
    b. John₁ thinks he₁ likes Mary
    c. *John₁ thinks Mary likes John₁
    d. John₁ thinks Mary likes him₁

Note that (34b) and (34d), where *he/him* is used instead of *John*, are perfect. However, the versions of these sentences with *John* ((34a) and (34c)) are not possible.

Compare (34a–d) with (35):

(35) ?After John$_1$ walked in, John$_1$ sat down

I take it that (35) is slightly odd, perhaps because of the desire not to repeat R-expressions. But the impossible cases in (33) and (34) are much worse than (35), so something more must be involved.

Another case to consider is (36):

(36) a. *John$_1$ can't stand John$_1$'s teacher
     b. John$_1$'s teacher can't stand John$_1$

This paradigm strongly suggests that c-command is involved in the constraint on R-expressions. We will discuss further evidence shortly. Notice that the impossibility of the cooccurrence of *John* with another *John* "nearby" in (36a) cannot be explained by the constraint against repetition alluded to earlier. This is because (36b), with equally close instances of *John*, is virtually perfect. In fact, (36b) can be made absolutely perfect if we substitute an "anaphoric epithet" for the second *John*; under the same treatment (36a) is still impossible. Thus:

(37) a. *John$_1$ can't stand the bastard$_1$'s teacher
     b. John$_1$'s teacher can't stand the bastard$_1$

Though anaphoric epithets are in some sense potentially "anaphoric," their reference being determined by another NP, they have the binding properties of R-expressions (see Lasnik 1976 for discussion). Note that the oddness that repetition might create disappears completely in these cases. This is further confirmed for a version of (35) with an anaphoric epithet in place of the second occurrence of *John*:

(38) After John$_1$ walked in, the bastard$_1$ sat down

Significantly, if we replace *John* with *the bastard* in all the really bad cases we have seen so far, the resulting sentences are still bad:

(39) a. *John$_1$ thinks the bastard$_1$ likes Mary
     b. *John$_1$ thinks Mary likes the bastard$_1$

As hinted before, in all of the bad cases with two R-expressions, binding is involved; that is, one of the pair of coreferential NPs c-commands the other. On the other hand, the good cases do not involve binding, since in all of them each R-expression is buried inside some phrase and therefore cannot c-command the other R-expression. This, together with the lack of GC involvement, indicates that we need a further binding requirement, one that is particular to R-expressions. Such a requirement had its roots in Lasnik 1976 and was incorporated into Chomsky 1981b as in (40) (usually referred to as Condition C):

(40) An R-expression must be free.

It is clear that (40) rules out all of the bad cases we have seen so far, since the R-expression in all of these cases is not free, being c-commanded by a coindexed NP.

An interesting question arises when we look at the nature not just of the bindee (as we have been doing so far) but also of the binder. Thus, consider (41):

(41) a. **He₁ likes John₁
     b. **He₁ thinks John₁ likes Mary
     c. **He₁ thinks Mary likes John₁
     d. **He₁ can't stand John₁'s teacher

The examples in (41) seem worse even than the versions of these examples with *John* in place of *he*. But nothing thus far predicts this, since our theory (essentially that of Chomsky 1981b) is constructed so as to constrain the distribution of a bindee irrespective of the nature of the binder. So the fact that *he* in (41) (a pronominal) and not *John* (an R-expression) is the binder of the illegal R-expression is irrelevant for our theory. In this respect, the theory seems to be missing a significant distinction. This speculation is further supported by facts from certain other languages. In Thai, for instance, examples in which an R-expression is bound by another R-expression are perfect:

(42) a. cɔɔn₁ chɔ̂ɔp cɔɔn₁
        'John likes John'
     b. cɔɔn₁ khít wâa cɔɔn₁ chàlàat
        'John thinks that John is smart'

This suggests that there is no Condition C in Thai. However, examples like those in (41) are still bad in Thai:

(43) a. *khǎw₁ chɔ̂ɔp cɔɔn₁
        'He likes John'
     b. *khǎw₁ khít wâa cɔɔn₁ chàlàat
        'He thinks that John is smart'

Evidently we are missing something involving properties of the binder. In Thai, apparently an R-expression may be bound (42), but it may not be bound by a pronoun (43). In English, since the more general constraint does hold, the more specific constraint is difficult to isolate. But the somewhat worse status of (41) as compared to the other Condition C cases examined suggests that English has both constraints. I will not explore a version of the theory embodying this distinction here, but the idea is worth pursuing.

2.1.3.2   Strong Crossover

Let us now consider a phenomenon first discussed by Postal (1971). Consider (44a), with its associated "semantic" representation in (44b):

(44) a. Who₁ t₁ thinks Mary likes him₁
     b. For which x, x a person, x thinks Mary likes x

Compare this example with (45a), with the same semantic representation:

(45) a. *Who₁ does he₁ think Mary likes t₁
     b. For which x, x a person, x thinks Mary likes x

(45) is completely impossible. Descriptively, *he* in (45) cannot be a bound-variable pronoun, as *him* is in (44). Instead, *he* in the context in question can only be used deictically. Postal called this phenomenon *crossover* because, as he put it, one of a pair of coreferential expressions crosses over another via *Wh*-Movement, which is not the case in (44).[4] We can easily see this if we examine the movement of the operator in each of the examples:

(46) a. Who   [*t* thinks Mary likes *him*]
　　　　↑___|

　　b. Who does [*he* think Mary likes *t*]
　　　　↑_____|

In (46b), but not in (46a), *who* "crosses over" the pronominal. Wasow (1972) proposed a way to deduce this constraint against crossover from independent properties of the constructions involved. Let us look at his analysis.

In accord with Trace Theory, let us assume that *who* leaves a trace when it moves. This trace is obviously an NP, a fact ensured by Trace Theory, which essentially says that, upon movement, an item leaves behind a syntactic silent copy of itself. Now, what type of NP is this trace? We have discussed three types of NPs: anaphors, pronouns, and R-expressions. Which of these does a *wh*-trace pattern like? Wasow observed that the ungrammaticality of (45) patterns exactly with the ungrammaticality of a more familiar case, (47):

(47) *He_1 thinks Mary likes $John_1$

In turn, Wasow observed that the grammaticality of (44) patterns with the grammaticality of another familiar case, (48):

(48) $John_1$ thinks Mary likes him_1

Wasow's point was that a *wh*-trace behaves like (what is now called) an R-expression. That is, a *wh*-trace must obey Condition C of the Binding Theory. This immediately accounts for (45a) because in that example the trace is bound by *he*. Note that this account of so-called strong crossover demands that Condition C be applicable to derived structure, a conclusion we reached on other grounds in section 1.3.2. Furthermore, to the extent that this analysis is successful, it provides a second argument for the basic tenet of Trace Theory—that movement rules leave traces.[5] If there were no traces, then there would be no R-expression for Condition C to constrain.

This analysis of strong crossover raises one obvious question. If a *wh*-trace is an R-expression, and if an R-expression must be free, then how do we allow a simple case like (49)?

(49) Who_1 t_1 left

Surely, the trace of *who* is bound here by this operator (in fact, this binding is obligatory, since otherwise the constraint against vacuous quantification would be violated). But then we are predicting that (49) violates Condition C as stated in (40), since, by hypothesis, the trace of *who* is an R-expression. The question is how to reconcile the grammaticality of (49) with the ungrammaticality of (45).

The standard way to do this is to state Binding Conditions in terms of A-binding, and not $\bar{\text{A}}$-binding. That is, we will assume that relevant binders for our purposes are NPs in argument position, not in operator position. Thus, a condition like (40) will be restated as in (50):

(50) An R-expression must be A-free.

By (50), an R-expression may not be bound by something in an A-position. This gives the correct results. (45) will be a Condition C violation, because there the trace of *who* is A-bound by *he*, an NP in subject position. (49), on the other hand, will be permitted, because there the trace of *who* is only $\bar{\text{A}}$-bound, by *who*, and is not A-bound by anything. It is harder to find clear evidence that the other Binding Conditions involve only A-binding as well, but, in the absence of counterevidence, I will adopt the simplest hypothesis here and assume that the Binding Conditions are uniform in this regard.

This provides an elegant analysis of strong crossover, though not an entirely unproblematic one (see section 5.2.5). Clearly, the best aspect of this analysis is that it does not add any new stipulation to the theory but makes use of an independently motivated principle, Condition C. It does rely on the claim that *wh*-traces are R-expressions. But if all NPs must be "something," R-expression seems a not unreasonable candidate.

2.1.4 The Binding Status of NP-Traces

We may now ask whether *all* traces are R-expressions. In particular, what are the traces of NP-Movement?

Consider (51):

(51) John$_1$ was arrested t_1

This is a perfectly well-formed sentence. *John* and its trace are coindexed, if movement entails coindexation (as Chomsky (1981b) assumes). Then we can establish one thing immediately: the trace of NP-Movement cannot be an R-expression; otherwise, it would violate Condition C in the perfect (51). We can go further than this: the trace of NP-Movement cannot be a pronominal either. Not only is the trace in (51) A-bound; it is in fact A-bound in its GC (namely, the minimal S including the trace and its governor, *arrested*). We are thus led to the conclusion that the trace in question is an anaphor, working under the assumption alluded to earlier that every NP must be something. In fact, Chomsky (1973, 1976) presented a certain amount of independent evidence that NP-traces are anaphors. Recall that a lexical anaphor must be bound in the domain determined by the TSC and SSC (that is, its GC). Chomsky showed, in effect, that exactly in these domains an NP-trace also must be bound. Thus:

(52) a. *John$_1$ believes that himself$_1$ is clever
   b. *John$_1$ was believed that t_1 is clever
   c. John$_1$ believes himself$_1$ to be clever
   d. John$_1$ was believed t_1 to be clever

As we have seen before, the subject of a finite clause can never be an anaphor, since it can never have an A-binder within that clause (its GC). Take then the interesting ungrammaticality of (52b). The θ-Criterion is not violated in (52b), since the infinitival version of (52b) in (52d) is perfect. So what could be going on? If the trace of NP-Movement is an anaphor, it cannot appear in subject position of a finite clause, as we see in (52a) for lexical anaphors: it will violate Binding Condition A. This is further confirmed by the grammaticality of (52c) alongside the grammaticality of (52d). As we have seen, the subject of an infinitival clause in an ECM site *can* be an anaphor (its GC is extended to the higher clause, because the exceptional governor is included in the higher, not the lower, clause). Thus, (52d) is perfect. But this is also the case with (52c), which is again what we expect if the NP-trace is an anaphor.

Once again, as in the Condition C treatment of strong crossover, we have evidence for traces. A Condition A account of constraints on NP-Movement demands that the structure contain an anaphoric element (in this case a trace). Furthermore, once again we have evidence for application of a Binding Condition to derived structure. If Condition A were only relevant to D-Structure, then obviously it could not capture the distributional similarity between lexical anaphors and NP-traces, since at D-Structure the latter do not even exist. There is, in fact, further evidence for this conclusion. We have just considered ungrammatical cases of NP-Movement that would not violate Condition A at D-Structure. Alongside these, there are *grammatical* cases of NP-Movement whose representations at D-Structure would *violate* Condition A. The grammatical (53) satisfies all binding requirements:

(53) The men$_1$ seem to each other$_1$ [t_1 to be clever]

But its D-Structure form, (53'), would have an anaphor *each other* that is not bound at all, hence not bound in its GC:

(53') e seem to each other [the men to be clever]

Once again, then, it is derived structure, rather than D-Structure, that is relevant to the Binding Conditions.

2.1.5   The Interpretation of Indices

Thus far we have been examining the syntax of binding, that is, the syntactic conditions under which various types of nominals must be bound or must be free. However, a "purely" syntactic theory cannot really explain certain facts, including most of the very facts that we set out to explain. For example, consider again a sentence like (54):

(54) a. *He$_1$ likes him$_1$
     b. He$_1$ likes him$_2$

We want to account for something about the meaning of this sentence, in particular that *he* and *him* are not coreferential. Under the indexation in (54a), the structure is ruled out because *him* is bound in its GC in violation of Condition B. But what does the theory say about the indexation in (54b)? Clearly, Binding Conditions do not have anything to say about this second representation, since nothing binds the pronoun; that is, no Binding Condition is violated. Now why can't that well-formed representation have the impossible coreferential reading?

- *Uriagereka:* But what do the indices mean?
  Lasnik: Whatever we say they mean, and so far we haven't said anything. So the problem is precisely that we haven't explained that the only possible interpretation of the sentence *He likes him* is that *he* and *him* are different people. We've explained that (54a) is out and (54b) is in, but not what (54b) means.   •

  I think the lack of semantic import for relations between indices is in fact a serious deficiency that ends up nearly undermining the Binding Theory in Chomsky 1981b. The theory is constructed in such a way that the facts we are considering are not explained. Chomsky suggests that this is a virtue in that the theory does not make use of difficult semantic notions like disjoint reference. But a theory that says nothing about semantics cannot explain a semantic fact.

- *Kawai:* So indices are simply integers that we assign randomly, and furthermore, we have to state explicitly that each NP needs an index.
  Lasnik: Yes. We clearly have to say that each NP needs an index since the theory makes crucial use of indices. An NP without an index could not be evaluated in terms of the theoretical devices we have been considering. For example, Conditions B and C would never take effect with unindexed NPs. As for the idea that indices are assigned randomly, that is the null hypothesis, as opposed to an algorithm saying "Give an NP a particular index in a particular configuration."   •

  An index by itself means nothing. Instead, the relationship between NPs in terms of whether they have the same or different indices is what has some theoretical weight. Consider for instance (55):

(55) a. John$_1$ left
     b. John$_{37}$ left

(55a) and (55b) are different formal objects in some sense, but the semantics will treat them as identical: it is not that we find all the Johns in the world and number them. I think this is the way we want things to be, since we use language to talk about objects that do not (or even cannot) exist, as well as about things that we cannot count.

In Lasnik 1981, I argued, first, that some semantic principles must be added to the theory if it is to be able to explain semantic facts, and second, that the syntax of the theory in Chomsky 1981b was designed in such a way that it was impossible to impose the right semantic principles to get the right results. This has to do with how complicated the mapping between the syntax and the semantics has to be. Apparently, it has to be rather more complicated than Chomsky suggested. Consider what one simple mapping might look like:[6]

(56) a. If two NPs have the same index, they are coreferential.

b. If two NPs have different indices, they are disjoint in reference.

We can now account for the fact that we set out to explain: that in (54) *he* and *him* cannot be coreferential. To satisfy Condition B, the indices will have to be distinct—but then (56b) will demand that these two NPs be disjoint in reference. Consider now (57):

(57) John$_1$ likes himself$_1$

Condition A guarantees that *John* and *himself* are coindexed here. But what tells us that (57) cannot mean "John likes Bill"? Nothing does, unless we add a "semantic" rule like (56a); and so forth.

We could imagine stating (56b) in terms of noncoreference, instead of disjoint reference. To compare these two proposals, we first need to understand these two notions more clearly. Consider the sets in (58a), where lowercase letters stand for individuals, and suppose the sets are designated by the NPs *A* and *B*:

(58) a. $A = \{a, b, c\}$ $\quad$ $B = \{d, e, f\}$
b. $A = \{a, b, c\}$ $\quad$ $B = \{a, b, c\}$
c. $A = \{a, b, c\}$ $\quad$ $B = \{c, d, e\}$

A and *B* in (58a) are disjoint in reference and consequently noncoreferential as well. To be coreferential means to designate exactly the same thing. But in (58a) there is no overlap between the sets (they are disjoint in reference), so of course they do not designate the same thing. Now consider (58b). There, since both sets include the same individuals, *A* and *B* are two coreferential NPs and hence are nondisjoint (that is, overlapping). If all the cases were like (58a) and (58b), the mapping between the syntax and the semantics would be trivial, and it would be easy to make the theory work (not without semantic rules, but with very simple ones). But there is one more relevant case. In (58c) *A* and *B* are not coreferential, because some individuals in A are not in B. Nor are they disjoint: some individuals are in both sets. If language makes crucial use of all these set-theoretic options, then our theory will be inadequate. If the theory has only an integer index, and if two NPs either have the same index or have different indices, then there is no way to describe three possibilities.[7] Notice that if we were dealing exclusively with singular NPs, there would be no problem, because for singulars, noncoreference and disjoint reference are equivalent. The interesting difficulties will arise with plurals.

Let us turn, then, to binding interactions involving at least one plural NP. First consider a case that works:

(59) *We$_1$ like me$_1$

       1   2

The oddness of such an example is a phenomenon discussed by Postal (1966). Under the first indexation, our theory has two ways of ruling this sentence out. Semantic rule (56a) rejects it because it contains two NPs with the same index, which must therefore be coreferential; but *we* and *me* by their lexical meanings cannot be coreferential. Binding Condition B also rules the representation out because *me*, which is a pronominal, is bound in its GC. The Binding Theory says nothing about the second indexation, since the pronominal is not bound. But semantic rule (56b) rejects the representation, because the NPs must be disjoint in reference. Yet if we look at the meaning of *we* (which includes the speaker and someone else) and *me* (which includes only the speaker), we can easily see that these two NPs are not permitted to be disjoint in reference in a particular utterance.

Now here comes the problem:

(60) We$_1$ think that I$_1$ will win

       1   2

I take it that (60) is perfectly well formed, in contrast with (59). Thus, the syntactic and the semantic rules must allow it. Consider the first indexation in (60). The Binding Theory says that the representation is fine, because the binder of the pronoun is outside its GC. But semantic rule (56a) creates the same situation as before, since *we* and *I* cannot be coreferential—that is, semantic rule (56a) contradicts the lexical requirements of these pronouns. Let us then try the second indexation. The Binding Theory says nothing about this case, since nothing binds anything. But now semantic rule (56b) still creates the same problem, since again the lexicon is contradicting a semantic rule. The problem is that (60) is perfectly grammatical, yet we have no representation left for it.

Will it solve the problem to change the semantic rules in (56)? Consider (56a′) as a possible modification to (56a):

(56) a′. If two NPs have the same index, the set denoted by one of the NPs includes the set denoted by the other NP.

This modification certainly permits (60) in the coindexation representation, since the reference of *we* does include the reference of *I*. But now consider (61):

(61) *We$_1$ like myself$_1$

(The interesting case is of course the one in which both NPs have the same index—the other one will be ruled out by Condition A.) This representation satisfies Condition A (the anaphor is bound in its GC). What about the semantics? The only relevant condition here is (56a′), but surely the reference of *we* (the speaker and some additional person or persons) includes the reference of *myself* (the speaker). Evidently, then, the stricter semantic rule (56a) was the right semantic rule. But such a rule was too strict to account properly for (60). The problem is really that we cannot both accept (60) and reject (61). If the semantic rule is (56a), we reject both; if it is (56a′), we accept both.

At first blush, it might appear that the problem of (61) can be solved in essentially morphological terms. Suppose that we adopt (56a′), thus allowing (61) by Condition A. In addition to binding requirements, anaphors are plausibly subject to an agreement requirement:

(62) An anaphor must agree in syntactic features with its antecedent.

(61) will now be ruled out for purely formal reasons (even though it would not be the Binding Theory that would reject it). Although this is reasonable, I do not think it is the general answer, in light of cases like (63):

(63) They$_1$ like themselves$_1$

Clearly, there is agreement here. Both the anaphor and its antecedent are third person plural. But now suppose that A in (64) is the reference of *they* and B is the reference of *themselves*:

(64) A = $\{a, b, c\}$ B = $\{b, c\}$

(63) clearly cannot grammatically describe that situation. But semantic rule (56a′) would not have a way of ruling out this representation—and in this case, as we just saw, we cannot appeal to some purely formal agreement requirement.

Let us finally look at the one other standard case where these kinds of considerations come into play—so-called split antecedents:

(65) John told Bill that they should leave

We know that *John* and *Bill* cannot have the same index, since that would violate Binding Condition C. We must give *they* some index, and there are three possibilities: the same index as *John*, the same index as *Bill*, or a different index from either of them. But now look at semantic rule (56b), which was motivated by (59). Since by (56b) NPs with different indices must be disjoint in reference, the third indexing possibility entails that *they*, *Bill*, and *John* are all disjoint in reference. That is fair enough: the sentence has a reading like that (where, say, Mary and Susan are the ones that should leave). But the other two indexations are hopeless if we assume semantic rule (56a). Neither *John* nor *Bill* can be coreferential with *they*. Even semantic rule (56a′), which we already had reason to reject, will not suffice here. With (56a′), we could get a reading of (65) in which *they* includes *John*, and another in which *they* includes *Bill*, but not one in which *they* includes both *John* and *Bill*. Such a reading would require that all three NPs be coindexed, clearly an absurdity. Thus, there is no way to represent split antecedence.

Clearly, the general problem is overlap in reference and, more specifically, *inclusion* (the relation whereby the reference of one NP includes the reference of another). There is simply no good way to deal with that situation in the simple indexing framework. In fact, this is an unsolved problem in the framework we are examining, that of Chomsky (1981b).[8]

• *McNulty:* So, going back to the conceptual issue about indices, do we want to explain *both* the fact that the sentences we have been discussing are or are not grammatical and the fact that they mean such and such, or only the latter?

Lasnik: Well, my view is that for lexical anaphors, pronouns, and R-expressions, the indices exist only to the extent that they let us explain what are essentially semantic facts. If they did not let us explain these facts, it would be unclear whether they exist at all. Thus, as we have seen, semantic rules assigning meaning to indexing relations are required—a complication, if you will, but a crucial one. Not everyone sees things this way. Chomsky (1981a) argued that the version of the theory he presented there (essentially the same as the one in Chomsky 1981b) is to be preferred to other imaginable alternatives (such as those in Chomsky 1980 or Lasnik 1976) on grounds of simplicity. The theory is simple in that it has only a two-way indexing distinction and it does not have rules referring to semantic notions such as disjoint reference. But to the extent that there are phenomena exactly involving these notions, the theory is empirically inadequate.   •

2.2   Explaining the Distribution of PRO: A Case Study

We have looked at NP- and *wh*-traces. These are examples of empty categories. They are categories that we know are there: they function as anaphors; the Projection Principle tells us they are there; and so on. But they are silent, hence the name "empty categories." We should probably call them "silent categories," because they are not really empty. They have every syntactic feature that other categories have—the only thing they lack is a phonetic matrix.

2.2.1   *Motivating PRO*

There are other empty categories besides traces. We discussed one earlier with respect to the *wanna* contraction paradigm, examining sentences like (66a):

(66) a. I want [*e* to visit you]
     b. They want [*e* to visit each other]

(Recall that *e* stands for empty category.) In Chomsky's (1973) model there was little conceptual basis for saying that examples like (66a, b) contain an empty category.[9] But in his (1981b) framework the Projection Principle demands the empty category under consideration. The θ-Criterion says, for instance, that *visit each other* in (66b) is a predicate that has a subject θ-role to assign, so there must be an argument that can receive that θ-role. Because of the Projection Principle, we know that this must be true even at S-Structure, so there must be some category in the position in question. What category is it? We know it is not a *wh*-trace; no *Wh*-Movement took place. Could it be an NP-trace? It could be just in case there was an NP that could have moved from this position. But the subject of the matrix clause could not have moved from there, because the subject position of the matrix clause is also a θ-position; thus, it must have been filled at D-Structure. And the same is true for *each other*. If no NP could have moved, then we are dealing not with a trace but with a different type of empty category, which Chomsky called *PRO*. PRO is an argument, obviously, since it receives a θ-role. Thus, we have motivated a base-generated argument empty category.

2.2.2   The Distribution of PRO

Next let us investigate the distributional properties of PRO. Consider (67):

(67) I tried [[PRO to understand the problem]]

Since *to understand the problem* has a θ-role to assign, there must be a subject of the predicate. Consider (68):

(68) It is important [[PRO to understand the problem]]

Again, the predicate in question must have a subject. But now notice the following contrast: whereas (66) and (67) involve something like binding (PRO has a structurally represented antecedent), PRO in (68) does not seem to have a structurally represented antecedent.

The null hypothesis would be that if PRO is an argument, it can be inserted in any position to which a θ-role is assigned. In fact, that is false. Consider (69):

(69) a. *PRO eats
      b. It is important [[PRO to eat]]

(69b) shows that PRO is the kind of argument that can receive the subject θ-role that *eat* assigns. However, (69a) is ungrammatical. Let us collect some more environments where PRO cannot occur but where the θ-Criterion is apparently satisfied:

(70) *I spoke to PRO

Neither (69a) nor (70) is incoherent. If, as is often claimed, the meaning of (68) is something like (71),

(71) It is important for somebody or other to understand the problem

why could (69a) not mean (72) or (70), (73)?

(72) Somebody or other eats

(73) I spoke to somebody or other

Evidently, something is going on here that must be explained.

2.2.3 Two Hypotheses on the Distribution of PRO

2.2.3.1 Case

One popular approach to the problem we have just seen is to say that PRO is not allowed to have Case. Although this is not implausible (given that PRO has no morphological realization), it does not seem to work completely. Observe that there are environments where lexical NPs are impossible exactly because they cannot have Case, but where PRO is still impossible. Consider (74):

(74) *I like very much Bill

A standard analysis of (74) is that *Bill* cannot receive Case, since it is not adjacent to *like* (see section 1.4). But then, under the Case approach, (74) should be fine with PRO. It is not:

(75) *I like very much PRO

There are more complicated examples illustrating the same general point. Consider a D-Structure form like (76):

(76) *e* was arrested PRO

This form can undergo NP-Preposing, as in (77):

(77) *PRO was arrested *t*

And if PRO is not permitted to receive Case, we know how to rule (77) out, since the subject position is (nominative) Case-marked in (77). But suppose we had not done the movement. There is a descriptive generalization that null expletives are not allowed in English, however that might be explained. (76) would run afoul of this generalization. But we can insert an overt expletive, as in (78):

(78) a. *It was arrested PRO
     b. *There was arrested PRO

What is wrong with (78)? PRO is an argument, and it is in an argument position receiving a θ-role. By hypothesis, PRO is not allowed to receive Case. But object of a passive verb is exactly a position to which Case is not assigned. So far, then, we have no explanation for (75) and (78). That is, descriptively, it does seem that PRO is not allowed to receive Case. But if that is the only principle, we have not explained the entire distribution of PRO.

- *Uriagereka:* Under Pesetsky's (1982a) analysis of *wanna* contraction, we have no explanation for a sentence like (79), if not having Case is the only requirement on PRO:

(79) *I believe [to be here PRO]

Lasnik: Yes. But the problem lies not so much with his analysis of *wanna* contraction as with his conception of the whole grammar. The basic idea that he borrowed from Stowell (1981) is that there are no phrase structure rules. Instead, various principles determine where the different elements have to be. But as long as we construct a structure consistent with all of those, then everything should be all right. (79) is consistent with all the principles we have, since PRO surely does not need Case. But then (79) should be grammatical.[10] So we now have three problematic cases.

2.2.3.2   Government

Do all of our unresolved cases have a common property? Chomsky argued that they do. It is related to Case but is more general. In fact, it is *government*. Unlike government, Case requires adjacency; it also requires a Case assigner. The unresolved examples either lack adjacency—that is the situation in (75) and (79)—or lack government by a Case assigner—that is the situation in (78). But all the ungrammatical examples we have considered so far do exhibit government. This is immediately obvious in the situations where Case was assigned, since Case is assigned under government. But it is also true in (75), (78), and (79). On the other hand, in all the grammatical cases PRO is not governed.

   This leads to the prediction that in a position where a lexical NP is possible, PRO should be impossible. But in fact there are constructions that allow both; for instance:

(80) a. I want John to win
      b. I want PRO to win

Verbs of the *try* type or of the *believe* type, on the other hand, fit nicely with the proposed generalization:

(81) a.   I tried PRO to win
      b. *I tried John to win

(82) a.   I believe John to have won
      b. *I believe PRO to have won

If PRO is ungoverned in (81a), then *John* will be Caseless in (81b), hence the ungrammaticality of the latter example. The reverse situation obtains in (82). But the *want* type verbs are a problem. Notice that the account in terms of Case would have exactly the same problem as the account in terms of government. One approach to this is suggested in note 8 of chapter 1. Another possible approach might be to suppose that with *want*, S'-Deletion is optional. There would then be three cases: obligatory S'-Deletion—*believe*; no S'-Deletion—*try*; optional S'-deletion—*want*. This too raises certain problems that I will put aside (see the discussion in section 1.5.1).

• *McNulty:* We can say either (83a) or (83b), and both are grammatical. Is that a problem?

(83) a. ?His running away upset Bill
    b. PRO running away upset Bill

Lasnik: It is. And again, neither approach (Case or government) really allows that. (83a) is somewhat worse than (83b), but surely not as bad as (81b).

There are two more cases in which the description in terms of government is more accurate than the one in terms of Case. Consider (84):

(84) a. John's destruction of the building
    b. John's destruction the building

Chomsky (1970) proposes that the *of* is inserted and that (84a) derives from something like (84b). A fancier way of saying this is that since *the building* needs Case, and nouns in English do not assign Case, then *of* must be inserted to assign Case. Obviously, in such an approach to *Of* Insertion, it must be considered optional. If it is considered obligatory, we have an unnecessary redundancy: if *of* is not inserted, the resulting representation violates the Case Filter. But if insertion is optional, it would be possible to generate (85) if the only requirement on PRO were that it cannot have Case:

(85) *John's destruction PRO

But this *is* a configuration of government. A noun governs its complement just as a verb governs its complement. The same kind of argument can be constructed with adjectives, the other major category that does not assign Case. For example, one standard analysis of (86a) involves a D-Structure representation like (86b):

(86) a. I am proud of John
    b. I am proud John

But if *Of* Insertion is optional, then PRO should be possible, under the account we first considered:

(87) *I am proud PRO
    (meaning something like "I am proud of someone or other")

Again, if PRO must be ungoverned, then (87) is ruled out, because this is a configuration of government.

Finally, in (88) *belief* presumably governs PRO in just the same way that *believe* does in (82b) (see section 6.4):

(88) *My belief [PRO to be intelligent]

A constraint forbidding governed PRO would account for all of these cases.

2.2.4 Deriving the Fact That PRO Must Be Ungoverned

If we only went this far, we would have made a fair amount of progress. To say that PRO must be ungoverned works descriptively, and it is not obviously more stipulative than to say that it must not receive Case. Chomsky (1981b) argued, though, that we can go further and deduce this principle, in the following way. We have anaphors, which must obey Condition A, and pronominals, which must obey Condition B. Suppose we had something that was both a pronominal and an anaphor. Then it would have to obey both Condition A and Condition B. Is it possible for something to be bound in its GC and free (not bound) in its GC? Chomsky suggested that this would be exactly satisfied by an item that had no GC. If something has no GC, then it trivially satisfies both the requirement that if it has a GC it is bound in it, and the requirement that if it has a GC it is free in it.[11] How can something fail to have a GC? That is actually fairly easy. If something is not governed, then it will not have a GC. Thus, if PRO is a pronominal anaphor, it cannot have a GC, for otherwise it would have contradictory requirements. But for it not to have a GC, it must be ungoverned, which is exactly what we are trying to deduce. We discovered that fact, but now we can explain it, if we are willing to accept that PRO is a pronominal anaphor. This deduction is often referred to in the literature as the *PRO Theorem*.

One significant consequence of this approach to the distribution of PRO is that the Condition A–like relation between, say, PRO and *I* in (81a) cannot follow from Condition A. That is, for PRO to exist in a structure at all, it must lack a GC. But if it lacks a GC, it trivially satisfies Condition A *no matter what its index is*. Hence, to explain the necessary coindexing in such examples, we must appeal to another module, often called *Control*.[12] The properties of Control are at the moment still unclear.

We have seen that there is a nonpronominal anaphor that is silent (an empty category)—NP-trace. Also, there are anaphors that can be heard (lexical)—like *each other* or *himself*. According to Chomsky (1982), there are also nonanaphoric pronominals that are silent—like the null subject in a pro-drop language such as Spanish or Italian. And there certainly are pronominals that can be heard—like *he*. We have now decided that there is a pronominal anaphor that is silent. So we might expect that there is also a pronominal anaphor that can be heard. However, none seems to exist. That fact, which might at first seem like an unexplained gap in the paradigm, is in fact quite easy to explain. An NP that is lexical needs Case, by the Case Filter, and Case is assigned under government. Something that is a pronominal anaphor would not be allowed to be governed, because of the conflicting Binding Theory requirements that would result. But if it were ungoverned, it would not receive Case, and it would violate the Case Filter. The gap in the paradigm is thus predicted on independent grounds.

Here is something to be cautious about. Often linguists claim that some structure is ruled out since a governed PRO violates both Condition A and Condition B of the Binding Theory.[13] We decided that nothing that is governed can simultaneously satisfy both Condition A and Condition B of the Binding Theory, because it would have to be free and bound in the same domain—a contradiction. But for something to *violate* Condition A and Condition B simultaneously, it would also have to be both free and bound in the same domain. It is no more possible to violate both of those conditions simultaneously than to satisfy both of them simultaneously. What these linguists really mean is that governed PRO violates *either* Condition A *or* Condition B. Let us check that, to make sure. Consider (69a), repeated as (89):

(89) [$_\alpha$ PRO$_x$ Agr eats]

The GC of PRO in (89) is the minimal S that contains it and a governor—hence, α. Whatever index we give to PRO, it would violate Condition A. It satisfies Condition B, though, by virtue of violating Condition A. If an element has a GC and is subject to both conditions, then whenever it violates Condition A it satisfies Condition B, and vice versa. Now consider (70), repeated as (90):

(90) [$_\alpha$ I$_1$ spoke to PRO$_x$]

The GC is again α in (90). Suppose PRO has index *1*. That violates Condition B—not A. Suppose PRO has index *2*. That violates Condition A—not B.

The PRO Theorem relies on two things. First, both Condition A and Condition B mention the same domain: GC. Second, *free* entails "not bound" and *bound* entails "not free." Given this, we have deduced that PRO must be ungoverned, and, as a consequence, we have deduced that PRO must be Caseless, assuming that Case is only assigned under government. So the Caselessness of PRO is just a lemma deduced along the way, with no central role in the theory.

2.3 On the Notion "Accessible SUBJECT"

At this point we should look in more detail at the Binding Conditions, and in particular at the proper characterization of GC. We have been using a simplified version that has worked well for most of the cases we have looked at so far, but there are some well-known cases for which something more needs to be said.

2.3.1 Problems with a Simple Version of GC

Perhaps the most famous case is one that Chomsky has been concerned with since the writing of Chomsky 1973:

(91) The men$_1$ think [that [[pictures of [each other]$_1$] will be on sale]]

Recall our definition of GC:

(92) The GC of α is the minimal NP or S containing α and a
    governor of α.

In (91) *each other* is free in its GC, the NP *pictures of each other*. But we did not even need to look at an example this exotic for (92) to fail. It fails equally in (93), as we had seen before for a similar example ((29) in section 2.1):

(93) They$_1$ liked [pictures of each other$_1$]

By (92), the GC of *each other* is the NP *pictures of each other*, and *each other* is free in that NP. Yet this example is perfectly grammatical.

Think of what we must do. We must build the effects of the SSC into the definition of GC and thus keep an NP without a subject from being a GC. Compare (93) to (94):

(94) *They liked [Mary's pictures of each other]

2.3.2 Toward a Proper Characterization of GC

Let us try something like (95) as a modification of (92)—in fact, the simplest possible relevant modification:

(95) The GC of α is the minimal NP or S containing α, a governor of α, and a subject.

(95) works for (93) versus (94). According to (95), in (93) the GC of *each other* will be the matrix clause. In (94), however, the object NP is the GC for *each other*, since that NP has a subject in it. Thus, (94) violates Condition A of the Binding Theory, whereas (93) does not violate anything. These are the correct results.

But (95) still will not help with (91). The GC of *each other* is the sentential complement, since that complement contains *each other*, a governor of *each other*, and a subject, namely, *pictures of each other*. (95) is still too "tight." Another imaginable case shows this. According to (95), a GC requires a subject. But (95) does not specify any particular relationship between the subject and α. Let us test whether any relationship is required. Consider (96):

(96) They like [[pictures of each other] and [Mary's dress]]

By (95), the coordinate object NP of *like* is the GC for *each other*, since it contains *each other*, a governor of *each other*, and a subject, namely, *Mary*. The subject has nothing to do with *each other*, but (95) does not require any relationship between the two. This result is incorrect, since (96) is grammatical even though *each other* is not bound in the object NP.

Let us correct that inadequacy by making the subject have something to do with *each other*. The minimal structural way to do this is for the subject to c-command *each other* (compare the discussion of "intervening subject" in section 2.1.2.2). Let us therefore try "a subject *c-commanding* α" in the definition of GC.

This has the desired consequence for (96), because *Mary* does not c-command *each other*. Thus, the GC for *each other* in (96) will be the root clause, since the only subject c-commanding *each other* in (96) is *they*. Condition A will correctly allow (96).

Now we can also account for (91). The GC for *each other* is not the sentential complement, because there is no subject of that S that c-commands *each other*. The subject *pictures of each other* dominates *each other*, and *c-command* is defined in such a way that if α dominates β, α does not c-command β (see (12)). Domination and c-command are mutually exclusive. In (91) this takes us up to the root clause, since *the men* is the only c-commanding subject.

Another case is now correctly accounted for as well, namely, (97):

(97) They₁ like [each other₁'s books]

The object NP in (97) contains *each other* and (arguably) a governor for *each other*, if we assume that Case assignment always takes place under government. Even though *each other* is a subject, it does not c-command itself, because c-command is irreflexive. (That, by the way, follows from the fact that c-command and domination are mutually exclusive. When we formalize phrase structure, we find that an item dominates itself. But if an item dominates itself, then, by definition (12), it cannot c-command itself.)[14] To find a c-commanding subject, then, we must go out to the entire clause. (97) is thus correctly predicted to be grammatical.

There are problems, however. (98) illustrates the most obvious one:

(98) *They think [that [each other are intelligent]]

Before we added the proviso about subjects to the definition of GC, we had an account for TSC effects; but now we have lost it. The GC for *each other* is not the lower S, because although it contains *each other* and a governor, it does not contain a c-commanding subject. Thus, the matrix sentence in (98) is the GC for *each other*, and (98) is incorrectly ruled in, all else being equal.

Other problems arise as well. Consider (99):

(99) *Each other left

(99) is now also ruled in. There is no subject that c-commands *each other* in (99); therefore, there is no GC for *each other*. Finally, (100) is ruled in as well:

(100) *PRO left

This is interesting, because it will force us to rethink some of our previous conclusions about the distribution of PRO. As a pronominal anaphor, PRO may not have a GC. Until this point, we thought that the only way for something not to have a GC would be for it not to be governed. But now there might be another way, namely, for it not to have a c-commanding subject. We will return to this issue.

2.3.3 Accessible SUBJECTs

The way to recover our account for the TSC effects—that is, to make a finite clause a GC—is to extend the notion "subject." Chomsky (1981b) introduced the concept *SUBJECT*, which includes standard subject and Agr. It is the second type of SUBJECT, Agr, that rescues the TSC. Consider a more detailed representation of (98):

(101) *They think [that [each other Agr be intelligent]]

Agr is a governor of *each other*. (Nominative Case assignment tells us that Agr governs the subject of a finite clause.) If Agr governs *each other*, then presumably Agr c-commands *each other*, since that is generally taken to be part of the definition of *government*.[15] Furthermore, Agr is a SUBJECT, by definition. That means the GC for *each other* is the lower S, and *each other* is free in that GC, in violation of Condition A— the result we wanted. In fact, now we have recovered not only the TSC but also the SSC. The theory is beginning to look very much as it used to look circa 1973 (section 2.1.2). The definition of SUBJECT has two parts. One part (Agr) gives essentially the TSC. The other part (subject) gives the SSC. So (101) is now accounted for, and so is (97). In the latter case the GC for *each other* is still the S, because the NP contains neither Agr nor a c-commanding subject. Similarly, in (93) the GC for *each other* encompasses the whole S, and the example is correctly ruled in. Finally, if Agr c-commands the subject position in finite clauses, the GC in (99) and (100) is the root sentence, and both *each other* and *PRO* are free in their GC in violation of Condition A.

But unfortunately we have now once again lost our account of (91), repeated here as (102):

(102) The men$_1$ think [that [[pictures of each other$_1$] Agr will be on sale]]

The GC for *each other* is not the NP *pictures of each other*, for that NP does not have a SUBJECT of either type. But the sentential complement does contain a SUBJECT (Agr), which c-commands *each other*; that is, by hypothesis, Agr c-commands *pictures of each other* and thus c-commands *each other*. (It is not difficult to show that if α c-commands β, and β dominates γ, then α c-commands γ.) Thus, the sentential complement is the GC for *each other*, and we are back in our initial quandary.

Contrast (102) with (103) and (104):

(103) *The men$_1$ think [that [[Mary's pictures of each other$_1$]
          Agr will be on sale]]

(104) *The men$_1$ think [that [I Agr like [pictures of each other$_1$]]]

The phenomenon does not seem to be that an anaphor inside a picture NP can be bound by anything anywhere. There do seem to be GC-type effects.

The final revision proceeds as follows. Somehow, we must say that

Agr in the complement in (102) does not count as a relevant SUBJECT, even though it does in (101). Chomsky (1981b) proposed that it does not count as a relevant SUBJECT in (102) because it is coindexed with something that contains α. Let us see how to state this precisely.

By convention, Agr is always coindexed with the subject. The condition we are working toward means that something inside a subject will never have Agr of that subject as a relevant SUBJECT. Consider the definition in (105), where *accessible* is defined as in (106):

(105) The GC of α is the minimal NP or S containing α, a governor of α, and a SUBJECT accessible to α.

(106) β is accessible to α if
    a. β c-commands α, and
    b. β is not coindexed with any category containing α.

(106b) (due to Kevin Kearney) is not precisely Chomsky's way of stating the condition we are adding, but it is empirically indistinguishable from it (and somewhat easier to understand). Later we will look at Chomsky's statement.

In (102) the embedded S does have a SUBJECT: Agr. But now we must ask whether that SUBJECT is accessible to *each other*. It satisfies (106a). But it does not satisfy (106b), since it is coindexed with a category containing α, namely, the subject of the embedded sentence. Notice also that now *pictures of each other* is not accessible to *each other* for two reasons: it does not c-command *each other*, and it is coindexed with a category that contains *each other*, since an item is coindexed with itself. The higher S *is* the GC for *each other*, however, since both *the men* and Agr are accessible to *each other*: both c-command *each other* and neither one is coindexed with any category that contains *each other*. We will have to be cautious, though. If "contains" means "dominates," and if something dominates itself as I claimed earlier, then we will have to be more subtle about this. In (106b), instead of "containing," we should say "properly containing," in a set-theoretic sense.[16] The reason is that Agr in the lower S of (101) (or even in (99)) *is* coindexed with a category containing *each other*, namely, *each other* itself. However, Agr is not coindexed with any category *properly* containing *each other* and hence is accessible to *each other*. Both examples violate Condition A, as desired.

Let us make sure that we still reject all the ungrammatical sentences. We need not look further at the grammatical ones, for we have made it *harder* for something to count as a relevant SUBJECT, hence *easier* for Condition A to be satisfied. Thus, if an anaphor conformed to Condition A before, even when it was easier for something to count as a relevant SUBJECT, it will still conform. The new definition allows *more* binding relationships with anaphors.

In (101) the GC for *each other* is the embedded S, since Agr is accessible to it (Agr c-commands *each other*, and it is not coindexed with any category that properly contains *each other*).[17] Similarly for (99). The GC for *each other* is the sentence, for Agr is a governor, and it is a SUBJECT that c-commands *each other*, and it is not coindexed with any category that properly contains *each other*. Finally, (103) and (104) are straightforwardly accounted for. *Mary* and *I* (or Agr) are the respective accessible SUBJECTs for *each other*.

2.3.4 Further Examples (and Counterexamples)

Let us look at one other fact that Chomsky was able to explain with (roughly) this set of definitions and principles:

(107) They$_1$ Agr$_1$ think [$_{S'}$ that [$_S$ it Agr$_3$ be likely [$_{S'}$ that [$_S$[$_{NP}$ pictures of each other$_1$]$_2$ Agr$_2$ be on sale]]]]

(107) exhibits quite long-distance binding, yet the sentence is grammatical. We want the expletive *it* not to be an accessible SUBJECT (henceforth, Accessible SUBJECT) for *each other*. If it were, then the GC for *each other* would be the complement of *think*, and (107) would violate Condition A. There are only two ways to prevent *it* from being an Accessible SUBJECT. One possibility is that *it* does not c-command *each other*. That seems hopeless, since *it* is a subject and a subject c-commands everything in its clause.[18] The second possibility is that *it* is coindexed with some category that properly contains *each other*. Is that plausible? Chomsky argued that an expletive and an associated so-called extraposed clause are in fact coindexed. That is, he assumed that (108a) and (108b) are related:

(108) a. It is likely that John is here
      b. That John is here is likely

The relationship between *it* and the extraposed clause in (108a) is almost like the relationship between the elements of a chain. It is as if the θ-role that the clause has to receive is the θ-role of the subject of *be likely*. *It* is in subject position, and somehow it must act like a trace and transmit the θ-role. Working out the details of that suggestion is hardly trivial, but I won't be concerned about the details at the moment.

With these assumptions, let us consider what the GC for *each other* in (107) is. It cannot be *pictures of each other*, because that NP does not contain a SUBJECT; nor can it be [[*pictures of each other*] *Agr be on sale*], for even though that S contains a SUBJECT, the latter is not accessible to *each other*—remember that, descriptively, inside a subject the TSC is locally inoperative. Specifically, Agr is not accessible to *each other* because it is coindexed with *pictures of each other*. The next possible structure is [*it Agr be likely* [*that* [[*pictures of each other*] *Agr be on sale*]]]. This contains two SUBJECTs, *it* and Agr$_3$, both of which c-command *each other*; however, they are both coindexed with S', a category that properly contains *each other*, by the extraposition hypothesis. As a result, neither of those is an Accessible SUBJECT either.

Thus, we must go all the way up to the root clause, and there we find two Accessible SUBJECTs—*they* and Agr_1—that are not coindexed with anything that properly contains *each other*. Notice that it is a correct consequence that *each other* must be bound in the root clause in (107). If we embedded (107) once more, as in (109),

(109) We said that they think that it is likely that pictures of
each other are on sale

each other would have to take *they* as its antecedent; it could not reach all the way up to *we*.

Chomsky shows that this theory accounts for a surprising contrast. Consider (110):

(110) *$They_1$ Agr_1 think $[_{S'}$ that $[_S$ it_2 Agr_2 surprised each other$_1$
$[_{S'}$ that $[_S$ Bill won$]]_2]]$

Each other is actually closer to its antecedent in (110) than in the grammatical (107). But the theory correctly predicts that (107) should be ruled in and (110) out. *Surprised* is the governor for *each other*. The first SUBJECT we come to is Agr_2, which is an Accessible SUBJECT for *each other*. *Each other* is not contained in the extraposed clause and hence is not properly contained in a category coindexed with Agr_2. Thus, the S containing Agr_2 is the GC for *each other*, which is free in that domain, in violation of Condition A, exactly as we want. Recently, Chomsky has been working on a revised version of the Binding Theory that we won't be able to examine here. It has both good and bad points. One of its bad points is that it loses the remarkable contrast between (107) and (110). This contrast is about the strongest argument I know of for the notion "Accessible SUBJECT."

- *Epstein:* If what you say about examples like (107) is true, then a predicate phrase like *be likely* must have two kinds of θ-roles to assign. This is so because in (111) we don't coindex *John* with the postverbal clause:

(111) John is likely to leave

Lasnik: The question is, what is the indexation in (111)? The existence of examples like (111) undermines the independent motivation for the analysis of example (107). The account we just gave cannot be relevant for (111), because *John* is not the kind of thing that transmits a θ-role. Surely, then, we do not want to say that *John* and the complement of *is likely* have the same index. The answer to the problem should be that *is likely* assigns a θ-role to an object and not to a subject. This would not render the coindexation that we need for (107) impossible—but it would take away much of its motivation.

- *Uriagereka:* Could we make it a principle that an expletive needs to be coindexed with "something," due to its nature?
Lasnik: That might be right. It would require a particular analysis of weather predicates; but others, including Chomsky, have argued for

such an analysis. That is, in sentences of the type *It is raining* this suggestion would require that *it* be analyzed not as an expletive but as a sort of argument (see section 1.9).

As long as we are exploring the implications of these constructions, let us look at one more potentially relevant configuration. It is a construction that Chomsky dealt with in Chomsky 1981b, albeit unsatisfactorily:

(112) *John$_1$ seems [that [it$_2$ Agr$_2$ is likely [t_1 to leave]$_2$]]

(112) violates Subjacency, but it is far worse than an ordinary island violation. When Chomsky introduced the notion of Accessible SUBJECT, he pointed out the following problem that (112) raises. If we follow through the logic of our previous discussion, (112) does not turn out to violate Condition A. *Likely* in (112) is the governor for the trace. (Recall that PRO cannot occur in that position.) Now we want to find the nearest Accessible SUBJECT. Recall that the "extraposed" clause must constitute a chain with the expletive. The same should be true here (the only difference being that we are dealing with an infinitive instead of a finite clause). Once the extraposed clause has index *2*, as shown in (112), then neither *it* nor Agr$_2$ is an Accessible SUBJECT for the trace, for the same reason we saw earlier: they are both coindexed with the clause that properly contains the trace. Thus, the root clause is the GC, and no Condition A violation takes place. There are two possible solutions to this problem. One is to assume Zubizarreta's (1982) proposal that only S' has an index. If S has no index at all, then Agr and *it* will be Accessible SUBJECTs. (That still tends to undermine the motivation for the coindexation in (107), for I would assume that an infinitival complement needs a θ-role just as much as a finite complement does: an infinitival clause cannot appear in a position to which no θ-role is assigned.) We will consider a second solution in section 4.1.6, when we examine the Empty Category Principle.

A further problem is that (113) is ungrammatical:

(113) *[Pictures of each other]$_1$ Agr$_1$ are on sale

Thus far our theory does not predict this, since there is no GC for *each other*—*each other* has no Accessible SUBJECT, since Agr is coindexed with the subject, which properly contains *each other*. Furthermore, (114) should also be judged grammatical:

(114) *[Pictures of PRO]$_1$ Agr$_1$ are on sale

If it were a theorem of the system that PRO had to be ungoverned, we would predict (114) to be ungrammatical. But the PRO Theorem tells us only that PRO is not allowed to have a GC. We have now found a way in which something can be governed and still not have a GC: when it does not have an Accessible SUBJECT.

Somehow it must be true that anything that is governed has a GC. If we could impose that requirement (by brute force), then both (113) and

(114) would be ruled out by Condition A. That is what Chomsky (1981b) proposes (following a suggestion of Norbert Hornstein):

(115) The root clause is a GC for a governed element.[19]

But, apart from its stipulative nature, (115)—often called the *Auxiliary Hypothesis*—still does not explain (112).

The final problem harks back to one we noted in section 2.1.2.3: the lack of complete complementarity between anaphors and pronouns. Thus, a paradigmatic Accessible SUBJECT environment such as (102) permits a bound pronoun as well as an anaphor:

(116) The men$_1$ think that pictures of them$_1$ are on sale

Given that the GC for *them* is the matrix clause, (116) should be immediately ruled out by Condition B.

2.3.5 Chomsky's Definition of Accessible

Let us look now at Chomsky's (1981b: 212) definition of Accessible SUBJECT. (Recall that we have been using Kearney's notational revision.) At first Chomsky's version looks somewhat strange, but keep in mind that empirically it is indistinguishable from (106):

(117) β is accessible to α if
    a. β c-commands α, and
    b. assignment to α of the index of β would not violate the filter $*[_{\gamma_i} \ldots \delta_i \ldots]$.

The filter in (117b), often called the i-*within*-i *Condition*, stars a structure where γ contains δ, and γ and δ have the same index. Let us see what (117) means. The modality of (117b)—the word *would*—is important. (117b) does not claim that α and β *do* have the same index. It does not claim that they *should*. It does not even claim that it is *possible* for them to have the same index. It simply says, "Pretend we found α and gave it the index of β; what would we then have?" Consider again the classic case, (102), repeated here as (118). Recall that we want it to be true that Agr$_2$ is not an Accessible SUBJECT for *each other*, even though Agr c-commands *each other*.

(118) The men$_1$ think [that [[pictures of each other$_1$]$_2$
                                     α (2)

    Agr$_2$ will be on sale]]
    $\overline{\beta}$

Now pretend that we have assigned to α (= *each other*) the index of β (= Agr$_2$). The index of β is *2*. Hence, we give *each other* a "pretend-index" *2* (in parentheses in (118)). With that imaginary indexing, we create a configuration that violates the *i*-within-*i* Condition. We will create such a configuration, in fact, whenever β is (in actuality) coindexed with any category that properly contains α. That is why the two versions of the condition, Chomsky's and Kearney's, are empirically indistinguishable.

Finally, let us consider an example that might seem to cause problems for this theory:[20]

(119) *John$_1$ Agr$_1$ said [$_{S'}$ that [$_S$[$_{NP}$ his$_1$ brother]$_2$ Agr$_2$ likes himself$_1$]]

We want the embedded S to be the GC for *himself*; that is, we want (119) to be a Condition A violation. Since *his* is a pronoun, it could have any index here. Suppose we freely give *his* the index *1*. Now, is Agr or *his brother* an Accessible SUBJECT for *himself*? (If one of them is, the other one is as well.) A problem would arise if neither were an Accessible SUBJECT, because then the GC would be the matrix clause and the sentence would be wrongly allowed. Given (119), suppose we pretend to change the index of *his brother* to the index of *himself*, as in (120):

(120) ...[$_{NP}$ his$_1$ brother]$_2$ Agr$_2$ likes himself$_1$
              (1)   (1)

Further, suppose that if we pretended to change the index of Agr, then we would also have to pretend to change the index of the NP. Given these assumptions, neither Agr nor *his brother* is an Accessible SUBJECT for *himself*, since the imaginary indexing has created an *i*-within-*i* configuration. But of course this line of reasoning fails: (117) does not say to pretend to alter the index of the element that is being evaluated as an Accessible SUBJECT, but only the index of the anaphor. (117) refers to "assignment to α of the index of β," where α is the anaphor and β is the SUBJECT. To create (120), we did the reverse, assigning to β the index of α. If instead we had taken (117) as stated, assigning to α (*himself*) the index of β (either *his brother* or Agr), there would be no *i*-within-*i* configuration. That means β *is* an Accessible SUBJECT and the lower S is the GC for *himself*. Example (119) thus provides support for a very specific detail of (117b).

- *Uriagereka:* This is just small point, but if Agr has to enter a c-command relationship with its governee, we need a different definition of c-command for that than for other parts of the Binding Theory.
  Lasnik: For the Binding Theory, in order to allow for constructions like (121),

(121)

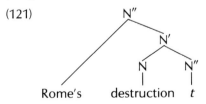

we need a "first branching node" definition of c-command. With a definition in terms of maximal projection, (121) would incorrectly be counted as a Condition C violation, since *Rome('s)* would be A-bound by *t*. We can also build an argument based on Condition B, as in *his* destruction, or even Condition A, as in *each other's destruction t*. In this last example both *each other* and its trace would incorrectly satisfy Condition A internal to the NP, since they would bind one another. All three problems disappear if c-command is based on branching rather than on maximal projections. But, as you just pointed out, for Accessible SUBJECTs, c-command will be based on "maximal projection" and not "branching," if we assume a sentential structure as in (122):

(122)

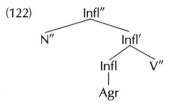

The first branching node dominating Infl/Agr is Infl', which does not dominate the subject. Merely changing (117a) to "β governs α" is no solution, since that would create problems for the SSC part of the account, as in (123):

(123) *We$_1$ believed [Mary to like each other$_1$]

This would mistakenly be ruled in. *Mary* does not govern *each other* in (123), since there is an intervening maximal projection boundary. It would thus not be an Accessible SUBJECT, and the whole S would have to be the GC. So (117a) would have to say "c-commands or governs." But beware of definitions including disjunctions. •

Chapter 3   Determination of Empty Categories

Let us begin this discussion with strong crossover. Consider (1):

(1) *Who$_1$ [does he$_1$ think [Mary likes t_1]]

As we know, this cannot be synonymous with (2):

(2) Who$_1$ t_1 thinks Mary likes him$_1$
    For which x, x thinks Mary likes x

We have been assuming, following Chomsky (who was following Wasow 1972), that (1) violates Condition C. (1) contains a variable (an R-expression) that is A-bound. Thus, (1) is analogous to (1'):

(1') *He$_1$ thinks Mary likes John$_1$

Koopman and Sportiche (1982) suggested another way of looking at the phenomenon, related to their view of variables:

(3) A variable is any element that is locally $\overline{\text{A}}$-bound by an operator.

"Locally $\overline{\text{A}}$-bound" does not mean bound by something nearby. It means that the nearest binder is an operator, even if that binder is quite distant. So a variable is anything whose nearest binder is an operator (in Comp or adjoined to S).

In (2) the trace is a variable, because its nearest binder is *who*, in Comp. *Him* is not a variable because its nearest binder is a variable, not an operator. Thus, (2) does not violate Koopman and Sportiche's Bijection Principle—the requirement that an operator bind exactly one variable—or anything else, apparently.[1] In (1) *he* is a variable because its nearest binder is an operator in Comp. There is again no violation of the Bijection Principle, because (1) is completely parallel to (2) in this respect: the operator does not bind two variables (in the sense of (3)). That is, the gap in (1) is not a variable, because its nearest binder is *he*, and not the operator in Comp. Since the gap is not a variable, under this definition, we must therefore determine what it is. In order for it to be PRO, it would not be able to have a GC, as we saw in section 2.2.4. The gap is a direct object, so it is certainly governed, and thus it will have a GC. (Notice that in our example PRO would violate Condition A since it would be free in its GC, the embedded S.) The gap is therefore not PRO. Nor is it pro, the null counterpart of lexical pronouns, proposed in Chomsky 1982. Since English is not a pro-drop language, pro must somehow be excluded. Even in standard Romance-type pro-drop languages, pro happens to be excluded from object position. So in our case, the gap could not be pro. Finally, it cannot be a pure anaphor, either. If it were, it would have to be A-bound in its GC—and it clearly is not. So the gap cannot be anything. If the theory contains a principle to the effect that "Everything must be something," then (1) violates that principle. Under this analysis, a slightly modified version of the one that Koopman and Sportiche presented, there is no need to appeal to Condition C to explain strong crossover.[2]

The theory that Koopman and Sportiche proposed came to be known as *functional determination of empty categories*. Until now we have been assuming a theory that has what we might call *intrinsic determination of empty categories*. Under this theory, an empty category is what it is: if we pull a PRO out of the lexicon and put it in D-Structure, then it is a PRO; if we generate an empty category by applying *Wh*-Movement, the result is a variable; and so forth. Koopman and Sportiche were suggesting another kind of theory: There is just one empty category, call it *e*. Its features are contextually or "functionally" determined by the environment in which it finds itself. If it is in the appropriate environment, then it will be determined as a variable— where "the appropriate environment" means being locally $\bar{\text{A}}$-bound by an operator in Comp. If the empty category is not in that context, then it is not a variable. And so forth. Chomsky developed this theory further in Chomsky 1982, and we will explore his extension of the theory as we go along.

In effect, we will be comparing three theories. The first might be called the theory of *intrinsic features*, and it may be tricky to characterize. Chomsky has often described it by saying that intrinsic features are simply in the lexicon. But of course traces must have features, and they are not in the lexicon but instead are created in the course of the derivation. So intrinsic features are those that an empty category has "at the moment of birth," whether that occurs in the lexicon or in the course of the syntactic derivation.

Another theory is that of *functional (or contextual) determination*. This theory posits one empty category, *e*, but then at a particular level in the derivation—S-structure, or perhaps LF—an algorithm applies to the effect that "If an *e* occurs in such and such a situation, then it is a variable; if an *e* occurs in such and such different situation, then it is PRO"; and so on.

A third theory, proposed by Brody (1984), might be called the theory of *free assignment*. Brody accepted the idea that there is only one empty category, *e*; but he rejected the idea that an algorithm is needed to determine its features. According to him, if we assign freely any combination at all of [±pronominal] and [±anaphor] (henceforth, [±p] and [±a]), independent principles will rule out all the bad constructions. If he is factually correct, that is a very strong argument for his approach, since his proposal is essentially the null hypothesis.

3.1 Functional Determination of Empty Categories

Consider the following algorithm (Chomsky 1982: 35):

(4) a. An empty category is a variable if it is in an A-position and is locally $\bar{\text{A}}$-bound [by an operator].

  b. An empty category in an A-position that is not a variable is an anaphor.

  c. An empty category [in an A-position] that is not a variable is a pronominal if it is free or locally A-bound by an antecedent with an independent θ-role.

We have to add *by an operator* to Chomsky's formulation in (4a); otherwise, intermediate traces will locally bind original traces and cause them to be variables, thus costing us our functional determination analysis of strong crossover.[3] Also, it is not clear that the word *antecedent* in (4c) does any work. I think Chomsky simply means "is bound by an A-binder." (4a), (4b), and (4c) apply in that order. In this theory, by *variable* we mean $[-a, -p]$. By *anaphor* we mean an empty category that has the feature $[+a]$—though not necessarily $[-p]$. By *pronominal* we mean an empty category that has the feature $[+p]$—though not necessarily $[-a]$. (4) clearly must be able to apply after transformations. If it applied only at D-Structure, it would never deal with traces at all, since traces do not exist at D-Structure.

Using (4), let us reexamine (1). The empty category in (1) is not locally $\bar{\text{A}}$-bound by an operator: its nearest binder is not an operator in an $\bar{\text{A}}$-position but instead is *he*. By (4a), *e* will therefore not be determined as a variable. Automatically, then, it is $[+a]$, given (4b). Finally, by (4c), it is $[+p]$, since even though it is not free, it is locally A-bound by an "antecedent" with an independent θ-role.[4] Hence, (1) violates Condition A, since its empty category is $[+a]$ (as well as $[+p]$) and is not bound in its GC.

Another strong crossover violation occurs in (5):

(5) *Who$_1$ [does he$_1$ like e_1]

By (4a), *e* is not a variable, because it is not locally $\bar{\text{A}}$-bound by an operator (its nearest binder is *he*). (4b), then, automatically makes *e* an anaphor.[5] Again, *e* in (5) is locally A-bound by an antecedent with an independent θ-role. Thus, by (4c), *e* is $[+p]$, which creates a violation of Condition B. So some strong crossover configurations will violate Condition A, and others will violate Condition B. All of them will violate one or the other, so we do not need Condition C, according to Chomsky.

Let us now see how (4) works to provide well-formed representations for grammatical sentences. Consider (6):

(6) Who$_1$ e_1 left

(4a) tells us that e is $[-a, -p]$, since it is in an A-position and is locally $\bar{A}$-bound by an operator. (6) does not violate anything, which is exactly what we want, since the sentence is grammatical. Now consider (7):

(7) John$_1$ was arrested e_1

By (4a), we know that e is not a variable—it is not $\bar{A}$-bound at all and hence is clearly not locally $\bar{A}$-bound. Then, by (4b), it is an anaphor. Finally, since e is not locally A-bound by an antecedent with an independent θ-role (nor, of course, is it free), (4c) tells us that e is $[-p]$. The theory thus accounts perfectly for (7). In this example e is correctly determined to be a pure anaphor. Since e is bound in its GC, (7) is well formed.

Now consider (8):

(8) Who$_1$ e_1 was arrested e_1

Here we must apply (4) to two empty categories. It does not matter which one we apply it to first, because (4) only cares about whether the empty category is in an A-position or an $\bar{A}$-position, whether an operator binds it or not, and whether it has an antecedent with an independent θ-role or not. Consider the first empty category first. (4a) directly determines it as a variable, that is, $[-a, -p]$. Next consider the second empty category. (4a) does not determine it as a variable. Thus, (4b) determines it as an anaphor, $[+a]$. Finally (4c) determines it as $[-p]$; it is not free, and, being in a passive construction, it is part of what Chomsky (1981b) called a chain. Thus, its A-binder has no *independent* θ-role. Note that the first e has no requirement whatsoever in this theory. The second has only the requirement that it be bound in its GC. So we have correctly accounted for (8).

Let us now look at PRO:

(9) John$_1$ tried [[e_1 to win the race]]

By (4a), e is not a variable; hence, by (4b), it is an anaphor. By (4c), provided that e and *John* do not constitute a chain, e is $[+p]$. The requirement on a $[+a, +p]$ empty category (PRO) is that it be both bound in its GC and free in its GC. That is possible only if PRO does not have a GC. PRO will fail to have a GC if it is not governed. And it will not be governed, in Chomsky's theory, just in case the embedded clause in (9) is an S'. We have independent evidence that that is true; namely, an overt NP cannot occur in this position (that is, it cannot receive Case from *try*). (9) thus satisfies all conditions.

Now consider a modification of (9):

(10) *John$_1$ tried [[e_2 to win the race]]

Again, by (4a), e cannot be a variable; hence, by (4b), it is an anaphor. Finally, it is a pronominal by (4c), since it is free. If e is $[+a, +p]$, then it must not have a GC, and in fact that requirement is satisfied in (10), just as it was in (9). The problem is that (10), unlike (9), is ungrammatical. This tells us something that we already suspected: in this theory not all

Control properties follow from the Binding Theory (see section 2.2.4). If we are going to derive the *distribution* of PRO by appealing to the Binding Conditions, then we cannot derive the *interpretation* of PRO by appealing to the Binding Conditions. Once PRO is allowed to exist at all, as far as the Binding Conditions are concerned, it is allowed to exist by virtue of having no binding requirement—that is, by having no GC. So it looks as if the model includes another module: Control Theory.

There are two schools of thought about this. One says that it's best to derive the distribution of PRO via the Binding Theory, as in the theory outlined, even though this requires adding Control Theory. The other school of thought says that it's best to derive the distribution some other way, perhaps via Case Theory, in which case the interpretation can be derived via the Binding Theory. But it is very difficult to derive the distribution, except by appealing to the Binding Theory. And it is even difficult to derive the interpretation solely via the Binding Theory. For now I will put this controversy aside and continue to follow the first school of thought.

Finally, let us look at a typical raising construction:

(11) John$_1$ seems e_1 to be crazy

We know that e is certainly not a variable, because it is not $\bar{\text{A}}$-bound at all, and that it is therefore an anaphor. Finally, it is not pronominal because it is not free, and its local A-binder does not have an independent θ-role—*John* and e share a θ-role. Brody (1984) pointed out a potential circularity here when he advocated his approach to the determination of empty categories. That is, how do we know whether *John* has an independent θ-role or not? We know it has an independent θ-role if the element it binds is not a trace; we know it does not have an independent θ-role if the element it binds *is* a trace. If that is correct, we cannot really use the algorithm as Chomsky intended, since the algorithm itself determines whether or not something is a trace, yet the algorithm also arguably depends on whether or not something is a trace. In any event, if the gap in (11) is somehow determined to be $[+a, -p]$, then everything is accounted for, because Condition A is satisfied.

The following example possibly further illustrates the circularity that Brody was concerned about:

(12) John$_1$ was arrested e_1 after e_1 leading the demonstration

The question involves the e subject of *leading*. Will it in fact be correctly determined as PRO? Suppose it is bound by *John*.[6] Is it bound by something with an independent θ-role? *John* is not in a θ-position, so there is a sense in which it does not have an independent θ-role. It does have a θ-role that is independent of PRO, but we do not know that it is independent of PRO until we apply the algorithm. Brody never gave an example of the circularity he suspected in the theory behind (4):

he simply said that it is conceptually circular. (12) suggests that this conceptual point has empirical ramifications.

Returning to the main issue, notice that (4) does not allow for the possibility of an empty category that is pronominal and nonanaphoric. At a later point in Chomsky 1982 this is modified, in a direction that Brody ultimately took further: it was to say that the feature $[+a]$ is simply *freely* assigned. One way of implementing this is to make (4b) optional. That, of course, would allow for pronominal nonanaphoric empty categories. In fact, Chomsky wanted this result for theory-internal reasons: there was a gap in the paradigm. If there are overt categories with the feature matrix $[-a, +p]$, why should there not be null categories with the same feature matrix? (The now standard name for such a null category is *pro*.)

Let us reconsider (1), repeated here (slightly modified) as (13), under this reformulation of (4):

(13) *Who$_1$ [does he$_1$ think [t_1 [Mary likes e_1]]]

In (13) e is in an A-position. Now, is it locally $\bar{\text{A}}$-bound by an operator?

- *Uriagereka:* Can we characterize an operator at the level of representation at which (4) applies?
  Lasnik: If you mean S-Structure, it's hard to tell. Chomsky's formulation does not have the bracketed proviso in (4a). So his formulation does not work, strictly speaking, where there is a trace in Comp. He mentions in the text that such traces are to be ignored. (4a) builds this into the definition. By reference to LF, we *can* define *operator*. It is an open question whether we can define it just in terms of properties of S-Structure. Notice what will not do. It will not do to say that an empty category cannot be an operator, to avoid the problem created by the intermediate trace. That would eliminate Chomsky's (1981b) analysis of (14):

  (14) John$_1$ is too dumb [Op$_1$ [PRO to talk to e_1]]

  Here, crucially, an empty category operator in Comp is needed.

Assuming that we can establish that *who* in (13) is an operator, whereas the trace in Comp is not an operator, then (4a) will not apply, because e is not locally $\bar{\text{A}}$-bound by an operator. Chomsky accomplishes the needed distinction between *who* and the trace in Comp by having the procedure ignore the latter. Then the e object of *likes* is locally A-bound. We then proceed to (4b), but at this point we have to consider two theories. In the early theory, whereby (4b) is obligatory, e is automatically an anaphor. Finally, by (4c), since e is locally A-bound by an antecedent with an independent θ-role, it will be determined as $[+p]$.[7] In the other theory, the assignment of $[+a]$ is optional. Since we have already explored the possibilities in which e is $[+a]$, let us try the opposite: let us say it is $[-a]$. For Chomsky, ignoring intermediate traces, (4c) determines that e is $[+p]$. The "pro-drop parameter" should account for the fact that this option is ruled out. But consider again (4), our version of functional determination. Here intermediate traces are not simply ignored. Rather, the proviso in (4a) defines the circumstances under which they will not count as relevant local binders. But then, by (4c), e will be $[-p]$, since e_1 is not locally bound by he. (This is particularly so if we assume that if a rule assigning a plus value of a feature cannot apply, the minus value of that feature is then assigned.) If we cannot simply ignore the trace in Comp, it seems that for strong crossover we do indeed need Condition C, even if we are assuming functional determination. For the first version of the theory (where (4b) obligatorily applies if (4a) fails to apply) we avoided the problem by adding the *by an operator* proviso. I do not see any analogous proviso for the second version of the theory (where (4b) is optional). If we want to maintain this analysis, then, dispensing with Condition C for strong crossover, I think we might be forced to say that traces in Comp are potentially there but that, even when they are present, the algorithm must ignore them, which does not seem particularly appealing.

- *Williams:* What exactly is the status of intermediate traces?
  Lasnik: They are presumably not any of the empty categories we are considering. We can view them as empty categories with no Binding Theory features. Recall that the notion "trace" does not play a role in this theory. The theory includes an algorithm determining the features $[\pm a, \pm p]$ and operations (such as the Binding Conditions) referring to these features. By saying that the *wh*-trace in Comp does not have any of those features, we are saying that the operations do not apply to *wh*-traces in Comp. Then, only if an element has these features is it realized as anything when it reaches semantic representation, since *wh*-traces in Comp are not interpreted at all.

Let us now investigate an example that Epstein (1984) brought to bear on the issue of functional determination and strong crossover:

(15) *Who$_1$ did he$_1$ try $[e_1 [e_1$ to win the race$]]$

(15) is not, a priori, incoherent. If it were grammatical, it would presumably mean something like what (16) means:

(16) Who$_1$ t_1 tried $[[$PRO$_1$ to win the race$]]$

However, (15) is completely impossible. Let us apply (4) to (15) to try to find out why (15) has the status that it does. The second empty category is in an A-position, and it is not locally $\bar{\text{A}}$-bound by an operator. Thus, it is not a variable. This means that, under Chomsky's first account, e is $[+a]$. It must also be $[+p]$ because, if the intermediate trace is ignored, it is locally A-bound by an antecedent with an independent θ-role, the subject of *try*. But now Condition A is not violated in (15) because e does not have a GC; yet the sentence is ungrammatical. In (13) we determined PRO functionally in much the same way we did here. However, there PRO had a GC, and hence we could explain the ungrammaticality of the example. But we cannot use the same explanation for (15), since in (15) PRO does not have a GC as it is not governed. This is a real asymmetry. On this basis, Epstein argued that functional determination simply cannot be used to explain the entire phenomenon of strong crossover, of which (15) is apparently an example. Before we accept this conclusion, we must investigate one other requirement for this case. PRO falls under the theory of Control. In particular, the subject of *try* must be coindexed with the subject of the complement of *try*. But that requirement *is* satisfied in (15). So it is not obvious that (15) violates anything, except Condition C.[8] Notice that (15) is not a problem for the more traditional theory we had been assuming, whereby features are determined intrinsically. In that theory *e* is automatically defined as a trace of *Wh*-Movement, which is a variable and hence subject to Condition C. That theory accounts for both (15) and (13), in fact. So what is interesting about these two cases is that functional determination sharply distinguishes them. Functional determination accounts for the ungrammaticality of (13) because PRO occurs in a position rendered impossible by the Binding Conditions. In (15), on the other hand, PRO occurs in a perfectly possible position.

3.2 Parasitic Gaps

In parasitic gap construction it appears as if one *wh*-phrase has somehow moved from two positions at once. Further, in most of the best cases it appears that one of the two positions is not even a position that a *wh* could have moved from, since it is inside an island (an adverbial adjunct). As is the case with so many interesting phenomena, this one was first pointed out by Ross (1967). Linguists have been intensively investigating it since the late 1970s (see especially Engdahl 1983 and Taraldsen 1981).

3.2.1 Properties of the Phenomenon

Here is one standard example of a parasitic gap:

(17) Which report$_1$ did you file e_1 without PRO reading e_1

(We will not be concerned for the moment about the Control of PRO.) Every English speaker I have asked finds (17) either fairly good or perfect. It appears that the *wh*-phrase came simultaneously from both *e* positions. But what kind of rule is that—a rule that can move one thing from two positions? The theory of transformations, as standardly formalized, does not allow for such a rule.[9] Furthermore, consider (18):

(18) *?Which book$_1$ did you file the report without PRO reading e_1

(18) is substantially worse than (17). I filled in the empty category after

filed in (17) with a lexical category, thus guaranteeing that movement took place from the position of the second *e* in (17). This feels like an island violation. That is, the second position under consideration is not a position from which movement can normally take place.

What are some other properties of this construction? One thing we must take into account is that (18) is not grammatical. Thus, the object position of *reading* does not freely allow an empty category, or even an empty category coindexed with a *wh*-phrase in Comp. Something special must be going on in (17), but not (18), that permits the empty category object of *reading*. This is often described by saying that "A trace licenses a parasitic gap." Such a gap is called parasitic because it depends on another gap: if the real gap did not exist, the parasitic gap could not exist. Notice that this property need not necessarily be stated directly in the theory. Ideally, it would be a consequence of independent properties. One would not expect parasitic gaps to have properties of their own since they seem to be such a peripheral phenomenon. That is, the data available for the language learner would contain very little evidence about their behavior.

Now consider (19):

(19) *Who filed which report$_1$ without reading e_1

At S-Structure (19) is much like (18): there is no trace that "licenses" the parasitic gap. But at LF it presumably contains a trace, after the object *wh*-phrase undergoes LF movement (see section 4.2); and the trace is in just the position of the "licensing" trace in (17). Yet the sentence is still ungrammatical. Let us state the descriptive generalization as follows: "A parasitic gap is licensed by an S-Structure trace."

A warning before we proceed. For some unknown reason, the best examples involve a gerundive (or infinitival) adverbial adjunct. We have to be cautious because—again, for some unknown reason—this gerundive construction requires its subject to be controlled by the subject of the matrix. That eliminates a lot of otherwise potentially revealing test cases. For example, Chomsky gives (20) to illustrate a property of parasitic gaps:

(20) *The report was filed *e* without PRO reading *e*

We know there is a trace after *filed* (the Projection Principle demands it), and Chomsky concludes, basically, that the trace that licenses a parasitic gap must be a *wh*-trace. An NP-trace, as in (20), will not suffice. So one could say, "A parasitic gap is licensed by an S-Structure *wh*-trace." Though this is essentially correct, descriptively, (20) is of no real relevance in establishing it. Remember that the subject of *reading* must be controlled by the subject of the matrix sentence. That, in (20), causes a number of violations, independent of any properties of parasitic gap licensing. First, unless a parasitic gap is a pure anaphor, which it surely cannot be in general, (20) will violate either Condition B or Condition C, since the second *e* is A-bound in its GC (hence, A-bound). In the latter case (20) would represent a strong crossover violation. Second, and less important, (20) violates selectional restrictions: reports cannot read anything.[10] Notice that PRO is coindexed with *the report*; since co-indexation, here, means coreference, PRO must be a report. (20) is thus ruled out independently of any property of parasitic gaps. It is ruled out in a way similar to (21):

(21) *The report fell on the floor after PRO reading the book

(21) is not ruled out for any reason having to do with parasitic gaps. There is no gap in (21), apart from PRO. But again, PRO in (21) is coindexed with *the report*, which means that PRO is a report. Compare (21) with (22):

(22) The teacher fell on the floor after PRO reading the book

The difference between (21) and (22) is not structural but selectional.

Since (20) turns out to have no real bearing on properties of parasitic gaps, we need another example to motivate the claim that NP-traces do not license parasitic gaps. Fortunately, there is such an example. Unfortunately, it does not give crystal clear judgments:

(23) ?Which report did you file *e* after you read *e*

(23) is not nearly as good as (17), but it is not too bad. The useful property of (23) is that it lacks the PRO that was causing interference unrelated to our analysis. (23) and (24) illustrate the desired contrast:

(24) *The report was filed *e* after Bill read *e*

Though (23) is not perfect, it is far better than (24), thus supporting the claimed difference between *wh*-traces and NP-traces with respect to the licensing of parasitic gaps.

- *Nakayama:* Can you consider (25)?

  (25) What *e* was filed *e* without PRO being read *e*

  Lasnik: Yes, that is perfect, as the theory predicts. There are two NP-traces, each created by passive in one of the clauses. Then there is a *wh*-trace in the matrix clause. Finally, PRO must be controlled by the subject of the matrix sentence, and it is. There is no binding violation (nor is there a violation of selectional restrictions because reports can be read). Notice that there is no parasitic gap in (25). The first empty category in the *without* clause is a PRO, and the second is an NP-trace. This predicts that the status of (25) would be unchanged even without a *wh*-trace or, in fact, without any trace at all. That prediction is confirmed by the cases in (26):

  (26) a. The report was filed t_1 without being read t_1
     b. The report disappeared without being read t_1

- *Uriagereka:* Can you consider (27)?

  (27) *The teacher$_1$ was fired t_1 without PRO$_1$ talking to e_1

Lasnik: The reason you bring up this example, I take it, is that, provided that teachers can both talk and be talked to, the sentence could not be ruled out purely for selectional reasons. In fact, we may want to compare it to (28):

(28) *The teacher$_1$ was fired t_1 after he$_1$ talked to e_1
   (meaning "after he talked to himself")

I also want to add to this paradigm (29):

(29) *The teacher$_1$ resigned after PRO$_1$ talking to e_1
   (meaning, again, "talking to himself")

These examples are all ungrammatical, obviously a significant generalization. Chomsky's description applies exactly to all three. A parasitic gap is licensed by an S-Structure *wh*-trace, and none of these sentences has a *wh*-trace. Keep in mind that the description still needs an explanation.

We must look at another example as well:

(30) *Who$_1$ t_1 resigned before we could fire e_1

If this were good, it would mean the same thing as the perfectly grammatical (31):

(31) Who$_1$ t_1 resigned before we could fire him$_1$

In a sense, (30) is the biggest mystery so far. It contains a *wh*-trace. And if licensing simply means coindexing, it exhibits licensing. So we must add to our descriptive generalizations. Chomsky (1982) proposed that in the ungrammatical cases the trace c-commands the parasitic gap, whereas in the grammatical ones it does not. He was assuming that gerundive adjunct phrases are outside the VP, which is plausible; they do not subcategorize verbs, for instance. The descriptive generalization now reads as follows: "A parasitic gap is licensed by an S-Structure *wh*-trace that does not c-command it."

• *McNulty:* An adverbial phrase adjunct can generally be fronted. But in these cases that doesn't seem true. For instance, I find (32) bad:

(32) *Without reading, which report did you file

Lasnik: Yes, which is interesting, and maybe very relevant. Notice that this is specifically a property of parasitic gaps. It is not a property of these gerundives, because as you said, they can generally be fronted:

(33) After visiting Bill, who did you hire

(33) is perfect. So parasitic gaps might exhibit some kind of left-right asymmetry, as well as the anti-c-command requirement. Or it might be that the c-command requirement we will see between the *wh*-operator and the gap is not satisfied in (32).

Consider one more paradigm, which Chomsky did not look at but which will lead us toward Chomsky's conclusion:

(34) ??Who$_1$ did you hire t_1 because Mary said e_1 would work hard

(34) is not particularly good, but it is much better than (35):

(35) *Who$_1$ did you hire t_1 because he$_1$ said e_1 would work hard

This contrast tells us something very significant about parasitic gaps—namely, that they are like variables. (35) is strongly reminiscent of a classic strong crossover effect. Actually, the issue is really theory dependent. If we believe in Condition C, this fact tells us that parasitic gaps are R-expressions. What is interesting about (35) is that it does not exactly fit into the descriptive generalization as it was presented. Every part of the descriptive generalization is true of (35). There must be an S-Structure *wh*-trace, and there is: the object of *hire*. The S-Structure *wh*-trace is not allowed to c-command the parasitic gap: by hypothesis, it does not. The *wh*-trace is inside the VP and, by hypothesis, the parasitic gap is outside. But (35) is still ungrammatical. This suggests that the requirement that the parasitic gap not be c-commanded by the real gap is simply part of a larger generalization, namely, that a parasitic gap is not allowed to be A-bound. In the classic ungrammatical cases, the ones that Chomsky gave, the parasitic gap was A-bound by the real gap. In this case the parasitic gap is not A-bound by the real gap, but it is A-bound by something, namely, *he*. So the true descriptive generalization is that a parasitic gap must be A-free.

3.2.2   Parasitic Gaps in Nonquestion Contexts

We have just been looking at *wh*-questions. We might digress to consider other constructions that allow parasitic gaps. We would certainly expect relative clauses to do so, because everything we know about relative clauses leads us to believe that they involve *Wh*-Movement.[11] And, in fact, parallel to (17) we also find (17'):

(17') The report which$_1$ I filed e_1 without reading e_1

Similarly, the ones that are unacceptable as questions are unacceptable as relative clauses. Observe the contrasts in (36):

(36) a. ??The man who$_1$ I hired e_1 because Mary said e_1 would
         work hard
     b. *The man who$_1$ I hired e_1 because he said e_1 would work hard

Two other constructions license parasitic gaps, and they are interesting in the following respect. Superficially, they do not look much like *Wh*-Movement constructions, but for theory-internal reasons, Chomsky (1977) argued that they do in fact involve *Wh*-Movement. Interestingly, they are like *Wh*-Movement constructions in this respect as well: they license parasitic gaps. Consider (37):

(37) This article$_1$ is too illogical PRO to read e_1 without PRO laughing
     at e_1

So-called *tough*-movement constructions (see section 6.2) pattern similarly:

(38) This article$_1$ is hard PRO to read e_1 without PRO laughing at e_1

Here too a parasitic gap is permitted. So whatever our theory of parasitic gaps ultimately looks like, it apparently should be consistent with Chomsky's analysis of *Wh*-Movement.

There are constructions—in particular, relativization—that greatly resemble *wh* constructions but lack a trace. As we would expect if our generalizations are correct, those constructions do not allow parasitic gaps. English does not provide the best examples of this, because the construction involves resumptive pronouns, which English does not allow very freely.[12] Some dialects of English do have them, however. Chomsky (1982) points out that even in an example where a resumptive pronoun is fairly acceptable, it cannot be used to license a parasitic gap. Thus, licensing seems to be a property at least indirectly—perhaps directly—tied to a trace, rather than to the binder of the trace. Resumptive pronoun constructions and trace constructions are often identical, except for the contrast between having a trace and having a pronoun.

Consider (39):

(39) a. ??The report which I filed it yesterday is over there
     b. *The report which I filed it yesterday without reading
        e is over there

The fact requiring explanation is that resumptive pronouns do not license parasitic gaps, even in those dialects allowing resumptive pronouns.

3.2.3   An Analysis

We are now ready to look at Chomsky's approach to these phenomena. Let us look first at (17), repeated here as (40):

(40) Which report$_1$ did you$_2$ file e_1 without e_2 reading e_x

Let us assume, with Chomsky, that the indexation in (40) is obligatory. Assuming that the last empty category is base-generated, we can give it any index we want. That is not established, but it is the null hypothesis. For the first two empty categories, movement or control forces the indexing in (40), but no such requirement holds for the last one. There are three possibilities to consider: x can be *1, 2,* or *3*. One of these, index *2*, will presumably violate selectional restrictions, assuming one cannot read a person, but we could solve that by changing the example (as in (27)). (40) would still be ruled out, as a Condition C violation, or the equivalent. Hence, let us put aside any concerns about selectional restrictions. With index *3*, the empty category will not be licensed. In Chomsky's (1982) terms, neither e_3 nor e_2 would be functionally determined as a variable. We will return to the consequences of this. Consider finally the value that gives a grammatical output, namely, *1*. Since the structure contains three empty categories, let us determine what they are by applying Chomsky's algorithm. The first empty category is locally $\bar{A}$-bound by an operator, so it is a variable. The second empty category is not a variable, since it is not $\bar{A}$-bound at all. Hence, it is $[+a]$.[13] By the third part of the algorithm, provided that the empty category is A-bound by something with an independent θ-role (the subject of *file* is a θ-position), the empty category must also be $[+p]$. Hence, it is PRO. (Even if the empty category had a totally different index—that is, if it were free—it would still be PRO.) Now, for the indexation *1* on the last empty category, we first must look for the nearest binder. The gap has only one binder—namely, *which report*. (Recall that, by hypothesis, the trace does not c-command the parasitic gap.) The binder in question is an operator in an $\bar{A}$-position, which makes the last empty category $[-a, -p]$.

Let us look now at (41):

(41) The report which$_1$ I filed e_1 without PRO reading e_1

The first gap must obviously be determined as a *wh*-trace; otherwise, even a simple construction like *the article which I filed* will be impossible. And in fact it is determined straightforwardly as such: it is locally $\bar{A}$-bound by an operator, so it is a variable. What about the last gap? Since the trace does not c-command it, its nearest binder is the operator *which*, in an $\bar{A}$-position. Hence, the gap is correctly functionally determined as a variable.

I regard this analysis of parasitic gaps as the great triumph of functional determination. I have never been convinced by the Condition C argument, because Condition C is apparently needed regardless. But functional determination really works well for parasitic gaps. It provides the beginnings of a theory that captures the observed descriptive generalizations. Notice that the theory itself did not have to refer to any of the descriptive generalizations—instead, the description follows from general properties. We did not even need to say anything about parasitic gaps. We have an algorithm that applies to empty categories in general.

Let us make sure, at this point, that we can rule out all of the ungrammatical examples of parasitic gaps we have looked at. But keep in mind the goal: we want to rule them all out without referring to any of the descriptive generalizations. If we succeed in that, we will have explained those generalizations. Consider (42):

(42) *The report$_1$ was filed e_1 after Bill read e_1

The first empty category in (42) must (or can, depending on which version of Chomsky's theory we are assuming) be $[+a]$, since it is not a variable. Moreover, since it is bound by something that lacks an independent θ-role (*the report* and the empty category constitute a chain), it is [−p]. It is thus the kind of empty category that must be A-bound in its GC, as we expected. The second empty category is not $\bar{\text{A}}$-bound either. Again, it can or it must be [+a]. Is it [+p] or not? Here is a case of potential circularity that Chomsky did not consider. The empty category is bound by the matrix subject. The question of whether the latter has an independent θ-role depends on what we mean by "independent θ-role." The subject does not have its own θ-role, so it is not clear whether the empty category will be determined as [+p] or [−p]. It will be determined as [+p] if we decide that by some definition the subject in question does have an independent θ-role. Otherwise, it will be determined as [−p]. Chomsky would presumably say that the subject does have an independent θ-role, which means that the notion must be relativized. But then the analysis becomes very tricky. We must know why the subject's θ-role is independent of the second, and not of the first, empty category. The answer would be because the first empty category forms a chain with the subject, whereas the second does not. But, as Brody (1984) argued, we do not know what empty categories form chains with what categories until we know what empty categories are traces and what empty categories are PROs. In any event, if the second empty category is determined either as PRO or as NP-trace, we are on the right track. In either case it will violate Condition A of the Binding Theory. If the assignment [+a] is optional, we must still consider making the empty category [−a]. If the correct interpretation of this theory is that the subject of the root clause has an independent θ-role, then the empty category will be determined as [+p], which will be ruled out for the usual (nonexplanatory, at this point) reason that English does not have pro. One final possibility is to interpret "independent θ-role" in the way we considered earlier whereby the matrix subject does not have an independent θ-role. Then the empty category will be determined as [−p]. Condition C can, of course, rule this option out, but only if the theory admits Condition C. Since the theory developed in Chomsky 1982 does not, presumably that theory must define "independent θ-role" in such a way that *the report* does have an independent θ-role. Then this problematic possibility will not exist.

For a parasitic gap, then, "being licensed" means being functionally determined as a variable. If an empty category is trying to exist in the constructions in question as a parasitic gap, and it cannot be functionally determined as a variable, then it cannot be anything. It cannot be an NP-trace, because it will not be A-bound in its GC; it cannot be PRO, because it will be governed; and it cannot be pro, because English does not have pro. Furthermore, even in languages that have pro, its distribution is heavily restricted (for reasons that are as yet unclear). We know under what circumstances the empty category can be determined as a variable: if it is locally $\bar{\text{A}}$-bound by an operator at S-structure.

Consider now a case where there is no real gap, but just a parasitic gap, or rather, an empty category vainly trying to be a parasitic gap:

(43) *I filed the article without PRO reading e

The empty category here cannot be determined as a variable because there is no operator. Once it is not a variable, it is nothing—the analysis is straightforward.

Let us consider some of the more interesting cases—for example, one in which there is an S-Structure *wh*-trace but in which the parasitic gap is not A-free. First consider (44a), which, if it were grammatical, would mean the same thing as (44b):

(44) a. *Who_1 e_1 left after you insulted e_1
      b. Who_1 e_1 left after you insulted him_1

The first empty category in (44a) can be determined as a variable, since it is locally $\overline{\text{A}}$-bound by an operator. The second empty category is bound by two elements, and in fact one of these is an operator. But is the empty category *locally* $\overline{\text{A}}$-bound by an operator? No, because its nearest binder is the first empty category. Thus, it will not be determined as a variable, and, as we have seen, there is no other viable possibility.

We have now ruled out the case where there is no "licensing" gap at all, the case where an NP-trace instead of a *wh*-trace attempts to function as licenser, and the case where the *wh*-trace c-commands the parasitic gap. At this point we should make sure that we can rule out examples like (35), repeated here as (45):

(45) *Who_1 did you hire e_1 because he_1 said e_1 would work hard

The first empty category is locally $\overline{\text{A}}$-bound by *who*, hence a variable. The second empty category is bound by *he* and by *who*. Again, it is not locally $\overline{\text{A}}$-bound by an operator, since its nearest binder is *he*, and it is therefore not a variable. In particular, that second empty category will be determined as a pronominal and (45) will constitute either a "pro-drop" violation or a violation of Condition A, depending on whether the empty category is determined as $[-a, +p]$ or $[+a, +p]$.

3.2.4 Problems with Resumptives: The Theory Extended

The theory rules out all the ungrammatical cases we have introduced, except for those that involve resumptive pronouns. Let us now consider (39b), repeated here as (46):

(46) *The article which_1 I filed it_1 yesterday without PRO reading
      e_1 is over there

(46) is superficially very surprising. The empty category is $\overline{\text{A}}$-bound by the relative operator, in fact locally $\overline{\text{A}}$-bound by that operator. Thus, it should be a variable. (46) should not be worse than any sentence with a resumptive pronoun and no parasitic gap, yet in dialects allowing resumptive pronouns the contrast is clear.

Let us see what we would like to happen and then how we can make it happen. Recall that parasitic gaps must be licensed at S-Structure. The way to be licensed is to be locally $\overline{A}$-bound by an operator and thus functionally determined as a variable. Suppose, then, that at S-Structure *which* had no index. Then the empty category would not be a variable because it would not be $\overline{A}$-bound. It would in fact not be bound at all. (The empty category would be determined either as PRO if assignment of [+a] is obligatory or possibly as pro if assignment of [+a] is optional. In the former case Condition A is violated; in the latter case whatever constraint instantiates the pro-drop parameter is violated.) The type of S-Structure representation we are considering, where *which* has no index, could not be optional, since if it were, the one with an index would still be possible and we would still generate (46). So we must force *which* not to have an index at S-Structure. But why should this be the only possible representation at S-Structure? That is, why should the operator not be *allowed* to have an index? Let us follow the logic of Chomsky's (1982) proposal for assignment of indices. Consider (47):

(47) a. Coindex via movement.
     b. Freely assign indices.

(47a) says that if an item is moved to another position, the moved item and its trace must be coindexed. Some elements do not move, but they are indexed nonetheless; that is case (47b). This case is crucial; otherwise, reflexives (for instance) would never be permitted. Without (47b), a reflexive that had not moved could never have an index, hence would always violate Condition A. Given (47), we would still have trouble trying to rule out (46), because we could freely assign index *1* to all the relevant categories in (46)—as in the representation I gave. Here is Chomsky's answer to the problem:

(48) a. Coindex via movement.
     b. Freely assign indices to A-positions.

The empty category is in an A-position: it is the object of *reading*. *It* is in an A-position: it is the object of *file*. But *which* is not in an A-position: it is in Comp. So by (48), as opposed to (47), it will not be freely assigned an index, under the assumption, of course, that no movement took place. (If movement did take place from the position of the empty category to Comp, then an island constraint, Subjacency, was ultimately violated.) If *which* cannot receive an index, then the empty category is not locally $\overline{A}$-bound by an operator and thus cannot be a variable. This is the correct result, since (46) must be ruled out. But what about dialects that allow (49) (that is, constructions with no parasitic gap but with a resumptive pronoun)?

(49) The article *which* I filed *it*...

Presumably, it is necessary to establish a relationship between the italicized positions in (49), if the structure is to be interpretable. How could that relationship be established? Not by movement, because there is no gap. Not at S-Structure, because by (48) we can assign indices only to A-positions at that level. Plausibly, then, the relationship could be established at LF. The whole proposal for indexation would then be as follows:

(50) a. Coindex via movement.
 b. Freely assign indices to A-positions at S-Structure.
 c. Freely assign indices at LF.

The fact that parasitic gaps must be licensed at S-Structure basically follows in this theory from two claims: that what goes wrong when a parasitic gap is not licensed is that a Binding Condition is violated, and that Binding Conditions must be satisfied at S-Structure (see sections 1.3.2 and 2.1.4).

But let us make sure that we can still generate the good examples like (17). There the parasitic gap receives an index at S-Structure because it is in an A-position. The real gap and the operator must be coindexed under movement. At least that is a possible derivation. It does not matter whether it is the only derivation, as long as it is possible. There is another imaginable derivation where the real gap is base-generated. (Recall that it is necessary to base-generate empty categories in general under this approach, or parasitic gaps would be impossible altogether.) The operator would then be base-generated in Comp. At S-Structure neither gap could be a variable, and thus we would have two Binding Condition violations.

This is a very important conclusion, for the following reason. Consider (51):

(51) *What$_2$ [did you meet [$_{NP}$ a man [who$_1$ [e$_1$ likes e$_2$]]]]

This is a classic island violation, an example of Subjacency. Our investigation of parasitic gaps has demonstrated that it is possible to base-generate empty categories. Suppose we base-generate the empty categories and the operators in (51) (or in (18)). Then suppose we could index these elements as in (51). That does not create a problem with respect to e_1, but it does with respect to e_2. The example would not violate Subjacency now, because movement is not involved and Subjacency is strictly a constraint on movement, in this theory. It would not violate the Binding Theory either, because e_2 is locally $\overline{A}$-bound by the operator *what*, hence a variable. But then the structure does not violate anything, which is clearly an incorrect result. We have found a good derivation for a bad sentence. We did find a derivation that ruled it out—namely, movement—but we also found one that ruled it in. Thus, the example can be generated, under the assumptions outlined. If we aren't able to exclude it, we will be able to base-generate the whole range of Subjacency violations. The proposal for indexation in (50) neatly solves this. Coindexation via movement cannot be relevant here because, by hypothesis, there was no movement. However, indices are freely assigned at S-Structure *to A-positions only*. The operator is not in an A-position, so it will not receive (by (50b)) an index at S-Structure. Functional determination obligatorily applies at S-Structure because the Binding Theory applies there—obviously, we cannot apply the Binding Conditions until we know what type of empty category we are dealing with. The empty category will then be functionally determined as either PRO or pro, depending, as usual, on the obligatoriness of the assignment of the feature [+a]. Both of those will be illicit, as before.

The theory of functional determination of empty categories has thus kept us from wrongly generating island violations. That is a nice result. In fact, I do not know how to keep from base-generating such violations without functional determination. What is particularly nice about this analysis is that everything we have used to explain this phenomenon was independently motivated by properties of parasitic gaps. We did not have to introduce any new machinery.

3.2.5 Summary and Residual Problems

To what extent have we explained the phenomena we considered? We have explained why resumptive pronouns do not support parasitic gaps. If a sentence contains a resumptive pronoun, no movement has taken place to Comp. A base-generated item in Comp will not have an index at S-Structure. We have explained why it is crucially a *wh*-trace that is involved. Comp, an $\bar{A}$-position, must be filled; hence, *Wh*-Movement must have taken place. We now have a dual explanation for the fact that a parasitic gap must be A-free. If it is not A-free, the vast majority of the time it will not be locally $\bar{A}$-bound by an operator. That is like Koopman and Sportiche's explanation of strong crossover. If an empty category is trying to be a *wh*-trace, but it is locally bound by a pronoun instead of by an operator, then it will fail to be a *wh*-trace. If in addition we believe in Condition C, we have another explanation for the phenomenon in question.

What did we have to stipulate to make this analysis work? Apparently, the only real stipulation is that free assignment of indices is limited to A-positions at S-Structure. Everything else that was novel involved the removal of stipulations. For instance, in this analysis there is no restriction on base-generating empty categories. A priori, that is an improvement over previous theories. Note too that the one remaining stipulation explains two independent phenomena: some problematic cases of parasitic gaps involving resumptive pronouns, and the impossibility of base-generating island violations.

Let us look at one last phenomenon involving parasitic gaps. Consider (52):

(52) Who$_1$ did you give a picture of e_1 to e_1

Either gap in (52) could be a trace, but not both simultaneously, because only one thing could have moved. Both positions are accessible to movement, however, as (53) shows:[14]

(53) a. Who did you give a picture of *t* to Bill
     b. Who did you give a picture of Bill to *t*

The problem, of course, is that Chomsky's theory lets (52) in. If I were Chomsky, I would have had trouble with that, since I find (52) totally ungrammatical. Back in the early 1980s, though, when linguists started taking this example seriously, a surprising result emerged. Almost half of the people asked about it thought that (52) was all right. But it turns out that most of them in fact disallowed it so extremely that they were turning it into something apparently inconceivable, syntactically. They were interpreting (52) as if it were (54):

(54) (*)Who did you give a picture of who to *t*

That is, they were taking it as a double *wh*-question, without a coindexed trace at all as the object of *of*. That is presumably illicit: we cannot just freely delete a *wh*-phrase in situ. But that is how these people, rather generally, were interpreting (52). That speakers would go to such lengths to avoid understanding (52) as a parasitic gap construction suggests that such an interpretation is strongly excluded.[15] Chomsky, though, gives example (52) as a well-formed parasitic gap construction, whose grammaticality is explained by the theory. But I think the reverse is actually true. That the theory we have developed lets (52) in, I regard as a problem. Both gaps can be functionally determined as variables, since they are both locally $\bar{A}$-bound. Since neither of these positions c-commands the other, (52) ought to be acceptable. We are obviously missing something. It has to be relevant that in cases like (52) either gap could be a trace, whereas in the good cases only one of the gaps could be a trace. But I do not know just how to make that fact relevant.

- *Yang:* So the operator in Comp can bind two variables?
  Lasnik: Yes, that has to be true in this theory, and, on some accounts, it is precisely what is funny about parasitic gaps altogether. These examples have a *wh*-phrase that is locally binding two different items. For instance, the Bijection Principle of Koopman and Sportiche (1982), which was proposed as an account of weak crossover, rules out configurations in which an operator (locally) binds two variables (see section 6.3 for discussion). The Bijection Principle would therefore rule out all parasitic gap constructions. (Koopman and Sportiche actually presented this as an argument *for* the Bijection Principle, because of the somewhat marginal status of certain parasitic gap constructions. But many such constructions are perfect.)

The descriptive problem is that (17), the standard case, is perfect, whereas (52) is quite bad. So if a certain principle is used to rule out (52), but it does not distinguish (52) from (17), we are right back where we started.

It is occasionally argued in other contexts that *to* is really not a preposition but a sort of Case marker. If that is so, then we do not really have a prepositional phrase in (52), but an NP of some sort, and then the first gap is arguably bound by the second gap. In that case the first gap would not be a variable. But I think (52) can be replicated with other prepositions that no one would argue are mere Case markers. It would be nice if we constructed such an example and it turned out to be much better than (52), but that does not seem to be true. Consider (55):

(55) (*)Who$_1$ did you put a picture of e_1 under e_1

In my view (55) is as bad as (52), and we have no way of explaining this. This represents an interesting problematic research area.

I want to reiterate, nevertheless, that the analysis of parasitic gaps is a triumph of functional determination. In recent years Chomsky has given up functional determination and gone back to intrinsic features, for what I regard as basically good reasons. But as a result he no longer has an analysis of certain central properties of parasitic gaps. For example, much recent work has no convincing account for the striking property of parasitic gaps that they cannot be A-bound.

3.3 Free Determination of Empty Categories

Let us consider now an idea basically due to Brody (1984), which differs both from Chomsky's proposal in Chomsky 1981b and from his proposal in Chomsky 1982. In the former proposal empty categories have inherent features. In the latter proposal empty categories are assigned features by an algorithm, say at S-Structure. Brody proposes that the features [±a] and [±p] are *freely* assigned. A priori, it is the right sort of theory, because it means fewer stipulations—basically, none. But the question is, does it work?

3.3.1 *Considering All Options*

Consider (56):

(56) Who *e* left?

There will always be four possibilities now, for there is no algorithm, and there are four combinations of two binary features. For the moment let us assume that *who* and *e* are obligatorily coindexed, though later on we will question even that assumption.

(57) Who$_1$ e_1 left
    a. $e = [+a, +p]$
    b. $e = [+a, -p]$
    c. $e = [-a, +p]$
    d. $e = [-a, -p]$

(57a) and (57b) violate Condition A of the Binding Theory, since in either case an anaphor is A-free in its GC. We know there must be an answer for (57c): somehow, we have to be able to say that English does not have (57c) because it is not a pro-drop language. But of course we do not really know what that means. Putting (57c) aside, we are left with (iv), which has to work out, because the sentence is grammatical. Conditions A and B are not relevant. Condition C could be,[16] but in fact e is not A-bound, so there is no problem with Condition C. There is also a requirement of no vacuous quantification. But as long as *who* and e are coindexed, e can be realized as a variable bound by the operator *who*; so (56) does not run afoul of vacuous quantification either.

If everything worked as well as this, then we would have to adopt this theory, since it is conceptually so attractive. Koopman and Sportiche could perhaps argue that the theory needs to *add* Condition C, but that seems wrong because it looks as though Condition C is needed apart from the treatment of empty categories (for instance, for anaphoric epithets, as in section 2.1.3.1).

Let us look at one more grammatical example and then at some ungrammatical ones. Logically, the grammatical ones won't tell us much, because any representation available under functional determination is also available under free determination. We simply have to pick the feature matrix that would be functionally determined as the right one and freely assign it. The problem, if there is one, will be *overgeneration* rather than *undergeneration*. Nonetheless, let's consider one final grammatical example, just to get the feel of the theory:

(58) John$_1$ was hired e_1

    a. $e = [+a, +p]$
    b. $e = [+a, -p]$
    c. $e = [-a, +p]$
    d. $e = [-a, -p]$

(58d) violates Condition C. (58c) violates both Condition B and the pro-drop parameter. (58a) violates Condition B. So (58b) is our only hope. Neither Condition B nor Condition C is relevant. Condition A is relevant, and it is satisfied in (58). Ultimately we will have to impose a further requirement on (58); namely, we will need a chain condition explaining the part of Chomsky's (1982) algorithm that depends on whether or not an element has an independent θ-role. (We will return to this.)

3.3.2 Chain Formation

Now let us look at more interesting cases, like (59). (I will stay at first with cases that functional determination accounted for.)

(59) a. *John$_1$ likes e_1
    b. *John$_1$ likes e_2

       Chapter 3

According to functional determination, *e* is not a variable in either (59a) or (59b). It is a pronominal in both, however, since it is locally A-bound by something with an independent θ-role in (59a), and it is free in (59b). But then in (59a) it will violate Condition B, no matter whether it is [+a] or [−a]. In (59b) the option [+a] violates Condition A, whereas the option [−a] violates the pro-drop parameter.

Free determination also rules out the options we have just considered for precisely the reasons we have adduced. Now we need to consider the possibilities that functional determination did not deal with at all. Two cases are relatively easy to rule out. The option [+a, −p] for (59b) will be ruled out by Condition A. The option [−a, −p] for (59a) will be ruled out by Condition C. But two other cases—[−a, −p] for (59b) and [+a, −p] for (59a)—are quite difficult to rule out. For the former case we presumably need some sort of principle stating that a variable must be bound by an operator—just as an operator must bind a variable. We might want to consider the cost of this principle in terms of the theory, whether it is needed independently, and so forth. For the second case we need some requirement on chains—something like "An NP-trace and its A-binder obligatorily form a chain." In that case the example in question would violate the θ-Criterion, since it would have a single chain with two θ-roles.

A methodological remark is in order here, with regard to adding conditions in order to account for difficult cases. One can imagine a theory that has more stipulations about what features empty categories have, but fewer stipulations of the sort considered above. A theory of that type might be one that says, "Any trace and something that binds it *optionally* constitute a chain." As far as I can see, in the above cases we needed to *force* the chain to exist. Thus, part of the cost of free assignment of features is perhaps the need for such a chain condition.

Now consider (60):

(60) **e* died

The empty category in (60) cannot be [+a], since that would violate Condition A. It cannot be [−a, +p] because of the English setting of the pro-drop parameter. For the option [−a, −p] we will have to use the "no free variables" condition suggested with respect to (59b). Thus, every possible representation for (60) is excluded, as required.

3.3.3 Free Indexation

Let us now begin to consider an even freer theory. Not only are all *features* freely assigned, but all *indices* are freely assigned as well. The only cases we will really have to look at now are cases of movement. In cases without movement, indices were already freely assigned. More-over, the only movement case we have to consider is one in which something is moved from a position and is not coindexed with the empty category it left behind; we have already explored the cases where it *is* coindexed. Consider then (61):

(61) Who$_1$ [e_2 left]

e cannot be [+a] at all, for it would then violate Condition A. Nor can it be [−a, +p], as usual. The option [−a, −p] violates the "no free variables" condition. In fact, (61) would also violate the "no vacuous quantification" principle. Thus, all possibilities are excluded, as desired.

Let us look next at a passive case:

(62) John$_1$ was killed e_2

e cannot be either [+a] or [−a, +p], for the usual reasons. [−a, −p] is then ruled out by the "no free variables" condition.

McNulty: But (62) also violates the θ-Criterion.
Lasnik: Right. *John* and *e* do not constitute a chain since *e* is not [+a, −p]; thus, *John* cannot be assigned a θ-role. (Recall that *John* is not in a position to which a θ-role is assigned).

Consider also (63):

(63) Who [e was killed e]

(63) offers many possibilities. Immediately, we can eliminate the option in which *who* and the first gap are not coindexed. In subject position in this configuration the gap can only be a variable—that is, [−a, −p]. But if it is not bound by the operator, it will violate the "no free variables" condition. On the other hand, the second gap, if it is coindexed with the first one, cannot be [+p] at all, since that would violate Condition B. If it is [−a, −p], then Condition C would be violated. So that leaves only [+a, −p], which does not violate the Binding Theory. Earlier we decided there is a condition on an empty category that is [+a, −p], namely, that it must form a chain with its A-binder. Only one θ-role can be assigned to the chain, but that is exactly what we have in (63), in the representation we are dealing with. Hence, that representation is correctly allowed.

We must still look at the possibility where the two gaps are not coindexed. In such a case the second gap cannot be [+a] at all, since it would violate Condition A. If it is [−a, −p], it is a free variable; and if it is [−a, +p], then the pro-drop parameter is violated. (Note also that in this case, as well as some of the earlier ones, the θ-Criterion is violated, since an empty category that is [−a, +p] must be an argument; that is, it cannot transmit a θ-role.)

We have considered a very large number of possibilities and have successfully narrowed the grammatical representation down to just one of those.

Let us now analyze (64):

(64) *John is illegal [[e to park here]]

All the options in which *John* and *e* are not coindexed are ruled out by the θ-Criterion, since *John* is neither in a θ-position nor part of a chain under these conditions. Next consider the case in which *John* and *e* are coindexed. If the latter is $[-a, -p]$, Condition C is violated. If it is $[-a, +p]$, the pro-drop parameter is violated. Ultimately, we will have to propose the converse of the idea of an NP-trace being able to transmit a θ-role. That is, as noted with regard to (63), no other empty category is allowed to transmit a θ-role. And that would create a θ-Criterion violation as well in the case we are considering, since *John* could not receive a θ-role. On the other hand, $[+a, -p]$ will not violate the chain condition. There is exactly one θ-role to be assigned, and (because of the formation of a chain) *John* would be licensed, incorrectly allowing the example. However, there is an additional requirement on traces, to be explored at length in chapter 4, that essentially requires them to be governed. This requirement, known as the *Empty Category Principle* (ECP), rules this option out. The subject of the complement of *illegal* is not governed, since there is no S'-Deletion.

Consider now the final option. The index assignment $[+a, +p]$ satisfies the Binding Conditions, for *e* does not have a GC, since it is not governed in (64). No principle developed so far is violated. In fact, this option would be fine, if *John* and the empty category could constitute a chain. As suggested earlier, we must rule out this possibility (though we do not want to prevent *John* from being part of a chain in general). We must keep PRO from being a nonhead of a chain. PRO is, of course, allowed to be the *head* of a chain, as in (65):

(65) John wanted [e to be arrested e]

$$\begin{bmatrix} +a \\ +p \end{bmatrix} \qquad \begin{bmatrix} +a \\ -p \end{bmatrix}$$

The requirement would have to be that for a category to be allowed to be a nonhead of a chain, it must have the features $[+a, -p]$. Descriptively, what I am saying is that NP-Movement can only leave behind a $[+a, -p]$ empty category. The way to rule out the representation in question, then, is by means of the θ-Criterion. *John* cannot receive a θ-role, since there is no chain it can be part of. This makes a strong prediction. If we had a category in the position of *John* in (65) that was not an argument and hence needed no θ-role, then the sentence would be grammatical. And that is true:

(66) It is illegal to park here

- *Hong:* Can we consider (67)?

(67) *John$_1$ tried [[e$_2$ to win]]

Lasnik: $[-a, -p]$ would be a free variable. $[+a, -p]$ violates the ECP. It also violates the θ-Criterion if we strengthen the chain requirement mentioned earlier to a requirement that a $[+a, -p]$ empty category must form a chain with a binder. That is, a $[+a, -p]$ empty category must "transmit" a θ-role. In turn, $[-a, +p]$ violates the pro-drop param-

eter. $[+a, +p]$ is the case you are probably interested in. Notice that
this option must also be excluded.

- *Kawai:* Is Control relevant?
  Lasnik: It has to be. Nothing other than Control would rule the representation out under our assumptions: neither Binding Conditions, nor
  any chain condition (because the gap is not an NP-trace), nor the ECP
  (because the gap is not a trace at all), nor the θ-Criterion (because PRO
  is always an argument and here it is in an argument position). (67) is
  customarily claimed to be a configuration of obligatory control, which
  means that *John* and the gap must be coindexed, even though the
  Binding Conditions do not entail that.

- *McNulty:* Can we dispense with the requirement that *wh*-trace needs
  Case in this theory?
  Lasnik: Let us investigate that. Consider (68):

(68) a. *Who_1 [is it likely [e_1 to win the race]]
   b. Who_1 [is it likely [e_1 will win the race]]

Consider the case where e is $[-a, -p]$. e is then an argument and is in
an argument position. It is $\bar{\text{A}}$-bound by an operator and not A-bound
at all. Thus, it does not look like it violates anything, except for the
requirement that *wh*-trace needs Case. Apparently, the latter is an
irreducible stipulation.[17]

3.3.4 Island Violations and Other Difficulties

One final consideration concerns how to block base generation of
island violations of the following form:

(69) $\text{Operator}_1 \ldots [_{BN} \ldots [_{BN} \ldots e_1 \ldots] \ldots] \ldots$
$$\begin{bmatrix} -a \\ -p \end{bmatrix}$$
  (BN = bounding node)

With functional determination, it is relatively easy to prevent this from
happening, as we saw in section 3.2.4. (The empty category will be functionally determined as PRO or pro at S-Structure, and either possibility
is straightforwardly excluded.) Without functional determination, it is
not so obvious, since we can give the gap whatever features we like,
including $[-a, -p]$, and then, when we reach LF, we must be able to
give the operator an index. (Recall that such assignment was necessary
even in Chomsky's (1982) account in order to license resumptive pronoun constructions.) So, at LF at least, we will have neither a free
variable nor a vacuous quantifier. Furthermore, it seems to me that
both of these requirements should be LF requirements. Thus, at LF the
construction in question would not violate anything. By hypothesis, it
would not violate anything at S-Structure, either, as long as the gap
could be $[-a, -p]$. Chomsky was able to keep the gap from having

those features because the algorithm could not have assigned them, since the operator did not have an index at S-Structure. But now it is not clear what the possibilities are of preventing this. Apparently, it simply must be stipulated that an operator cannot be base-generated in Comp. But there certainly seem to be resumptive pronoun languages, and some of them at least seem to have base-generated operators in Comp. Chomsky has occasionally denied that, claiming that resumptive pronoun constructions never contain an operator. But that seems incorrect. Certainly the English dialects that allow resumptive pronouns seem to allow relative clauses with overt operators, as well as those without. Thus, these dialects allow both of the sentences in (70):

(70) a. The man that I wonder whether he will win the race
     b. The man who I wonder whether he will win the race

It is true, however—and this is what Chomsky is basing his claim on—that resumptive pronouns with questions are much rarer than resumptive pronouns with relative clauses; and questions undeniably contain an operator. Compare (71a) and (71b):

(71) a. The man who you wonder whether he will win the race
     b. ?*Which man do you wonder whether he will win the race

But if it is ever possible to have an operator with a resumptive pronoun, the theory must be capable of base-generating operators in Comp. However, if the theory base-generates operators in Comp and has free assignment of features instead of functional determination of empty categories, then it runs into trouble when the assignment $[-a, -p]$ shows up in the case under consideration.[18]

    Finally, let us not forget the problem we saw with an example brought up by Epstein (1984) (see example (15)):

(72) *Who_1 did he_1 try [e_1 [e_1 to win the race]]

Recall that the lower *e* does not have a GC, rendering Binding Conditions A and B irrelevant. Control Theory does not reject (72), nor, presumably, does Case Theory. Thus, if we freely assign $[+a, +p]$ to the lower *e* in (72), we will have no obvious way of accounting for the ungrammaticality of the example. I know of only one theory that straightforwardly does not allow the gap in question to be PRO: namely, the theory with intrinsic determination of features. In that theory the gap must be a variable because it is a *wh*-trace, that is, an empty category created by *Wh*-Movement. I regard this as an unfortunate consequence, because Brody's free assignment theory is conceptually appealing in a number of respects.

Chapter 4   The Empty Category Principle

4.1   On the Distribution of Traces

4.1.1   Introduction

Consider a D-Structure representation like (1):

(1) [[*e* is crucial [[John to see this]]]]

I assume that (1) is a perfectly well-formed D-Structure representation. *Crucial* takes an S′ complement and does not assign a θ-role to a subject. *See* assigns a θ-role, and there is an argument, *this*, to receive it; *see this* assigns a subject θ-role, and there is an argument, *John*, to receive it. If we try to convert (1) directly into an S-Structure form without doing anything else, except for inserting *it*, we get (2):

(2) *[[It is crucial [[John to see this]]]]

(2) will be ruled out by the Case Filter, since *John* would not receive Case. But I want to make things more difficult. Consider (3):

(3) *[[John is crucial [[*t* to see this]]]]

Can we explain the ungrammaticality of (3)? It certainly does not violate the Case Filter: *John* is in a position where it does receive Case, and it moved from a position where it would not receive Case. It does not violate the Projection Principle because it was well-formed at D-Structure and we have not created or destroyed any arguments or argument positions along the way. So we might hope that it violates Condition A—but it does not. What is the GC of the trace? It does not have one; that position is not governed. But if something does not have a GC, then it satisfies Condition A. That was how we allowed PRO to exist (see section 2.2.4). Thus, nothing we have said so far explains the ungrammaticality of (3).

   Let us compare (3) with a similar but grammatical example:

(4) John is certain [*t* to see this]

Notice that (5) would be ungrammatical:

(5) *It is certain [PRO to see this]

((5) is perfectly coherent: if we pick some person at random, it is certain that he or she can see this. But the example cannot mean that.) Something interesting is going on here. Where trace is grammatical, PRO is ungrammatical, and vice versa. Neither PRO nor NP-trace needs Case, so we cannot appeal to Case Theory to explain this fact. Nor can Condition A explain these effects. In (3), as in well-formed instances of

PRO, Condition A is trivially satisfied since there is no relevant GC. In the ungrammatical cases of section 2.2.4 we ruled out PRO by deducing that it must be ungoverned. If it is true that wherever PRO can occur, trace cannot—and that is the way things are shaping up descriptively—obviously the generalization is this: trace must be governed. This is not quite parallel to the requirement that PRO must be ungoverned, because the latter we were able to deduce from independent principles, in particular, from the interaction of Conditions A and B. It does not appear that we can deduce from anything the requirement that trace must be governed. When we have something that is descriptively true, either we can deduce it from something else, in which case it is a theorem, or we cannot deduce it from anything else, in which case it is a principle. The fact that a trace must be governed seems to be a principle. This requirement is commonly called the *Empty Category Principle* (ECP); it was first proposed by Chomsky (1981b). (This is not actually a very good name. For one thing, the ECP is only about traces and not, crucially, about PRO. If PRO had to be governed, then PRO could never occur, since Conditions A and B conspire to guarantee that it *not* be governed.) Our first version of this principle must be something like (6):[1]

(6) A trace must be governed.

Let us see how this would work in the examples above. In (3) the trace is in an ungoverned position, so our new principle directly rules the sentence out. In (5) PRO is apparently in an illegal position. The best way to explain that is to say that the position is governed. Thus, the trace in (4) is perfectly all right. But why should that position be governed? It will be governed exactly if no S' boundary separates *certain* from *t*. When an S' intervenes, PRO, not trace, is allowed. When no S' intervenes, trace, not PRO, is allowed. We came to a similar conclusion earlier, in the case of *believe*, where it was easy to show the absence of S' because of Case assignment (see section 1.4.2). With an adjective, as in (4), the argument must be indirect, because adjectives do not assign Case.

We know some respects in which NP-trace behaves differently from a lexical NP. But here we have one respect in which it behaves like a lexical NP. Not exactly like it, since it has a slightly weaker requirement: the lexical NP must be governed by a Case assigner. All we have concluded about an NP-trace is that it must be governed. Obviously, we cannot say that an NP-trace must be governed by a Case assigner, because then we would prohibit passive or raising constructions entirely. It would be nice to deduce (6) from deeper principles. So far no one has been able to do that completely, though there have been several interesting attempts. But it should be clear that we haven't yet achieved much explanatory depth. We have a fact that needs to be explained—namely, (6)—and we have essentially called that fact a principle.

4.1.2 The That-Trace Effect

Let us consider some additional facts that Chomsky tried to explain with a principle along the lines of (6). One of these facts is the *that-trace* paradigm, first discussed by Perlmutter (1971) and later investigated by a variety of linguists, including Bresnan (1972) and Chomsky and Lasnik (1977). The basic phenomenon is illustrated in (7) and (8):

(7) a. Who do you think [that [John saw *t*]]
    b. Who do you think [[John saw *t*]]

(8) a. *Who do you think [that [*t* saw Bill]]
    b. Who do you think [[*t* saw Bill]]

(7b) and (8b) illustrate a perfect extraction of an object and a subject, respectively. In these cases the complementizer of the embedded clause is null. Interestingly, when this complementizer is overt (*that*), the extraction of the object is possible but not the extraction of the subject, as shown in (7a) and (8a), respectively. Informally, when *that* is immediately followed by a trace, ungrammaticality results, hence the descriptive name of the phenomenon.

From the point of view of (6), (7a) is no problem. The trace is a direct object, and direct objects are governed. (7b) is likewise no problem. (8b) is all right because the trace is governed by Agr—it is the subject of a finite clause. But by this same reasoning, the trace in (8a) should also be licensed. Thus, (6) does not yet account for the paradigm in question.

Here is Chomsky's modification of (6):

(9) A trace must be *properly* governed.

There are two ways in which a trace can be properly governed. The first might be called *lexical government*, the core case of which is defined as follows:

(10) A head lexically governs its complements.

Before considering the other way in which a trace can be properly governed, let us see whether (10) helps us at all with the paradigm under consideration. The examples in (7) are still ruled in, since we are dealing with a direct object—the complement of a verb. And (8a) is now accounted for as well. The trace in (8a), though it is governed, is not lexically governed—it is not the complement of any head. But now (8b) is a problem. It is excluded for the same reason as (8a). (9) and (10) correctly rule out (8a) but incorrectly rule out (8b) as well. For the trace in (8b), we need a special exemption. Further, the special exemption we grant to the trace in (8b) mustn't carry over to (8a); if it does, we will lose the account of the paradigm again.

4.1.3 Antecedent Government

Here is the special exemption: a second way in which a trace can be properly governed is called *antecedent government*, informally defined as follows:

(11) α antecedent-governs β iff α binds β and α and β are not too far apart.

We will have to collect data to determine how far is "too far."

Let us look now at our problematic case, (8b). The trace there is not lexically governed. It does have an antecedent; that is, it has a binder. Now suppose that the structure in (8b) is of the type that satisfies the ECP requirements of the trace in question. Then (8a) is once again incorrectly allowed, for there the binder is exactly as far away from the antecedent as it is in (8b). We must make use of the difference in the complementizers, something we have not yet done. One way to say this, though not exactly Chomsky's way, is as follows: if Comp contains *that*, then it cannot contain anything else. Otherwise, there could be an intermediate trace.[2] Let us repeat the structures in (8) to see this more clearly, including the intermediate trace where it is possible:

(12) a. *Who$_1$ do you think [that [t_1 saw Bill]]
      b.   Who$_1$ do you think [t_1 [t_1 saw Bill]]

Now we need to be able to say that the intermediate trace in (12b) is not "too far" from the subject trace, whereas *who* in (12a) is "too far" from the subject trace.

Let (13) be our first attempt to characterize "too far":

(13) α is "too far" from β iff β is contained in an S' that does not contain α.

In other words, "S' is a barrier to antecedent government." A conceptually more appealing claim would be that any maximal projection is a barrier to antecedent government. But we will see that that option does not work.

This machinery will handle the *that*-trace phenomenon. Now the trace in (12a) is not antecedent-governed, because its nearest binder is outside the S' that contains it. However, the trace in (12b) is antecedent-governed, because its nearest binder—the intermediate trace—is inside the same S'.

- *Hong:* Does the intermediate trace have to be properly governed?
  Lasnik: That's a good question. I've been carefully directing your attention to the traces I wanted you to look at. But there are some other potentially relevant traces, or at least one other. In (7b), perhaps there is not another trace in Comp. We do not need another trace there, for ECP purposes, because the initial trace is lexically governed. But we need a trace in Comp in (12b). Crucially, if such an intermediate trace were not present, then the initial trace would not be antecedent-

governed. And now your question arises: if a trace must be properly governed, how does the intermediate trace satisfy the requirement? Apparently, it doesn't. It is not a complement to anything and, even though it is bound by *who*, we are back in trouble, given the definition of "too far" in (13), since there is an intervening S'. The trace in Comp violates the ECP.

4.1.4 Intermediate Traces

Let us consider the problem of intermediate traces in more detail. We have to say that the trace in Comp in (12b) is not too far from *who*, while keeping in mind that we still want the subject trace in the lower clause to be too far from *who*, in order to maintain our account of the *that*-trace paradigm. One proposal has been made by Lasnik and Saito (1984). Several linguists investigating government in recent years have come to the conclusion that for government of any sort, a maximal projection is a barrier, but that there is one kind of exception to that constraint. The head of a maximal projection can be governed by something outside the maximal projection (Belletti and Rizzi 1981; Kayne 1980). This notion can help us. The trace in (12a) is clearly not the head of S'; but if S' is a projection of Comp,[3] then we can say that the trace in (12b) *is* the head of S'. Extending those proposals from government to proper government, the head of S' is accessible for proper government from outside that S'. (12b) could then be a case of antecedent government.

The immediately preceding analysis is not exactly what Chomsky proposed for this example. In fact, Chomsky avoided the problem by ignoring traces in Comp. But Lasnik and Saito (1984) pointed out evidence from several languages that traces in Comp do have to be properly governed. Therefore, they cannot be ignored, and the problem must be solved somehow. I have not yet given any evidence that traces in Comp have to be properly governed. But we will come back to this.

- *Long:* You said that in (7b) it's not necessary to leave a trace in Comp. How does that behave with respect to Subjacency?
Lasnik: To answer this, we have to look at what Subjacency is. Chomsky has argued that Subjacency is a constraint on movement—that each step of movement cannot be too long. Freidin (1978) has argued that, on the contrary, Subjacency is a sort of binding principle. To apply it, we look at S-Structure (or some level of derived representation) and judge whether or not a trace is too far away from its antecedent. If the analysis we are considering is right, then Freidin is wrong. I am relying on the claim that in (12a) there cannot possibly be a trace in Comp. But if there cannot be a trace in Comp in (12a), there cannot be a trace in Comp in (7a) either, because the Comps are indistinguishable. And if

there cannot be a trace in Comp in (7a) and we check Subjacency by looking at S-Structure, then (7a) should be ungrammatical.

Now you may ask how we can make (7a) consistent with Subjacency on any interpretation of that constraint. Suppose the D-Structure form of (7a) is roughly (14):

(14) [[You think [[John saw who]]]]

Suppose we move *who* in two steps, as in (15):

(15) a. [[You think [who [John saw t]]]]
$$\uparrow_____\rfloor$$
    b. [Who [you think [t [John saw t]]]]
$$\uparrow_____\rfloor$$

Now suppose we insert *that* at S-Structure, assuming something along the lines of Davis's (1984) proposal for inserting *it* or *there* at S-Structure. The idea is that expletive-like elements, those with no semantic content, can be inserted into any position of the right syntactic type. The result is (16):

(16) [Who$_1$ [you think [that [John saw t_1]]]]

We might raise the question of Recoverability here, if there were a trace in (15b) that was later obliterated.[4] But there is an easy answer to that: why should we leave a trace in Comp in (15b)? True, we moved through the position, but we may assume that in doing so we did not leave a trace. This was the proposal of Lasnik and Saito (1984).[5] The standard assumption was, and still is, that movement by definition creates a trace. The problem is that if an element moves but does not leave a trace, almost invariably it will violate some independent constraint— except in cases like the ones we are considering. But if it is essentially always true that independently needed principles dictate when an element must leave a trace, then our theory is massively redundant if, in addition to these principles, we stipulate that a moved element must leave a trace. The trace we are considering, the one in Comp in (15b), is not demanded by the θ-Criterion, because it is not in a θ-position; it is irrelevant to vacuous quantification, because such a position is never interpreted as a variable. No independent principle forces us to leave a trace there, so I would prefer to say that leaving such a trace is simply optional. In (12b), on the other hand, an independent principle *did* ultimately demand that a trace be left, namely, the ECP.

4.1.5 *Lexical Government versus Antecedent Government*

If the previous arguments are on the right track, some conclusions suggest themselves. In particular, it appears that S' is a barrier to proper government, except that the head of S' is accessible. The *except* clause allows intermediate traces. If S' were an absolute barrier, then these traces could not be properly governed (and later we will see that they must be). So the difference between intermediate and initial traces is that the former are in the head position of S' and the latter are not.

There is a problem with trying to strengthen the above conclusion to "All maximal projections are barriers to proper government." Again, it will be a theory-internal argument that depends on intermediate traces needing to be properly governed. Actually, we already have a relevant example. In (12b) a maximal projection—the VP headed by *think*—intervenes between *who* and the trace in Comp. If this maximal projection prevented *who* from properly governing the intermediate trace, then the sentence would incorrectly be ruled out (again, under the assumption that *all* traces must be properly governed). Notice that the trace in question surely is not the head of VP, so that exemption is unavailable.

If, as is widely assumed, all maximal projections are barriers to government, it appears that the notions "government" and "proper government" diverge, at least for the case of antecedent government. Government sort of goes along with Case. Proper government is more mysterious; we do not know what it goes along with. Aoun (1982) argued, plausibly, that it goes along with the Binding Theory, because it concerns binding (see section 5.1). Others have claimed that there is really only one kind of proper government, and it is binding; but as far as I can tell this is usually a stipulation. How is an object properly governed? Consider (17):

(17) Who$_1$ did you say [that [John likes t_1]]

Here the trace must be lexically governed by the verb. The binding account says that a verb and its complement are coindexed—so the verb "binds" the complement. But that seems rather like a notational trick. The coindexation in this case cannot be interpreted in anything like the normal way. We know how to interpret coindexing: namely, as some form of coreference or variable binding (see section 2.1.5). But neither of those interpretations is remotely plausible for the relationship between a verb and its direct object. The real problem is that there seem to be two distinct ways in which a trace can be licensed: one is to have a binder nearby; the other is to be the complement of a head. This suggests that we are missing something, but at present I know of no viable alternative.

4.1.6 Raising and Super-raising

Now consider (18):

(18) *John$_1$ is believed [[t_1 is intelligent]]

(18) is redundantly ruled out by the ECP, since it also violates Condition A. (In the old days we might have said it violates the Nominative Island Condition or, older still, the Tensed Sentence Condition.) Recall that the ECP also applies to NP-traces. (This is how we ruled out NP-traces in

positions that allow PRO, which are not governed positions—see (3).)
Given the representation in (18), the trace is not properly governed. It is
certainly not a complement to any head. Furthermore, its nearest binder
is too far away, in that *John* is outside the minimal S' containing *t*, and
t is not the head of that S'. So (18) does violate the ECP. It is just like a
that-trace violation, really, except that there is not even a *that* in Comp.
But that does not matter in this case. For *Wh*-Movement, it does
matter, because if there is no *that*, then there could be a trace in Comp.
But NP-Movement is not allowed to go through Comp.[6]

Interestingly enough, the PRO versus *t* paradigm that originally motivated the ECP will now not receive the analysis we gave it when we first
looked at the principle. Let us look back at (4), repeated here as (19):

(19) John$_1$ is certain [t_1 to see this]

Chomsky accounted for this example by saying that the trace is properly
governed by *certain*. PRO is impossible in that position because it is
governed by *certain*; thus, Chomsky argued, we might say it is not just
governed but in fact *properly* governed. Then, we cannot get PRO and
we can get trace. However, we have seen considerable evidence now
that government and proper government are not exactly the same
notion. In fact, with the definitions I have given, the trace in (19) is *not*
properly governed by *certain*. The only way something can be lexically
governed thus far is by being a complement to a head. But this trace
is not a complement to *certain*. It does not receive any θ-role from
certain. The whole complement sentence does, but not the subject of
that sentence. So (19) is problematic, or would be if we did not have the
notion of antecedent government, independently motivated by the
that-trace paradigm. Notice that the trace is not too far away from its
nearest binder: the only S' that contains the trace is the entire S',
because (19) is an S'-Deletion configuration. We know it must be,
because if there were an S' in (19), PRO would be allowed, since subject
position would then not be governed. Thus, reducing lexical government to the relationship between a head and a complement does allow
us to eliminate some redundancy. The trace in (19) is not properly
governed in two ways, as it would have been under Chomsky's proposal. Chomsky asserted that the trace was properly governed by the
adjective but did not mention that it was also properly governed by the
NP that moved. In our theory it is *only* antecedent-governed.

Evidence for a restrictive definition of lexical government along the
lines we have been considering comes from (20) (first discussed in
chapter 2, example (112)):

(20) *John$_1$ seems [that [it is likely [t_1 to leave]]]

Chomsky assumed that what I have been calling lexical government
was simply government by a lexical head. Then, since *likely* governs the
trace in (20), it would lexically govern this trace. Explaining why (20) is so
much worse than a mere Subjacency violation then becomes very

difficult. Lasnik and Saito (1984) proposed a more restrictive definition of lexical government. Under that definition, *likely* cannot properly govern the subject position of the lower clause because it assigns neither a θ-role nor Case to it. We proposed that lexical government only obtains when there is some relation between the governor and the governee—θ-assignment, which we have already considered, or Case assignment.[7] Under this narrower conception of lexical government, then, (20) would be an ECP violation. Chomsky could not call upon that, because he had a broader notion of lexical government, essentially the same as government.

- *Uriagereka:* The antecedent-trace relationship in (19) crosses a VP. Maybe (19) illustrates again that not all maximal projections are barriers to antecedent government.
  Lasnik: Yes, it does. It is the same conclusion as the one we reached before. In fact, the conclusion is even clearer here. Before, it relied on something I have not demonstrated yet: that intermediate traces must be properly governed. But, given that lexical government does not obtain in (19), here the conclusion relies merely on the fact that *initial* traces must be properly governed, which we already know to be true. So the claim that VP is not a barrier to antecedent government seems well supported now. •

- *Williams:* But all maximal projections *are* barriers to lexical government.
  Lasnik: Correct, with one exception. Maximal projections other than S are barriers to government, and lexical government is a special case of government. The way I put it is: for α to lexically govern β, α must assign a θ-role or Case to β (and α must be a lexical head).[8] And both θ-role and Case are assigned under government. •

4.2 Superiority

Let us look now at some other standard examples before proceeding to more recent ones. The analysis I'm about to illustrate is originally due to Aoun, Hornstein, and Sportiche (1981). I will present a modification developed by Huang (1982b), with some further refinements that I will introduce. The phenomenon in question is Superiority, named and explored by Chomsky (1973). Consider a D-Structure representation like (21a), which is obviously well formed, and the S-Structure forms we might derive from it:

(21) a. Who will read what
   b. Who$_1$ [t_1 will read what]
   c. *What$_1$ [will who read t_1]

A priori, (21c) should also be possible. Chomsky proposed a constraint to handle this: if a construction has two sources of *Wh*-Movement, and one is superior to the other (in the sense of "higher" in the tree), then *Wh*-Movement must pick the superior one. The notion of c-command had not yet been developed (though it is essentially the inverse of the relation "in construction with" proposed by Klima (1964)), but *superior* should probably be defined in terms of c-command. For example, if α and β are potential sources of the same movement on the same cycle, and α asymmetrically c-commands β, α rather than β moves. The subject asymmetrically c-commands the object; hence, movement has to pick the subject. That is essentially the Superiority Condition, brought up to date with modern terminology. In fact, Chomsky's original definition of Superiority already has very much the flavor of asymmetric c-command:

(22) "... the category *A* is "superior" to the category *B* in the phrase marker if every major category dominating *A* dominates *B* as well but not conversely." (Chomsky 1973:246)

Aoun, Hornstein, and Sportiche suggest that all of this can be made to follow from the ECP. To see this, we must look in some detail at *wh*-questions and their LF representations. Let us first look at a grammatical double question like (21b). What should its LF representation be? There are two possibilities. One is to directly translate the S-Structure form into the LF representation, by essentially calling S-Structure LF, calling something in Comp an "operator," calling a trace a "variable bound by an operator," and so on. This results in (21d):

(21) d. For which x, x will read what

That does not sound right, though. It sounds as if we are questioning *who* but not *what*. In fact, we are questioning both; that is why sentences like (21b) are called multiple questions. We want a set of pairs as an answer. Thus, (23a), and not (23b), is a possible answer to (21a):[9]

(23) a. John, *Syntactic Structures* and Mary, *The Sound Pattern of English*
     b. John

But (23b) ought to be a sensible answer to (21a) if (21d) is its LF representation, because there the only thing we are questioning is x, the subject. Why would we say that (23b) is not a good answer to (21a)? Presumably because both the subject and the object are being questioned, even though, as it happens, only one of them is in Comp at S-Structure. For those who are native speakers of languages other than English, it might not come as a surprise that something that is not in Comp at S-Structure can be questioned, because there are many languages where no *wh*-phrases are in Comp at S-Structure at all, where they are all "in situ" (unmoved, hence "in place"). So, for instance, speakers of Chinese, Japanese, Korean, and many other languages would say something like (24a) with the meaning that (24b) has in English:

(24) a. You will read what
    b. What will you read

There is evidence, though, that at LF the *wh* must be in Comp. For one thing—this is Huang's argument—in Chinese it is possible to say the equivalent of (25a) but not the equivalent of (25b):

(25) a. I wonder you will read what
    b. I wonder you will read the book

Apparently, there must be a *wh* there, just as in English. English has an S-Structure requirement: at S-Structure the *wh*-phrase must already be in Comp. But in Chinese-type languages, which lack overt *Wh*-Movement, this S-Structure requirement does not exist. Surely, we do not want to say that the English version of (25a)—namely, (26)—

(26) I wonder what you will read

and (25a) have different LF representations, because they have exactly the same LF requirements: there must be a *wh*-phrase, and the complement of *wonder* must be understood as a question. Now the question is, at what level of representation can we capture the similarity between English and Chinese? Not at S-Structure, patently. But how about at LF? We can capture the similarity by saying that there is a rule just like *Wh*-Movement, except that its results are silent. In some models of grammar that would not make any sense. But in the model we have been examining it does. Recall the picture of the model (from chapter 1, example (1)):

(27)

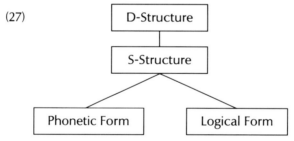

It makes perfect sense to say that there are some "syntactic" operations in (27) whose results can be heard. Those are operations forming S-Structure. And there are some operations whose results cannot be heard. Those are operations in LF. According to this model, if we perform some operation between S-Structure and LF, its results will not be heard.

A priori, the difference between English and Chinese could reflect the setting of a parameter, a sort of two-position switch—something like "Every language has *Wh*-Movement and every language has to make a choice: it either happens between D-Structure and S-Structure or between S-Structure and LF." Evidently we do not want to say that, however. If we do, then it is unclear how to translate (21a) into the appropriate LF representation. Or, if (21b) is the LF representation of

(21a), it is very unclear how to translate this into the actual semantics of the sentence. We really want to say that both *who* and *what* in (21a) are being questioned. That is, we want a semantic representation along the lines of (28):

(28) For which x, for which y, x will read y

We know how we got "for which x." That was easy: we had a *who* in Comp and we changed it into "for which x." We also know how we got "x" in an A-position. We had a trace bound by *who* and we made it an instance of the appropriate variable. But how do we get "for which y" and "y"? We can get those by doing exactly what Chinese does: take a *wh*-phrase and move it into Comp, but not in any way that can be heard. That is, instead of moving it in the syntax, we move it in LF.

Apparently, then, some languages allow syntactic *Wh*-Movement (in other words, movement that takes place before S-Structure); additionally, every language we have talked about so far allows LF *Wh*-Movement. If (28) is the interpretation of (21a), we may want to say that the representation immediately prior to this translation looks roughly like (29):

(29) Who$_1$ what$_2$ [t_1 will read t_2]

Then we would just have to translate *who* into "for which x," *what* into "for which y," t_1 into "x," and t_2 into "y."

This sort of analysis of *Wh*-Movement was hinted at in the last part of Chomsky 1973 and developed in detail in Huang 1982a,b.

Now we are ready to look at the details of the analysis. Roughly along the lines of Aoun, Hornstein, and Sportiche, Huang introduced a further device: when an item moves into Comp, Comp receives the index of that item. Let us adopt this idea, which I will substantiate later. Given this, (21a) should be more precisely represented at S-Structure as (30):

(30) [$_{Comp}$ Who$_1$]$_1$ [t_1 will read what]

Now what will the LF representation look like? Various proposals exist, but let me develop the one made by Lasnik and Saito (1984), according to which there is only one position in Comp. How is (29) produced if there is only one position in Comp? Let us suppose that *what* adjoins to Comp by *Wh*-Movement in LF. Let us ignore the question of whether *what* adjoins to the right or the left, since that is irrelevant to our concerns. Here is the result, assuming left adjunction:

(31) [$_{Comp}$ What$_2$ [$_{Comp}$ who$_1$]$_1$]$_1$ [t_1 will read t_2]

(32) is the tree diagram corresponding to the labeled bracketing:

(32)
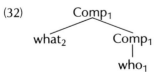

Since we left-adjoined *what* to a Comp with index *1*, the result is again a Comp with index *1*.

Now, are the traces in (31) properly governed? t_2 is properly governed because it is lexically governed—not in any other way. There is another element that bears the same index as t_2, but since it is buried inside another category, it does not bind t_2. Now let us look at t_1. It is antecedent-governed—not lexically governed. It is bound by the higher node with the label Comp. Hence, both traces are properly governed.

Now let us look back at the ungrammatical (21c).[10] First consider its S-Structure representation (33):

(33) $[_{Comp}$ What$_2]_2$ [will who read t_2]

(33) violates nothing. But now consider the LF representation for (33):

(34) $[_{Comp}$ Who$_1$ $[_{Comp}$ what$_2]_2]_2$ [will t_1 read t_2]

Now Comp has index 2, which follows, according to our assumptions, from *what*'s having moved into Comp first (that is, before S-Structure). Since I continue to assume that there is only one position in Comp, let us say that that position is the head, assuming that every category needs a head. Now let us suppose, as part of the formalism, that a category and its head are coindexed. *Who* adjoins, by LF *Wh*-Movement. And now, finally, let us ask whether anything is violated. t_2 is lexically governed by *read*, and it is antecedent-governed by Comp. But t_1 is not properly governed at all. It is not lexically governed because it is not a complement, and it is not antecedent-governed because it is not bound. So (34) violates the ECP. In this way, we deduce Chomsky's Superiority effects from an independently needed principle.[11]

4.3 Adjuncts

4.3.1 Complement-Noncomplement Asymmetries

So far we seem to be dealing with some sort of subject-object asymmetry. As far as I know, Huang was the first to argue that it is not really a subject-object asymmetry but a complement-noncomplement asymmetry. The case of subject-object asymmetry is simply part of a wider generalization. We already know something about complement-noncomplement asymmetries: that is exactly what lexical government is about. Hence, we should not be surprised to find a paradigm like the following:

(35) a. Why$_2$ did you read what t_2
   b. *What$_1$ did you read t_1 why

What is a complement and *why* is not, and this apparently correlates with the possibility of having the item in situ.

Let us explore the details of the account for these contrasts. Consider the LF representation of (35b), following the Comp-indexing assumptions we discussed earlier:

(36) $[_{Comp}$ Why$_2$ $[_{Comp}$ what$_1]_1]_1$ [did you read t_1 t_2]

And now let us hope that (36) violates something. t_1 is fine—in fact, it has an embarrassment of riches, being properly governed both ways. Since it is the complement of the verb, it is lexically governed; and since Comp binds it, it is also antecedent-governed. That precisely does not leave any way for t_2 to be properly governed. Crucially, t_2 is not a complement of anything, nor is it bound.[12] Thus, the ungrammaticality of (35b) follows directly.

Now let us look at the LF representation of the well-formed (35a):

(37) $[_{Comp}$ What$_1$ $[_{Comp}$ why$_2]_2]_2$ [did you read t_1 t_2]

t_1 is now fine: it is not antecedent-governed, but it is lexically governed, since it is the complement of *read*. t_2 is not lexically governed because it is an adjunct, but it is antecedent-governed by Comp, since Comp binds it and is surely close enough to it. This is a much more equitable arrangement of proper government wealth than we found in (36).

Thus, it seems that the real asymmetry is between complements and noncomplements. One kind of noncomplement is a subject—as we saw in the case of Superiority and the *that*-trace effect. The other kind of noncomplement is an adverbial adjunct, as we just saw. The generalization is then that noncomplements must be antecedent-governed. That is why both examples in (38) are impossible:

(38) a. *Who$_1$ t_1 left why
　　 b. *Why$_1$ did who leave t_1

No matter which *wh*-phrase moves to Comp first, hence to head position, the other will violate the ECP, because, ignoring ECM constructions, traces of noncomplements, by definition, cannot be lexically governed. We are assuming that only one particular trace can be antecedent-governed by a complementizer, since the complementizer cannot have the same index as two distinct (initial) traces.

4.3.2 Intermediate Traces of Adjuncts

We are now ready to examine the type of example that indicates that intermediate traces must be properly governed. There is a conceptual argument for this, of course: a theory in which *all* traces must be properly governed is a simpler theory than one that must distinguish two types of traces with respect to the ECP. But there are empirical arguments as well. The first example we will consider is of a type discussed by Huang (1982b). Huang did not consider every possible derivation of this example, and we will see that one derivation he omitted must be prevented.[13] Here is the crucial example:

(39) *Who$_1$ t_1 said John left why

This seems to be just as bad as (38a). Suppose the LF representation of (39) is (40):

(40) $[_{S'}[_{Comp}$ Why$_2$ $[_{Comp}$ who$_1]_1]_1]_1$ $[_S$ t_1 said [[John left t_2]]]]

This can later be translated into (41):

(41) For which x, x a reason; for which y, y a person; y said that John left for x

t_1 in (40) is licit: it is antecedent-governed. t_2 is not, as desired, because it is neither lexically governed nor antecedent-governed. But now look more carefully: the Comp position in the embedded sentence is available. We could have moved *why* through that slot, as in (42):

(42) $[[_{Comp}$ Why$_2$ $[_{Comp}$ who$_1]_1]_1$ $[t_1$ said $[t_2'$ [John left t_2]]]]

Consider t_2. This time it *is* properly governed, by the intermediate trace t_2'. Since the sentence is ungrammatical, we need an additional assumption to explain its ungrammaticality. Because no other principle seems to be relevant here, we can deduce that intermediate traces must be properly governed. t_2' is not bound (the matrix Comp is headed by *who*), so it cannot be antecedent-governed. This is one of the arguments I have been promising for the assumption that *all* traces, not just initial ones, must be properly governed.

4.4 Move *Wh* in Languages with/without *Wh*-Movement

4.4.1 The ECP and LF Movement of Adjuncts

Let us change to a slightly different subject now, but one that will ultimately return to the main theme. The data—which are from Chinese—are delicate; but it is my understanding that the relative judgments are firm.[14] Huang (1982b) examined what at first seems to be a major difference between English and Chinese:

(43) a. ?*What$_1$ do you believe the claim that Lisi bought t_1
    b. Ni   xiangxin Lisi mai-le   sheme de shuofa
       you believe Lisi buy-Asp what   claim

(43a) is a standard example of a (complex NP) Subjacency violation. On the face of it, given that (43b) is good, it seems that there is a major difference between the two languages. At first one might think that of course (43b) should be fine because nothing has actually moved. But that cannot be why it is fine. I have given several reasons for thinking that *wh*-phrases must move, even if the results of the movement cannot be heard. In fact, I can prove this more directly by embedding (43b) under *wonder*, which we know needs a *wh*-phrase in its complement Comp, as in (44):

(44) Zhangsan xiang-zhidao ni   xiangxin Lisi mai-le   sheme de shuofa
     Zhangsan   wonder you believe Lisi buy-Asp what   claim
     'Zhangsan wonders what you believe the claim that Lisi bought'

The conclusion then might seem to be that English has Subjacency whereas Chinese does not. Huang argued that this is not, in fact, the right conclusion. Consider the following sentences of English:

(45) a.   Who$_1$ [t_1 believes [the claim [that [Mary read what]]]]
     b. ?*What$_1$ [do you believe [the claim [that [Mary read t_1]]]]

(45a) is essentially perfect, and surely much better than (45b). Thus, the exemption from Subjacency that we saw in the Chinese example (43b) obtains in English as well. So the difference, rather than being one between English and Chinese, seems to be one between syntactic movement and LF movement. Apparently, syntactic movement obeys Subjacency, whereas LF movement does not. This was the heart of Huang's argument.

Huang pointed out an even more interesting fact as well. In Chinese, movement of an adjunct *does* seem to obey Subjacency. Consider (46) as compared to (43b):[15]

(46) *[Ni   xiangxin [[Lisi weisheme likai] de shuofa]]
      you believe   Lisi why   leave   claim
      ('Why do you believe the claim that Lisi left *t*')

But it is difficult to see how the contrast between (46) and (43b) can be explained by Subjacency, because we already have evidence that Subjacency does not constrain LF movement. Further, in both (43b) and (46) the movement spanned the same distance. But now look at these facts from the perspective of proper government: the trace of *what* in (45b) is lexically governed. What about the trace of *why* in (46)? Being an adjunct, it is not lexically governed. However, assuming that movement through the embedded Comp in (46) is possible and that we can leave a trace there, then the initial trace is antecedent-governed by the intermediate trace. But is the intermediate trace properly governed? We would hope not, but according to what we have said so far, it is, because it is bound and no S' barrier intervenes between *why* in LF and its trace in Comp. (Recall that the head of S' is subject to proper government from outside that S', and notice that there is only one intervening S' in (46).) Suppose that what is going on is that NP is also a barrier to government. There is in fact an intervening NP, which then would account for why the intermediate trace is not properly governed. This is essentially the conclusion reached by Lasnik and Saito (1984), following Huang.

So the basic phenomenon that Huang was trying to explain did not have anything to do with Subjacency. The real generalization, he argued, is this: if a complement moves in LF, it can do whatever it pleases; but if a noncomplement moves, then it is constrained by a locality condition that is not Subjacency (even though its barriers and those for Subjacency are quite similar), namely, the ECP.

Significantly, (47) is grammatical in Chinese:

(47) [[Mali   renwei [[Yuehan weisheme likai]]]]
    Mary think   John   why   leave
    'Why does Mary think John left t'

Suppose (47) had an LF representation like (48)—I will use the English equivalent. Subjacency does not constrain a movement like the one in (48), since the movement in this case takes place in LF.

(48) [Why$_1$]$_1$ Mary thinks [[John [left] t_1]]

But the trace violates the ECP under this representation, since *why* cannot antecedent-govern its trace, because of the intervening S', of which the trace in question is not the head. Consider, however, (49):

(49) [Why$_1$]$_1$ Mary thinks [t_1 [John [left] t_1]]

Aoun, Hornstein, and Sportiche (1981) claimed that LF movement is never allowed to take place from Comp to Comp. (49), which shows how we derive a grammatical representation for (47), suggests that they were wrong. The traces in (49) all satisfy the ECP. The grammatical derivation crucially relies on the intermediate trace, so it must be true that Comp-to-Comp LF movement is possible, which in fact is the null hypothesis. A special stipulation would be needed to prevent such movement. The contrast between (46) and (47) confirms, or reconfirms, several claims. LF Comp-to-Comp movement must be allowed, LF movement must satisfy the ECP, and intermediate traces must be properly governed.

Before we go on, let us consider some of the analogues in English of the examples we investigated in Chinese. Consider (50):

(50) a.   Who$_1$ [t_1 believes [the claim [that [John hit who]]]]
    b.   *Who$_1$ [t_1 believes [the claim [that [John left why]]]]

(50) illustrates the same phenomenon we saw earlier. In (50a) the trace of LF movement of *who* will be lexically governed by *hit*. No intermediate traces are necessary. In (50b) lexical government will not obtain. The initial trace of *why* in (50) could be properly governed by an intermediate trace,[16] but the intermediate trace could not be properly governed, since *who* is the head of the matrix Comp.

We can also try to construct English analogues using syntactic movement. But then we should not be able to front either of the types of *wh*-phrases above, since syntactic movement must obey Subjacency. However, we might expect that an example like (51b) should be worse than one like (51a), since the former would violate the ECP in addition to Subjacency. This prediction is borne out:

(51) a.   ?*Who$_1$ [does Mary believe [the claim [that [John hit t_1]]]]
    b.   **Why$_1$ [does Mary believe [the claim [that [John [left] t_1]]]]

(51b) is totally inconceivable. Of course, that string of words is a well-formed sentence of English, but with a different structure in which *why* is associated with the matrix. But with the interpretation in (52), which is the one that corresponds to (51b), there is no way to salvage it:

(52) What is the reason such that Mary believes the claim that for that reason John left

Thus, once again, we find the familiar complement-adjunct asymmetry.

Huang also investigated another Subjacency-type phenomenon in Chinese, the *Wh*-Island Constraint. Consider the Chinese S-Structure representation in (53):

(53) Mali xiang-zhidao Yuehan weisheme da-le   shei
     Mary   wonder John   why   beat-Asp who
     'Mary wonders John hit who why'

There are several possibilities to explore, depending on the scope of the operators. We can immediately reject the alternative whereby *who* and *why* both have matrix scope. That is not well formed because *wonder* needs an embedded question. The other three combinations of matrix and embedded scope we must consider further.

Consider the following LF representation. (For ease of exposition, I will again use the English equivalents.)

(54) [Who$_1$ [Mary wonders [why$_2$ [John hit t_1 t_2]]]]

This is a well-formed LF representation. The movement of *who* is not constrained by Subjacency, since the movement takes place at LF. Further, the ECP is satisfied, since the trace of *who* is lexically governed by *hit*, and the trace of *why* is antecedent-governed by the lower Comp, since *why* itself occupies that position.

Now consider the reverse case:

(55) [Why$_2$ [Mary wonders [who$_1$ [John hit t_1 t_2]]]]

The interpretation that (55) would have, though perfectly coherent, is not grammatical.[17] Let us find out why. t_1 is licit because it is both lexically governed and antecedent-governed. t_2 is not lexically governed (it is an adjunct); nor is it antecedent-governed (its nearest binder is outside the S' that contains it). Hence, (55) is correctly ruled out.

The next to last case to consider is (56):

(56) Mary wonders [[who$_1$ [why$_2$]$_2$]$_2$ [John hit t_1 t_2]]

Huang claimed that (56) is ungrammatical; however, Saito found the Japanese analogue to be grammatical. When Saito asked Huang about this, he conceded that (56) is not as bad as might be expected of an ECP violation. Our theory claims that (56) obeys the ECP. If *why* is the head of Comp, the trace of *why* is bound by the Comp and hence is antecedent-governed.

Finally, there is a representation whereby *who* is the head of the intermediate Comp and *why* is adjoined to that Comp. In that case our theory predicts that the representation should be ruled out, since nothing would keep the trace of *why* from violating the ECP. This prediction cannot really be tested, because there is no phonetic or semantic difference between this case and the preceding one.

4.4.2 The ECP and Syntactic Movement of Adjuncts

Let us see what happens in English with syntactic movement across an ECP barrier. We should expect all the sentences to be at least some-what ill formed since all of them will violate Subjacency. But some should be worse than others. The contrast between (51a) and (51b) has already lent some substance to this view, with respect to complex NP island effects. *Wh*-islands show the same behavior:

(57) ?*[Who$_1$ [does Mary wonder [why$_2$ [John hit t_1 t_2]]]]

I think that (57) is a "mere" Subjacency violation. Compare it to (58):

(58) **[Why$_2$ [does Mary wonder [who$_1$ [John hit t_1 t_2]]]]

(58) is completely impossible. Once again, this is the expected result, since t_2 in (58) violates the ECP, but neither trace in (57) does.

Given the similarity that we keep finding between Subjacency islands and ECP barriers, let us examine further how Subjacency does or does not relate to the ECP. Rizzi (1982) argued that there is a parametric difference in Subjacency. In English the bounding nodes are S and NP, and that is why English exhibits *wh*-island effects. In Italian and Spanish the bounding nodes are S' and NP. That allows movement to occur somewhat more freely; in fact, it allows movement out of a *wh*-island. Consider the English example (59):

(59) ?*[$_{S'}$ Which worker$_1$ [$_S$ don't you know [$_{S'}$ why$_2$ [John fired t_1 t_2]]]]

If the lower Comp is filled by *why*, *which worker* cannot use it as an "escape hatch," so it must move in one fell swoop, the result of which is a standard *wh*-island violation, reduced to Subjacency in terms of crossing two bounding nodes. The example is not totally unacceptable. Rather, it has the marginal status associated with Subjacency violations that are not ECP violations. Imagine, though, a language where the bounding node was not S but S'; then the equivalent of (59) in that language should violate neither Subjacency nor the ECP. That is exactly what happens in Spanish:

(60) [A qué trabajador$_1$ [no sabes   [por qué$_2$
      to what worker   not know-you for what
      [despidió Juan t_1 t_2]]]]
      fired   John
      'Which worker don't you know why John fired'

Given the view that we have taken of the ECP, its similarity to Subjacency is striking: they both respect bounding nodes, which more-over are virtually the same bounding nodes, and so on. It certainly seems as though we ought to be able to deduce one phenomenon from the other. However, it turns out that they diverge in a crucial way. As noted, (60) is perfectly all right in Spanish; but if we try to move an *adjunct* out of a *wh*-island, as in (61), the result is as ill formed as it is in English:

(61) **[Por qué$_2$ [no sabes   [a qué trabajador$_1$
      for what not know-you to what worker
      [despidió Juan t_1 t_2]]]]
      fired   John
      'Why don't you know which worker John fired'

Neither (60) nor (61) will violate Subjacency in Spanish. But (61) apparently violates the ECP. The conclusion that Saito and I reluctantly reached, then, was that the ECP and Subjacency must be different principles.

4.5 Lack of *That*-Trace Effects with Adjuncts

So far we have looked at the simple cases the ECP can handle. Other facts must be considered, however. For instance, Huang (1982b) mentioned a kind of case that worked so badly that (he said) his whole theory might have to be rethought. An example of the general type that worried him is (62a), the S-Structure form of (62b):

(62) a. [Why$_1$ [do you think [that [John left t_1]]]]
    b. Why do you think that John left

(62b) is perfectly grammatical. It is clear why Huang would have been so concerned about this: (62a) should be a *that*-trace violation. There is a *that* in Comp, and we already know that when there is a *that* in Comp, the Comp cannot be a proper governor. That is how we explained the *that*-trace paradigm. Furthermore, we know that adjuncts are not lexically governed. So why does (62a) not violate the ECP?

Before I suggest an explanation, let me present a more recently discovered example that patterns abstractly in the same way as (62a):

(63) [Who$_1$ [do you think [that [Mary said [t_1 [t_1 won the race]]]]]]

(63) is also perfectly grammatical, and it also poses a problem. The initial trace is the subject of a finite clause. There is no way it can be lexically governed, so it must be antecedent-governed. Since the trace in the lower Comp is the antecedent of the initial trace, the latter is fine. But we know that the intermediate trace must also be properly governed— in particular, antecedent-governed.[18] But *who* is too far away, and the Comp with *that* cannot be a proper governor. Abstractly, then, (62a) and (63) pose the same type of problem.

Lasnik and Saito (1984) argued that (62a) and (63) have essentially the same solution. Suppose that there is a distinction between arguments and nonarguments. (This is not the same as the distinction we have been relying on so far between complements and noncomplements. A subject, for instance, is an argument, but it is not a complement.) Suppose further that the theory includes a process along the lines of (64) to instantiate proper government:

(64) a. Assign $[+\gamma]$ to a trace that is lexically governed or antecedent-governed.
 b. Assign $[-\gamma]$ to all other traces.

Finally, suppose that the theory includes a filter along the lines of (65):

(65) *$[\ldots[-\gamma]\ldots]$

(65) will be the ECP. So far I have just provided a notation for what we have been developing all along. Suppose now that (66) is true:

(66) γ-assignment applies at S-Structure and at LF.

This is a natural assumption, since we want to constrain S-Structure movement and LF movement. Finally, suppose we stipulate (64')—this is, in fact, the heart of the new proposal:

(64') At S-Structure, γ-assignment applies only to arguments.

We can come close to making (64') follow from the Projection Principle. Arguments (subjects, objects) are exactly the positions the Projection Principle covers. Adjuncts and intermediate traces are exactly the positions it does not. The idea is that certain positions (nonarguments) are potentially invisible to γ-assignment at S-Structure because they need not even be there at that level, since the Projection Principle does not require them to be there.[19] For present purposes, though, we will simply maintain (64') as a principle.

Now consider the S-Structure form (63), repeated here:

(63) [Who$_1$ [do you think [that [Mary said [t_1 [t_1 won the race]]]]]]

The initial trace is an argument; therefore, by (64'), (64) will apply, marking the trace $[+\gamma]$, because it is antecedent-governed. The intermediate trace is not an argument. Given (66), nothing happens to this trace at S-Structure. Next consider (62a), repeated here:

(62) a. [Why$_1$ [do you think [that [John left t_1]]]]

Nothing happens to the trace at S-Structure, because it is an adjunct, not an argument. (It is important to note that the proposal is not that nonarguments are marked $[-\gamma]$ by default or something of that sort; literally nothing happens to them.) Consider also (67), which is the type of case we still want to rule out:

(67) *[Who$_1$ [do you think [that [t_1 left]]]]

The trace in (67) *is* an argument, so it will be assigned $[-\gamma]$ by (64), since it is not properly governed. We might say that (67) is already ruled out at S-Structure, if filter (65) applies at S-Structure and at LF. Returning to (62a) and (63), let us work out more of the details of the analysis.

As mentioned in chapter 1, Chomsky has proposed that there is a general syntactic process, Move α, which means "Move any constituent anywhere in the structure." If it moves to the wrong place, some general principle will reject the representation. That is still largely a promissory note, of course. It has not yet been made to work in full generality. But it is clearly the right sort of idea. So let us assume it is right. In fact, let us generalize it. Why should it be restricted to movement? Why not say, "Do anything to any constituent in the structure"? Instead of "Move α," let us say that "Affect α" accomplishes the mappings from D-Structure to S-Structure and from S-Structure to LF. The difference would be that the first mapping would be constrained by Subjacency, whereas the second would not. What would "Affect" include? Of course, it would include movement. But let us suppose it includes deletion too. So why could we not generate *Left* from *John left*? That would be a paradigm case where a general principle, say Recoverability of Deletion, blocks application of a rule. That is, a rule cannot simply eliminate something with lexical content.

How will all of this help us? Suppose we apply Affect α to *that* in (62a) and (63) in the mapping from S-Structure to LF. Then, as far as PF is concerned, *that* is present, but as far as LF is concerned, it is absent. I assume that complementizer *that* has no lexical content. (This is why we are able to insert it in the middle of a derivation, just as we can insert *it*.) So let us simply delete *that*, a process apparently available in the syntax—hence, on the null hypothesis, available in LF also.[20] So far that does not buy us anything. But suppose that we now apply movement. Suppose, in particular, that we move the *wh*-phrase in (62a) or (63) down to the former position of *that*. If we do nothing else, that does not help; in fact, it violates the semantic requirements of *think*. Whereas *wonder* demands an embedded question, *think* does not tolerate one. (We might instantiate these requirements via a selectional restriction on the head of the complement, that is, the Comp: for *wonder* the requirement would be [+ wh], whereas for *think* it would be [− wh].) So let us not leave it there; let us move it back up, leaving a trace. We then have exactly the LF structure we need:

(68) a. [Why$_1$ [do you think [t_1 [John left t_1]]]]
    b. [Who$_1$ [do you think [t_1 [Mary said [t_1 [t_1 won the race]]]]]]

The intermediate traces will now be marked [+γ] by (64), as will the initial trace of *why* in (68a), since they all now have antecedent governors. (The initial trace of *who* in (68b) was already marked [+γ] at S-Structure.) What is particularly interesting about the sort of derivation I have just made possible is that I did not add any stipulations; rather, I eliminated some: for instance, the stipulations that movement is the only possible operation and that movement can only go up, not down. Of course, in general, if something moves down, it ends up violating one principle or another—for example, it results in a trace that is not

S-Structure:

$$[_{S'} \text{wh}_1 [\ldots [_{S'} \text{that} [\ldots [t_1 [t_1 \ldots]]]]]]$$
$$\quad\quad\quad\quad\quad\quad\quad\quad {}_{[+\gamma]}$$

Delete *that*:

$$[_{S'} \text{wh}_1 [\ldots [_{S'} e [\ldots [t_1 [t_1 \ldots]]]]]]$$
$$\quad\quad\quad\quad\quad\quad\quad {}_{[+\gamma]}$$

Move *wh* downward without leaving a trace:

$$[_{S'} e [\ldots [_{S'} \text{wh}_1 [\ldots [t_1 [t_1 \ldots]]]]]]$$

Move *wh* upward, leaving a trace:

$$[_{S'} \text{wh}_1 [\ldots [_{S'} t_1 [\ldots [t_1 [t_1 \ldots]]]]]]$$

γ-mark:

$$[_{S'} \text{wh}_1 [\ldots [_{S'} \; t_1 \; [\ldots [t_1 [t_1 \ldots]]]]]]$$
$$\quad\quad\quad\quad\quad\quad {}_{[+\gamma]} \quad\quad {}_{[+\gamma]} \; {}_{[+\gamma]}$$

Figure 4.1
LF derivation for example (63)

properly bound, in the sense of Fiengo (1974). But that does not mean that there should be a ban on downward movement. Rather, it means that there should *not* be such a stipulation, since it would be redundant. In the special case at hand downward movement would be allowed precisely because it does not result in an improperly bound trace. We also eliminate the stipulation that movement requires leaving a trace. Earlier I argued that we do not need or want such a stipulation. Thus, the derivations producing the LF structures in (68) involve no new theoretical apparatus. Rather, they reflect the elimination of certain devices. Given this new streamlined theory, the LF derivation for (63) can be schematized as in figure 4.1.

Conceivably, we can also derive (63) differently. Suppose that on the way from S-Structure to LF we delete the intermediate trace (after γ-marking the initial trace at S-Structure). Apparently, that would not violate anything. Whether this derivation exists depends on whether or not we are allowed to delete traces. So far, we have no evidence one way or the other. In general, a constraint that says "Do not delete traces" is redundant. We would have to examine the range of cases to make this conclusive. Some of the long movement cases from Chinese—for instance, (46), repeated here as (69)—could be relevant:

(69) *[Ni xiangxin [[Lisi weisheme likai] de shuofa]]
you believe Lisi why leave claim
('Why$_1$ do you believe the claim that Lisi left t_1')

Suppose we have an LF representation like (70) (as usual, I use the English equivalent):

(70) [Why$_1$ [you believe [the claim [t_1 [Lisi left t_1]]]]]

The initial trace is marked $[+\gamma]$ by the intermediate trace at LF, but the intermediate trace itself is marked $[-\gamma]$. If the intermediate trace did not exist at LF, then the initial trace would be $[-\gamma]$. Thus, both possibilities are ruled out, and no particular stipulation is required here.[21] As far as I know, all cases have this abstract character. Whenever deletion of a trace must be prevented, the presence of the trace is independently demanded.

If we adopt the trace deletion analysis of (63), it becomes even more plausible that we can do away with the only real stipulation we have, namely, (64'). In cases like (62b), repeated here,

(62) b. Why do you think that John left

we want to say that it is as if the initial trace were not there at S-Structure. Let us try simply saying that. Does that violate anything? We know that an LF representation like (71) violates something:

(71) [Why [do you think [that [John left]]]]

In particular, (71) violates the requirement that an operator must bind a variable. But that sounds as though it should be strictly an LF requirement. If that is the only requirement (62b) violates, then presumably it would not violate anything at S-Structure. (As pointed out earlier, the Projection Principle is not violated.) Then, on the path from S-Structure to LF we can move *why* downward, adjoining it to the lower S, as in (72):

(72) [[You think [that [[John left] why]]]]

(72) looks like a D-Structure representation. And if it does, we can just go ahead and do the derivation we want to do: delete *that*, move into the lower Comp, and then move from Comp to Comp. Only this time we will make sure we leave the necessary traces so that no principle is violated.

- *Davis:* Nothing that you've said prevents *why* in (62b) from adjoining to the matrix S, instead of the embedded one, in which case it would be modifying *think* and not *leave*.
  Lasnik: That's exactly right, but that particular case is not a problem, because S-Structure is the sole input to LF (which is, in turn, the sole input from the grammar to semantic interpretation) in this model. In the derivation you indicate, nothing is violated if *why* modifies *think*, nor do we want there to be a violation, apparently. But there *is* a problematic case along the lines you point out. In principle, we can first adjoin to the embedded clause, then adjoin to the matrix clause, and finally move through Comp. However, (71) could never mean something like (73):

(73) What is the reason such that you have thoughts for that reason, and the thoughts are about John leaving for that very same reason

Given that (73) is coherent, I do not have an explanation for the fact that it cannot be expressed by (62b). I have the feeling that it is something like a Condition C violation, but that is idle speculation at present. •

As I hinted earlier, for the one other example in which we made use of stipulation (64′) about γ-assignment, an alternative account is available

(74) [Who$_1$ [do you think [that [Mary said [t_1 [t_1 won the race]]]]]]

We cannot say that the subject trace is not there at S-Structure, since the Projection Principle requires it to be there. If that trace must be there at S-Structure, then the intermediate trace must be there as well, in order to antecedent-govern it. And now this intermediate trace is going to be assigned [$-\gamma$], in the absence of (64′). But, as suggested, we can say that this trace in Comp is deleted in the LF component. We would probably have to assume something like that, if we wanted to use the above account to eliminate (64′).

- *Davis:* And then we would have to say that filter (65) applies only at LF. *Lasnik:* Right. In such a case, the γ filter would have to be prevented from applying at S-Structure, because otherwise the perfectly grammatical (74) would be ruled out at that level. So far we've been assuming that the filter applies both at S-Structure and at LF,[22] but you've just presented a reason to reconsider that assumption. •

Chapter 5   Extensions and Alternatives to the Binding Theory

5.1   Generalized Binding Theory

Though we have seen that the notion "Accessible SUBJECT" is somewhat problematic, we will now examine a very interesting version of the Binding Theory due to Aoun (1982, 1986) based crucially on just that notion. Aoun tries to eliminate the ECP and recast all ECP violations as violations of Condition A of the Binding Theory. One reason why this is the right kind of thing to do is that, as we have seen, the ECP has a curious disjunction: a trace must be either lexically governed or antecedent-governed, and these two kinds of government seem dissimilar. Binding conditions, however, are needed independently. So the prospect of reducing the ECP to the Binding Theory is quite appealing. The proposal will be very reminiscent of the first modern approaches to the *that*-trace effect (Kayne 1980, Pesetsky 1982b, and Taraldsen 1978; see chapter 4 for an ECP treatment of this effect). These proposals attempted to deduce this effect from the Nominative Island Condition (NIC), which was Chomsky's (1980) revision of the earlier Tensed Sentence Condition. In essence, the NIC states that a nominative anaphor must be bound in the minimal S' containing it. (1) thus violates the NIC, with *t* the nominative anaphor:

(1) Who do you think [$_{S'}$ that [$_S$ *t* won the race]]

In current terms, if *t* in (1) were an anaphor, it would violate Condition A of the Binding Theory. Freidin and Lasnik (1981) argued that that cannot be right, because the trace of *Wh*-Movement must be a variable and variables obey Condition C rather than Condition A. (A variable must be A-free, as the strong crossover effect indicates.) Aoun attempted to accommodate both positions by proposing that a variable is both an R-expression and an anaphor. Although this is not consistent with standard versions of the theory presented in Chomsky 1981b, in which R-expressions are an "elsewhere" case, neither pronominal nor anaphoric, it is not conceptually problematic a priori. Compare, for example, Chomsky's proposal that there is an item, PRO, that is both an anaphor and a pronominal.

5.1.1   Condition A Generalized

Let us consider the details of Aoun's proposal. Aoun claims that there are two kinds of anaphors: A-anaphors and Ā-anaphors. A-anaphors are reciprocals, reflexives, and NP-traces. The only $\overline{\text{A}}$-anaphor we will consider is *wh*-trace, though Aoun argues that there are others. Aoun's Condition A is stated roughly as follows:

(2) An X-anaphor must be X-bound in its governing category, for X ranging over A and $\overline{\text{A}}$.

That is, Aoun claims that all the elements we are considering are anaphoric by nature and thus need a binder. But also, the type of position the binder must occupy in each case depends on the specific nature of the anaphor.

Does our definition of governing category (GC) work for this proposal (see section 2.3)? Consider (3):

(3) [$_{S'}$ Who [$_S$ *t* Agr left]]

(3) tells us immediately that the GC cannot be restricted to S, since the trace in (3) is by nature an $\overline{\text{A}}$-anaphor but is not $\overline{\text{A}}$-bound in the minimal S that contains it, a governor, and an Accessible SUBJECT.[1] Apparently, the GC must be allowed to include S'.

- *Epstein:* Is (4) then a problem?

(4) *John$_1$ believes [$_S$ Mary to like himself$_1$]

Lasnik: Yes, it is. Recall that because of S'-Deletion, the only S' in (4) is the root clause. *Himself* is thus bound in the minimal S' that contains it, a governor, and an Accessible SUBJECT, but (4) is nonetheless ungrammatical.

So perhaps things are not quite as easy as in (2). It looks as though we must say something along the lines of (5):

(5) a. An A-anaphor must be A-bound in the minimal NP or S . . .
    b. An $\overline{\text{A}}$-anaphor must be $\overline{\text{A}}$-bound in the minimal NP or S' . . .

(4) will now be correctly excluded.

5.1.2   That-Trace Effects

Now consider *that*-trace effects, as in (6):

(6) *Who do you think [$_\alpha$ that [*t* Agr left]]

Being an $\overline{\text{A}}$-anaphor, *t* must be $\overline{\text{A}}$-bound in its GC, namely, α. But it is free there, since this Comp contains only *that*. Thus, (6) violates Condition A, and we do not need the ECP to rule it out. (Notice that we cannot let Agr be a relevant binder of the trace, since that would rule (6) in.) Aoun in fact claimed that Comp contains both *that* and a trace and that because of the former the trace is not a binder. Whether this claim is tenable depends on just how c-command is defined. We will put that issue aside.[2]

The grammaticality of (7a) and (7b) follows straightforwardly from Aoun's account. The intermediate trace in both cases is the required $\overline{\text{A}}$-binder:

(7) a. Who do you think [*t* [*t* left]]
   b. Who do you think [*t* [Mary saw *t*]]

The harder case is (8):

(8) Who do you think [$_\alpha$ that [Mary Agr saw *t*]]

By Chomsky's definition of GC, even if we allow S', as in (5b), α in (8) would be the GC, and *t* is free in that domain, exactly as in (7). Thus, the theory as developed so far incorrectly rules (8) out, since the trace is not Ā-bound in its GC. To keep the embedded S' from being a GC for the trace in question, we need a revision in the definition of GC, which apparently will not have anything to do with c-command or with *i*-within-*i* type indexing possibilities, since neither is at issue here. Here is Aoun's proposal (slightly modified along the lines of section 2.3):

(9) β is accessible to α iff
   a. β c-commands (or governs) α and
   b.   assignment to α of the index of β would not
        violate (i) the *i*-within-*i* Condition
              or (ii) Condition C of the Binding Theory.

As in Chomsky's notion of Accessible SUBJECT, the indexing in (9b) is imaginary, not real. Having added (9bii) to the definition of Accessible SUBJECT, let us look at (8) again. Assigning the index of *Mary* to *t* would violate Condition C, since *t* is, by hypothesis, an R-expression. Similarly, since *Mary* and Agr in the embedded clause are coindexed, assigning the index of Agr to *t* would also ultimately create a configuration that violated Condition C. Thus, α contains no SUBJECT accessible to *t*, and α in (8) is not the GC for the trace. So Aoun not only accepts the claim that a *wh*-trace is an R-expression but in fact requires it: it is crucial for his whole analysis. If a *wh*-trace were not an R-expression, then the hypothetical indexing would not create a Condition C violation in (8).

With a proviso along the lines of (9bii), *you* in the upper clause of (8) is not an Accessible SUBJECT for *t* either, since Condition C would be violated if we were to assign the index of *you* to *t*. Similarly for Agr (*do*) in the upper clause. In fact, then, there is no Accessible SUBJECT for *t* in (8). Now there are two possibilities to keep in mind: (a) *t* has no GC; (b) the *Auxiliary Hypothesis* holds, namely, that the root sentence is the GC (see section 2.3.4). We will return to this issue. Notice, then, that *wh-t objects* in this theory never have Accessible SUBJECTs. *Wh-t subjects*, on the other hand, do. Coindexing Agr in a clause with the subject of that clause would not cause a Condition C violation, since Agr is never an A-binder. In fact, Agr and subject are *really*, not just *hypothetically*, coindexed. Thus, hypothetical coindexing creates no violation.

5.1.3 Superiority Effects

Consider now (10) (discussed in terms of the ECP in section 4.2):

(10) a. *What will who read t
b. Who t will read what

At S-Structure (10a) does not violate anything, since there is no Accessible SUBJECT for the trace. Now consider its LF representation:

(11) [Who$_2$ [what$_1$]$_1$]$_1$ [t_2 Agr will read t_1]

The object trace in (11) is fine, since either it has no GC (and hence trivially satisfies Condition A) or the root S' is its GC and it will be bound in that GC. What about the subject trace? It has an Accessible SUBJECT, namely, Agr. Agr is also a governor for t_2. Thus, S' is the GC for t_2. But this trace is not bound in its GC, assuming a Comp-index algorithm along the lines proposed by Aoun, Hornstein, and Sportiche (1981) or Lasnik and Saito (1984). Hence, Condition A rules (11) out. The grammatical (10b) is more interesting. Again, it is fine at S-Structure. But consider its LF representation (12):

(12) [What$_2$ [who$_1$]$_1$]$_1$ [t_1 Agr will read t_2]

The subject trace presents no problem, since it is bound by Comp. We have been assuming that a sentence containing an object *wh*-trace can be grammatical for two reasons: (a) the trace has a GC by the Auxiliary Hypothesis and is bound in that GC; (b) the trace has no GC, because it has no Accessible SUBJECT. (12) apparently resolves the issue: (b) must be the right option, in order to allow (12), since t_2 is an $\overline{\text{A}}$-anaphor but is not $\overline{\text{A}}$-bound.

5.1.4 The Auxiliary Hypothesis

This conclusion has the following consequence. If object traces cannot have an Accessible SUBJECT in this theory, and if the Auxiliary Hypothesis is unavailable, then object traces never have a GC. Let us consider now whether Aoun's theory might need the Auxiliary Hypothesis. Take (13):

(13) a. *[Pictures of each other] are on sale
b. [Pictures of each other$_{(i)}$]$_i$ Agr$_i$ be on sale

If we want (13a) to violate Condition A, then *each other* must have a GC. But *each other* in (13a) does not have an Accessible SUBJECT, since assignment to *each other* of the index of Agr would yield an *i*-within-*i* configuration, as (13b) shows. Previously we accounted for sentences like (13) by invoking the Auxiliary Hypothesis, whereby the root clause becomes the GC.

- *Hong:* Perhaps we can say the Auxiliary Hypothesis applies at S-Structure, but only at S-Structure.

Lasnik: Yes, that is conceivable. It would correctly distinguish between the S-Structure anaphor in (13) and the LF anaphor in (10b). Notice that this would work better than simply distinguishing between lexical and nonlexical anaphors. At S-Structure we want Condition A to be relevant not just for lexical anaphors but for governed anaphoric items in general, since we do not want to allow (14):

(14) *[Pictures of PRO] are on sale

And if we want to rule it out by Condition A, we must call upon the Auxiliary Hypothesis. But, as (12) showed, the Auxiliary Hypothesis is not applicable in the case of an LF *wh*-trace.   •

• *Willim:* Is a structure like (15) a problem for this theory?

(15) *John$_1$ is believed [that [[pictures of t_1] are on sale]]

Lasnik: Yes, as you imply, that example is incorrectly permitted, in the following way. Assignment to t of the index of Agr in the embedded clause, as in (15'), would create an *i*-within-*i* configuration:

(15') ...[[pictures of $t_{(i)}$]$_i$ Agr$_i$ be on sale]]

Thus, there is no Accessible SUBJECT for t in that clause. *John* in the matrix clause *is* accessible to t. Hence, the matrix S is a GC for t, and t is bound in that GC by *John*. (Note that assignment to t of the index of *John* would not violate Condition C, since an NP-trace is not an R-expression.) Of course, there is a Subjacency violation in (15), but the sentence is much worse than a mere Subjacency violation. So this looks like a very interesting problem. But notice that the ECP does not solve it either, since t seems to be lexically governed. It is not a problem specific to Aoun's theory. The difficulty, as far as Binding Theory–type conditions are concerned, is that an NP-trace should behave just like an anaphor. But whereas there are "picture NP"–reflexives and "picture NP"–reciprocals, there are no "picture NP"–NP-traces. The violation of Subjacency is only half an explanation for that. In fact, try to put a *wh*-trace in place of the NP-trace in (15):

(16) ?*Who does John believes [that [[pictures of t] are on sale]]

This is pretty bad, but I take it that (15) is even worse. Some additional constraint is evidently needed for (15). We will not pursue this issue.   •

5.1.5 Constraints on Adjuncts

Having looked at subject traces and object traces, we will now look at the most interesting traces of all. To my mind, the *that*-trace effect is a rather marginal ECP phenomenon. The really central one involves adjunct movement. Consider (17):

(17) *What did you read t why

(17) does not violate anything at S-Structure. But consider its LF representation:

(18) [Why$_2$ [what$_1$]$_1$]$_1$ [you Agr read t_1 t_2]

The object trace does not have a GC, according to the account we have developed. But what about the adjunct trace? It must have a GC, and it must be free in that GC, because the only other way we can rule out (18) is by invoking the ECP, and Aoun's theory, as a point of principle, does not have the ECP. The Auxiliary Hypothesis will not work, because we are now at LF. (Recall the discussion of (10b).) So the trace in question must have an Accessible SUBJECT. Suppose we were to assign to it the index of one of the SUBJECTs in the sentence, either *you* or *Agr*. That would not violate the *i*-within-*i* Condition. But the more interesting question is, will it violate Condition C? And for this there is no pretheoretic answer. We must simply decide. If it would not violate Condition C, then, according to Aoun, Agr and *you* would be Accessible SUBJECTs, t_2 would have a GC, and (18) would violate Condition A. But why should this imaginary assignment to t_2 of the index of Agr not violate Condition C? Aoun's answer is that *why* is not an NP; hence, its trace is not either. That is plausible: if an object moves, the trace it leaves behind is an NP; but if an adverbial moves, it does not leave behind an NP. Condition C is about NPs, then. This is not conceptually necessary, but the theory has forced us in that direction.[3] Now we have a GC (namely, S'), and the question is, is the trace bound in this GC?

- *Willim:* But we lack a governor.
  Lasnik: If we make the reasonable assumption that adjuncts are not governed, then in this case we do not want "governor" to be part of the definition of GC. (We will return to potential problems with this decision.)

Assuming then that S' is somehow the GC for the trace under consideration, we can easily claim that the latter is not bound in its GC, by the reasoning of Lasnik and Saito (1984) (compare the discussion of (11)).

Let us now look at more traditional Condition A effects:

(19) *John thinks that himself will win

Aoun's explanation for the ungrammaticality of (19) is exactly the same as his explanation for the ungrammaticality of (6). In each case an anaphor is free in its GC, an A-anaphor in the present case and an $\overline{\text{A}}$-anaphor in (6). Here Aoun makes a major typological claim. There are languages, like English, where both (6) and (19) are ungrammatical. In both cases Agr establishes a GC by being an Accessible SUBJECT. There are also language, like Chinese, where both (6) and (19) are grammatical. Aoun claims that in such languages Agr does not count as a SUBJECT. Put differently, in a language like Chinese, where both (6) and (19) are good, the sentence contains no Agr at all. At least superficially, that seems in accord with the facts of Chinese.[4] The claim would be that a parameter is responsible for these typological differences. In Chomsky's theory, on the other hand, since the ECP is completely independent of whether or not Agr is potentially an Accessible SUBJECT, we would expect four kinds of languages, not just two. It should be kept in mind, however, that Aoun's conclusion that there are only two kinds of languages in this regard is based essentially on an examination of two languages, English and Chinese. We would hope to establish a wider empirical basis for the typology.

Now consider the following Chinese structure:

(20) Yuehan renwei Mali xihuan ziji
　　　John　　think　Mary like　　self
　　　'John thinks that Mary likes himself'

(20) is grammatical in many Chinese-type languages and, in particular, for many speakers of Chinese. We have already seen that for Aoun's theory, Agr does not count as a SUBJECT in Chinese. Now (20) indicates that a *subject* does not count as a SUBJECT either, if we want to rule the sentence in. So far this is not a problem, even if it sounds bizarre. What we are saying, then, is that in Chinese there are no Accessible SUBJECTs, hence no GCs. However, remember that Huang's discussion of LF *Wh*-Movement was based upon ECP effects in Chinese. Aoun's theory is directed toward eliminating the ECP and replacing it by Condition A. By Aoun's theory, if a language has no GCs, then it cannot have ECP effects. That is a bad problem, which I now illustrate.

Consider the following Chinese S-Structure form (essentially from Huang 1982b):

(21) Bier xiang-zhidao weisheme Yuehan mai-le　　sheme
　　　Bill Asp-wonder why　　　John　bought-Asp what
　　　'Bill is wondering what John bought why'

We will try to derive from (21) the following LF representation:

(22) *Why_1 [Bill is wondering [$what_2$ [John read t_2 t_1]]]

Since neither Agr nor subject is an Accessible SUBJECT in Chinese (at least for the dialect in question), neither trace has a GC; thus, both traces are bound in their GC by virtue of having no GC (the same thing that happens with the PRO Theorem). But then (22) should be a well-formed LF representation for (21), which it is not. That is, there are speakers who accept (20) but reject (21) with LF representation (22). I do not see a solution to this problem. It simply seems that such ECP effects are not amenable to a Condition A treatment.

5.1.6　The Distribution of PRO

Let us return to the notion that the definition of GC cannot mention *government*, if the trace of an adjunct is ever to fall under Condition A. One might think that immediately causes the theory to collapse. The collapse is not quite as immediate as it appears, however. PRO is potentially problematic because, in Chomsky's theory, it is allowed to exist as long as it has no GC (in other words, when it is ungoverned). If the definition of GC does not mention government, however, an empty category can have a GC even if it is ungoverned. Consider (23):

(23) John$_1$ tried [[PRO$_1$ to leave]]

Under this theory, the GC for PRO in (23) is the root sentence, not the lower sentence (since there is no Accessible SUBJECT in the latter); and PRO is then A-bound in its GC. The reason why the theory does not immediately collapse is that we have not yet given Condition B. In Chomsky's theory, Condition A and Condition B specify identical domains: one says a category must be bound and the other that a category must be free, but the rest of the statement is exactly the same. That would clearly be unacceptable in the theory under consideration, because once a category has a GC, if it must be both free and bound in it, (23) could never exist. Aoun's alternative (reminiscent of a proposal by Huang (1982b), though for a different reason) is that the definition of GC is different for anaphors and pronominals. (In section 5.1.7 we will see a different treatment of PRO.)

Let us imagine three logical possibilities for defining the GC for pro-nominals and explore which one might work for (23): (a) for Condition B, PRO in (23) has no GC (Chomsky's approach); (b) the GC for Condition B is more inclusive than the GC for Condition A; (c) the GC for Condition B is less inclusive than the GC for Condition A. (b) will not help because then PRO will certainly be bound in its governing category in (23): if it is bound in the root clause (its GC for Condition A), and if its GC for Condition B is even wider, it certainly violates Condition B. (c), however, might help: PRO could be free in any domain that is less inclusive than the root clause.

In Aoun's theory, there is apparently only one way now not to have a GC: not to have an Accessible SUBJECT. And PRO surely has an Accessible SUBJECT in (23). Consider, then, possibility (c), with (24) as a revised definition of GC for Condition B:

(24) The GC-B [GC for Condition B] of α is the minimal S containing α.

According to (24), (23) now does not violate Condition B, because PRO is free in the minimal S that contains it.

- *Kawai:* But we allow (25):

(25) *She$_1$ believes [PRO$_1$ to be clever]

Lasnik: True. PRO is bound in its GC-A (the root sentence). And it is free in its GC-B (the embedded S). PRO satisfies both Condition A and Condition B, yet (25) is ungrammatical.

Let us then try to revise GC-B, as in (26):

(26) The GC-B of α is the minimal S' containing α.

We can still account for (23) with (26), and now we also account for the ungrammaticality of (25). But here is an example that causes trouble:

(27) John$_1$ believes [Mary to like him$_1$]

By (26), (27) should be ruled out, because the minimal S' that contains *him* is the root clause, and *him* should be free in that domain. We have now lost the contrast between the subject and the object of the complement of an S'-Deletion construction.

- *Uriagereka:* What if we try (28)?

  (28) The GC-B of α is the minimal NP or S containing α and a governor of α.

Lasnik: (28) is the type of definition we had before we began to explore Accessible SUBJECTs (see section 2.1.2.3). In a way, it is not surprising that we are back to that for Condition B. Recall that Accessible SUBJECTs were proposed to let in funny cases of long-distance binding of anaphors. But I pointed out that there remains a bad problem with the new definition of GC, because in the cases where long-distance binding of an anaphor can take place, a bound pronoun can generally occur as well (see section 2.3.4). So if the GCs for Condition A and for Condition B are going to be different, we may as well go back to something like (28) for Condition B.

    Under (28), (23) (repeated as (29)) is fine:

(29) John$_1$ tried [[PRO$_1$ to leave]]

The GC-A of PRO in (29) is the root clause; thus, PRO satisfies Condition A. Now, according to (28), PRO does not have a GC-B, since PRO is ungoverned here: *try* does not trigger S'-Deletion. Thus, PRO trivially satisfies Condition B, as desired. What about (25)? There, the GC-B for PRO according to (28) is the root clause—but PRO is bound in the root clause. So we account for the ungrammaticality of (25). PRO, a pronominal, is bound in its GC. Finally, (27) is allowed, since the GC-B for *him* is the embedded S.

    It will be quite unexpected under this theory if PRO has to be ungoverned—an entailment that Chomsky's theory is constructed to make. We might expect that according to this theory there are either cases of governed PRO that are grammatical or cases of ungoverned PRO that are ungrammatical. There is of course one case that will be a problem, but in a sense we needn't worry about it right now because it was already a problem. Recall (13). (14), repeated here as (30), still presents the same problem that (13) did:

(30) *[Pictures of PRO] are on sale

PRO in (30) does not have a GC, since there is no Accessible SUBJECT, so it satisfies Condition A. The subject NP [*pictures of PRO*] is the GC-B for PRO, so it also satisfies Condition B. What is happening is that Condition A is mistakenly letting (30) in. But that is a problem we already knew we had, which appeared as soon as we abandoned the Auxiliary Hypothesis. Sungshim Hong's suggestion, though, would salvage the proposal we are considering, since the Auxiliary Hypothesis would rule (30) out at S-Structure. The root clause would be the GC-A for PRO in (30), and PRO is not A-bound in that GC.

- *Hong:* Could we consider (31)?

(31) *John$_1$ wants [[PRO$_2$ to leave]]

Lasnik: Yes. In fact, the revision of Aoun's theory that we are considering does better than Chomsky's in a case like (31). PRO in (31) does not have a GC-B, since it is not governed. But the matrix clause is the GC-A, and thus PRO violates Condition A in (31). That is arguably the correct result. Chomsky's Binding Theory cannot explain the ungrammaticality of (31)—he has to appeal to another module of the theory, Control, to solve this problem (see chapter 2, note 12).

- *Kawai:* Does Aoun have a Control Theory?
Lasnik: He doesn't really discuss that question. In fact, he does not pursue the theory in quite the way we have done. But if we adjust things in the manner I've just outlined, possibly his theory can dispense with Control Theory, at least for the cases we have considered so far.

- *Kawai:* Can we consider (32)?

(32) I told John$_1$ [[PRO$_1$ to leave]]

Lasnik: PRO in (32) has no GC-B, since it is ungoverned. The matrix S is the GC-A for PRO, and it is bound in that GC. So (32) is ruled in.

- *Kawai:* What about (33)?

(33) *I$_1$ told John [[PRO$_1$ to leave]]

Lasnik: Yes, that is the problem. In (33) PRO is bound in its GC. So it seems that Aoun's theory cannot dispense with Control Theory, after all. Something has to specify what the controller must be. With an "object control" verb like *tell*, control must be exercised by the object.

5.1.7 Solutions (and Further Problems)

Let me mention briefly Aoun's solutions to some of the problems we have found. He claimed, based on (10b), that the Auxiliary Hypothesis does not exist. That left (13) unexplained. He then proposed, in addition to Condition A, the following requirement:

(34) An anaphor must be bound.

(34) would rule out (13), because *each other* is not bound in (13). It seems, however, that there is a redundancy between (34) and Condition A.[5]

One might think that Aoun also intended (34) as a means of accounting for (14). He did not, for the following reason: (35) is grammatical:

(35) [[PRO losing the race]] would be unfortunate

PRO has no GC-A in (35). But by (34), PRO should be bound even if it lacks a GC. PRO is not bound in (35), yet (35) is grammatical, contrasting sharply with (14). Aoun's solution to (35) is to claim that PRO is not an anaphor.

- *Willim:* But that does not account for the ungrammaticality of (14). *Lasnik:* True. Aoun's proposal in this case is a familiar one: PRO is not allowed to be Case-marked. But that raises a number of problems we have discussed before (see section 2.2.3.1). For example, consider (36):

(36) *It was arrested PRO

PRO in (36) is not Case-marked, since passive participles do not assign Case. By hypothesis, PRO is not an anaphor; its only further requirement is that it be free in its GC—and it is, since it is entirely free. (36) then does not violate anything except, conceivably, something about Control.

Notice that in our version of Aoun's theory we were getting much of Control Theory (though not all of it) for free. But in Aoun's own version none of Control Theory comes for free, because if PRO is not an anaphor, then Condition A will not be relevant.

Returning briefly to adjuncts, let us look in particular at the status of their intermediate traces. (We will ignore for this purpose the problem raised by (20) and pretend that subjects, even in Chinese-like languages, count as Accessible SUBJECTs.) Consider first (37a), with the LF representation (37b):

(37) a. Ni   renwei Yuehan weisheme likai
        you think   John   why   leave
        'Why do you think John left'
     b. [Weisheme$_1$]$_1$ [ni renwei [t_1 Yuehan t_1 likai]]

The lower t has a GC, since the embedded subject is accessible to it, and it is bound in its GC by the intermediate t in Comp. (37) does not tell us what the status of that intermediate trace is. Suppose it has no status: the Binding Theory does not care about it at all. The example is grammatical, so that is fine. Now, is there an example that has a trace in Comp that can act as a binder of a lower trace, and yet is ungrammatical? Lasnik and Saito (1984) dealt with just such cases (see section 4.4.2). For instance, consider the Japanese example (38a), with the LF representation (38b):[6]

(38) a. *[$_{NP}$[$_{S'}$ Taroo-ga   naze sore-o te-ni ireta] koto]-o
            (you) Taro-nom why it-acc obtained fact-acc
         sonnani okotteru no
         so-much be-angry Q (question marker)
         'Why are you so angry about the fact that Taro obtained it t'
     b. [$_{S'}$[$_S$[$_{NP}$[$_{S'}$[$_S$ Taroo-ga t_1 sore-o te-ni ireta]$_S$ t_1']$_{S'}$ koto]$_{NP}$-o
         sonnani okotteru]$_S$ naze$_1$]$_{S'}$ no

As far as I have been able to determine, (38) is about as bad in Japanese as the corresponding sentence would be in English. The lower trace is perfectly all right. Thus, it must be the trace in Comp that is causing the problem. Hence, by Aoun's theory, the trace in Comp must be violating Condition A, so it must have a GC. We thus need an Accessible SUBJECT, and—except for the problem that there might be no Accessible SUBJECTs in the languages we are looking at—(38) does have one, namely, *you*. Then the question is whether the trace under consideration is bound in its GC, the matrix clause. It is. But that is a wrong result, because the sentence is ungrammatical. Aoun has an answer to this, adapted from proposals by Huang (1982b). It is the claim that a noun can be an Accessible SUBJECT. We are dealing with an NP, *the fact* . . . . If a Noun can act as an Accessible SUBJECT, then the GC will be the entire NP and the trace will be free in its GC. But, as we see from the grammaticality of (39b), this incorrectly predicts that in Japanese and Chinese something like (39a) should be ill formed:

(39) a. I read a book about myself
     b. Wo du-le   yi-ben guanyu ziji de shu
        I   read-Asp one   about self book

Since (39b) is grammatical, *shu* 'book' cannot be a SUBJECT, for if it were, the NP would incorrectly be the GC for the reflexive, and the reflexive is not bound within that NP. So, of the three candidates we have been considering for SUBJECT, in at least a subset of the languages under consideration, none of them really ever counts as a SUBJECT. In such a language, then, there should be no GCs at all, which means that anaphors should have but one requirement: that they be bound, with no locality condition on the binding. For the traditional anaphors, such as *caki* in Korean and *zibun* in Japanese, that is true. But intermediate traces or initial traces of adjuncts are subject to a much stronger ECP-like requirement: being bound in the minimal NP or S'. The symmetry that Aoun was interested in capturing does not obviously exist.

- *Hong:* In Chinese (40a) is good, with (presumably) the LF representation in (40b):

(40) a. Ni   xiangxin Yuehan mai-le   sheme de shuofa
        you believe John   buy-Asp what   claim
        'What$_1$ do you believe the claim t_1 John bought t_1'
     b. Sheme$_1$ [ni xiangxin [[t_1 [Yuehan mai-le t_1]] de shuofa]]

Is this further evidence that nouns are not Accessible SUBJECTs?
Lasnik: There is a potential problem with the intermediate trace, as in (38). But there we were dealing with the trace of an adjunct. Here we are dealing with the trace of a complement, and the sentence is grammatical. If the complex NP is the GC, the trace under consideration will not be bound in its GC. But we can simply eliminate the trace that is causing the trouble, as in Lasnik and Saito 1984 (see section 4.1.4). The

intermediate trace could be deleted, or never created in the first place, since no principle requires its existence. The initial trace, as usual, will have no GC, because, by (9bii), it will have no Accessible SUBJECT. Hence, the problem you raise could be solved. The problem about adjunct traces remains, however. Hence, there appear to be major obstacles standing in the way of any attempt to reduce the entirety of the ECP to Condition A.

•

5.2 Linking Theory

Let us turn next to Linking Theory, an alternative to Binding Theory originally introduced by Higginbotham (1983) and developed further by Montalbetti (1984).

5.2.1 The Notion "Linking"

The basic idea is this. In Binding Theory all NPs have indices, and the core syntactic relation among NPs is coindexation. In Linking Theory indices play no role; rather, linking obtains. Coindexation is a symmetric relation (if α is coindexed with β, then β is coindexed with α). The relevant property of linking is that it is not a symmetric relation. The notation that Higginbotham uses for this is an arrow, with a head and a tail:

(41) β α

     ↑_____|

"α is linked to β"

Let us investigate some of the phenomena Linking Theory was designed to account for. Consider the case of "split antecedents":

(42) John told Bill that they should leave

Recall why Binding Theory, as articulated by Chomsky (1981b), fails for (42). *John* and *Bill* must have different indices. But what index does *they* have? If it has an index different from those of both *John* and *Bill*, then it is disjoint in reference from both of them. If it has the same index as *Bill*, then it will be disjoint from *John*, and vice versa. So there is no way that the reference of *they* can include the reference of *John* and the reference of *Bill*—clearly an incorrect result.

Since this is the basic case we want Linking Theory to account for, let us design a theory that works here. In particular, following Higginbotham, let us design a theory in which (43) is a well-formed representation (that is, where *they* is linked to both *John* and *Bill*):

(43) <u>John</u> told <u>Bill</u> that <u>they</u> should leave

Notice that it must be true that an item may be linked to more than one other item. Otherwise, the analysis will never get off the ground.

Let us tentatively begin developing the semantics. In particular, what is the semantic import of linking? It cannot be the same as the semantic import of coindexation; that is, linking must not entail coreference. (*They* is not coreferential with *Bill*, nor is it coreferential with *John*.) Something along the lines of (44) is what we need:

(44) If α is linked to β, then the reference of α includes the reference of β.

Now consider (45):

(45) John likes him

Clearly, we want this representation to be ruled out. There are two possibilities we could try, but both will have to involve something rather like Binding Condition B. Let us first try something that looks a lot like such a condition, and see how far we can push it:

(46) A pronominal cannot be linked within its GC.

(46) correctly excludes representation (45) but incorrectly excludes (45′):

(45′) John's mother likes him

Soon we will modify (46).

Next consider an analogue of Binding Condition A:

(47) An anaphor must be linked within its GC.

- *McKee:* Does that allow (48)?

  (48) *John likes themselves

  Lasnik: Yes, it does. In (48) *themselves* is an anaphor and hence must be linked in its GC. *John* is in that GC.[7] So our only hope is that the linking in (48) violates the semantic interpretive rule (44)—but it doesn't. We will return to this issue.

- *McKee:* Is that the same type of problem as we find in (49)?

  (49) John told Bill that they should leave

  Lasnik: (49) is fully grammatical with *they* meaning, say, Bill and Mary. Thus, the grammaticality of (49) as compared with the ungrammaticality of (48) raises an interesting problem, since we must be allowed to link a plural to a singular.

- *Epstein:* Does linking by definition entail c-command?
  Lasnik: No. In fact, Higginbotham does not want linking per se to entail c-command, since he wants to be able to have linking in cases like (50):

(50) a. His mother loves John
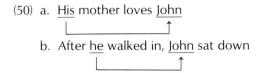

   b. After he walked in, John sat down •

- *Epstein:* But do we need c-command in any of the definitions we've seen?

  Lasnik: Well, we need c-command *somewhere.* Consider (51):

(51) *Himself likes him

Nothing that we have said so far disallows this representation. We are going to need a general condition of the following type:

(52) If α c-commands β, then α cannot be linked to β.

(51) will violate (52). Further, the articulated analogues of the Binding Conditions will also involve c-command, as we will see directly. •

5.2.2 Condition A Effects

In this theory, there are two ways to establish links. One is to link automatically under movement. The other is to link arguments freely at S-Structure. Again, this is analogous to the assignment of indices in Binding Theory.

   Given this, let us look at exactly how Higginbotham states these processes and why he states them as he does. Consider first his version of Binding Condition A:

(53) If A is an anaphor, then there is exactly one B in G(A) [governing category of A] such that B c-commands A, and A is linked to B.

There are two differences between (53) and our earlier simplified version (47): the "exactly one" requirement and the c-command requirement. The latter is needed to rule out cases like (54):

(54) *[John's mother] likes himself

By (47), (54) should be well formed. *Himself* is an anaphor; it is linked in its GC, for its GC is the whole S. But it violates (53), for even though *himself* is linked to something, it is not linked to something that c-commands it. This bears again on the issue of c-command that we just discussed.

   What about the "exactly one" requirement in (53)? Here is an interesting case. It is well known that whereas pronouns display "split antecedent" phenomena, anaphors generally do not. Thus, (55) is ungrammatical:

(55) *John asked Mary about themselves
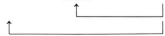

Here (53) is violated, since *each other* is multiply linked in its governing category.

Consider now (56):

(56) *John said that Mary likes themselves

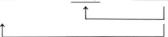

Themselves is multiply linked. Surprisingly, however, (56) does not violate (53), because (53) does not say that anaphors cannot be multiply linked. Notice that the anaphor in (56) is linked to exactly one antecedent *in its GC*. The additional link is to an NP outside the GC. Suppose, then, that we augment (53) with a requirement such as (57):

(57) An anaphor cannot be multiply linked.

Then (56) would be ruled out, as desired. Condition (57) is of further interest since, as noted by Finer (1984), it could provide a solution to the problem of "illicit NP-Movement" examined in Lasnik 1985 (see section 6.4 for discussion).

5.2.3 Condition B Effects

Consider now Higginbotham's Condition B, which will rule out (45) in the same way that (46) did, but will allow (45').

(58) If A is pronominal and B c-commands A in G(A), then B is not an antecedent of A.

The notion "have as an antecedent" is much like "be linked to," but only the former is transitive. It can be defined as follows:[8]

(59) a. If A is linked to B, then B is an antecedent of A.
    b. If B is an antecedent of A, and C is an antecedent of B, then C is an antecedent of A.

Thus, by (59a), B in the configuration C   B   A is an

antecedent of A, and C is an antecedent of B. By (59b), C is also an antecedent of A.

We have seen that the mention of c-command makes (58) somewhat weaker vis-à-vis (46). On the other hand, the reference to antecedence in place of linking makes (58) somewhat stronger. This can be seen in (60):

(60) *After he walked in, he hit him

Here *him* is not linked to the second *he*, so (46) would be ineffectual. But by (59b), the second *he* is an antecedent of *him*. (58) can thus successfully rule out this representation.

By this theory, an item can have more than one antecedent even apart from classic split antecedent phenomena. In (60) both *he*'s are antecedents of *him*. Consider also a construction such as (61):

(61) John thinks he washed himself

On the relevant reading, *himself* has two antecedents: *he*, which it is linked to; and *John*, which *he* is linked to.

- *McKee:* What about coreference? If A is an anaphor linked to B, and if B is linked to C, then are A, B, and C coreferential?
  Lasnik: Let us look at (61), which illustrates your case. Have we guaranteed that *John* and *himself* are coreferential, if the link between *he* and *John* does not entail coreference? Put differently, do we want to guarantee that? In fact, we do not. Consider (62):

(62) John told Bill that they should wash themselves

Themselves must be linked to *they* to satisfy (53). Furthermore, we want to allow *they* to be linked to *John*. And now, since the sentence is grammatical, we don't want a condition that would force *John* and *themselves* to be coreferential (since they cannot be). Hence, antecedence does not entail coreference. That is what we want the theory to say, because if the notion "antecedent" carries any force at all, we would certainly want it to be true that in (43) *they* has two antecedents. But, clearly, *they* is not coreferential with either *John* or *Bill*.   •

5.2.4   Condition C Effects

Now consider (63):

(63) He thinks John is intelligent

```
   |_____↑  (a)
   ↑_____|  (b)
```

We have disallowed (63a) by (52), because *he* c-commands *John*. But we have not yet dealt with anything that rules out (63b). There are a couple of possibilities. One would be something along the lines of Binding Condition C. For instance:

(64) An R-expression cannot be linked.

What Higginbotham says sounds at first totally different from that:

(65) The interpretation of an expression is given in one and only one way.

Intuitively, the idea is clear. The interpretation of *John* is given internally, and if we link it to something, then its interpretation is also given by that link—because a link has semantic significance. But then in (63b) it would be getting its interpretation in more than one way, in violation of (65). There are potential difficulties with this. First, it is not entirely true that an R-expression cannot have an antecedent. There are relevant phenomena that Higginbotham did not address. Consider the case of anaphoric epithets (discussed in section 2.1.3.1):

(66) *John thinks the bastard is intelligent

(66) is not a problem: (65) correctly rules it out. (67) does pose a problem, however:

(67) After John walked in, the bastard hit me

In (66) *the bastard* is behaving like something that is not allowed to have an antecedent. In Binding Theory terms, it is behaving like an R-expression. In Linking Theory terms, it is behaving like an expression whose interpretation is given internally—hence, like an expression that is not allowed to be linked. But in (67) it is behaving like something that *is* allowed to have an antecedent. Evidently, the difference is c-command, but the basic semantic principle that is supposed to be giving these results does not, and cannot, say anything about c-command. Whether an element is allowed to receive an interpretation in more than one way should not be a structural fact. For the Condition C approach (as in section 2.1.3.1), (67) is not a problem. *The bastard* causes ungrammaticality when it is c-commanded by something that it is coindexed with. Binding Theory correctly does not say anything about R-expressions that are not bound. But (65) is apparently too broad a principle to account for this paradigm. If we gave up (65), we might consider modifying (64) to allow it to account for (66) and (67). As it stands, (64) is too general. An appropriate narrowing might be (68):

(68) An R-expression cannot be linked to something that
      c-commands it.

Of course, this would weaken one of Higginbotham's arguments for Linking Theory: that it obviates the need for Condition C. (68), in effect, *is* Condition C.

Condition (65) faces another potential problem, which was first noticed by Paul Gorrell. Consider (69):

(69) John likes himself

Here *himself* apparently receives an interpretation in more than one way. It receives one aspect of its interpretation by virtue of being linked, but it also seems to have some internal meaning: third person, singular, masculine. However, we could avoid this difficulty by claiming that these features are just an agreement fact and not part of the meaning of *himself*; agreement would be needed precisely because the reflexive is getting all of its meaning from *John*. I don't know if this is right, but it doesn't sound implausible.

There is, however, a related problem that cannot be avoided so easily. Consider (70):

(70) a. They like themselves

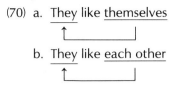

b. They like each other

In both (70a) and (70b) linking obtains, and in both cases the linking is crucial; without it, (53) would be violated. We can analyze (70a) just as we did (69): the anaphor is given an interpretation in exactly one way, via its antecedent. Now in (70b) the anaphor is surely also given an interpretation via its antecedent. But one aspect of its interpretation—reciprocity—must be given internally. If this were not so, (70a) and (70b) would have to be synonymous. Thus, *each other* is an expression that receives its interpretation in more than one way. This is a very strong argument against (65), I believe. The fact that *each other* appears in (70b) cannot be a low-level agreement fact. It is a real semantic fact: reciprocity carries semantic force.

Consider now (71), a case discussed in Wasow 1972 and later reconsidered in Lasnik 1976:

(71) *[The woman who loved him] [told him [that John was nice]]
α β

The first *him* is linked to *John*, and the second *him* is linked to the first. Under a Binding Theory approach as in Lasnik 1976 (see section 2.1.3.1), it is clear why (71) is ill formed. For *him*, *him*, and *John* to be coreferential, they must be coindexed, but that representation violates Condition C since the second *him* would bind *John*.[9]

Now consider the links in (71). Both instances of *him* have *John* as an antecedent, whereas *John* itself, not being linked to anything, has no antecedent. So far (71) does not violate anything we've discussed. The issue is that (52) claims that α cannot be linked to β if the latter c-commands the former. (52) is not violated in (71) because α and β in (71) are not linked at all. Thus, we have to make (52) stronger, as in (72):

(72) If α c-commands β, then β cannot be an antecedent of α.

(72) would rule out (71), since β is an antecedent of α.[10] (α is linked to an item that is linked to β. Hence, by (59b), β is an antecedent of α.) The only way to keep β from being an antecedent of α would be to erase one of the links in (71). If we do that, we presumably are in a position to account for the relevant fact: namely, that the NPs in question cannot all be coreferential. I say "presumably," since Higginbotham did not explicitly discuss the semantic import of lack of antecedence.

• *Uriagereka:* How does Linking Theory deal with (73), where both instances of *John* refer to the same person?

(73) John hit John

Lasnik: There are three possibilities to consider:

(74) a. John hit John
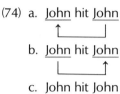

b. John hit John

c. John hit John

For Higginbotham, (74a) is ruled out by (65).[11] (74b) is ruled out both by (65) and by (72). (74c) is not ruled out, and Higginbotham claims that this is the correct result, even when the two instances of *John* are coreferential, for his theory says nothing about coreference.

This sort of approach to such Condition C effects is in line with a now prevalent view (not necessarily Higginbotham's). It is frequently claimed that there is an extragrammatical explanation for an example like (74c): namely, that it is grammatical and yet somewhat unacceptable because there is a simpler way of saying the same thing, with a reflexive instead of the second *John*. I find this rather dubious. Consider a contrast like the following:

(75) a. John walked in, then John hit me
b. John walked in, then he hit me

For (75a), too, there is a "simpler" way of saying the same thing, namely, (75b). And in fact there is something right about that. It is slightly odd to say (75a). The question is whether the oddness of (74c) can be reduced to the oddness of (75a). And that is where people seem to disagree in their judgments.

For a test case, we can even build a more exact parallel for (75a):

(76) John thinks John is clever

Both in (76) and in (75a) the preferred option is to use a pronoun. But is the oddness of (76) exactly like the oddness of (75a)? (76) seems far worse, yet the theory does not distinguish these two cases. The non-linked representation is equally available for both.

Consider (67) once again. (67) is perfect, contrasting sharply with (66) on the relevant reading. This constitutes another problem for the version of the theory we have been considering. Whatever weak pragmatic effect we might have been appealing to for (75) is clearly off the mark in the case of an anaphoric epithet. But (66) is, I believe, exactly as bad as (76). As far as I know, this contrast is not addressed in the recent literature. (77) is also incorrectly allowed, in just the same way as (66):

(77) John hit the bastard

Again, the relevant case is the one where the two NPs are coreferential, but neither is linked to the other. (77) is impossible on that reading, but it is not clear how Linking Theory could rule it out.[12]

5.2.5 *Strong Crossover*

• *Epstein:* Can we consider cases of strong crossover?
Lasnik: Your question, I take it, is whether Linking Theory can handle strong crossover, since it lacks a precise analogue of Condition C. Though it is true that there is no obvious way for Linking Theory to reduce strong crossover to the same phenomenon as (63), I do not regard that as a major argument against the theory. This is because I do not believe Condition C of Binding Theory can handle the full range of strong crossover–type effects, even though Chomsky 1981b and its immediate predecessors took it for granted that it can. For purposes of exposition, I have gone along with that assumption, but perhaps this is a good time to call it into question.   •

For several years now Higginbotham has been pointing out cases, which have largely been ignored, of strong crossover–type effects that cannot be handled by Condition C (see, for example, Higginbotham 1980a). Consider the following paradigm:

(78) a. *Who_1 does he_1 like t_1
   b. *$[Whose_1 \text{ mother}]_2$ does he_1 like t_2
   c. *$[\text{Which picture of } [\text{which man}]_1]_2$ does he_1 like t_2

(78a) is the standard case. It can be accounted for straightforwardly by Condition C under the assumption that a *wh*-trace is an R-expression. *t* is A-bound by *he*. Condition C does not seem to say anything about (78b), however, since the variable is not A-bound. Examples like (78b) motivate the process called *Reconstruction* (see Chomsky 1976, Freidin and Lasnik 1981). Chomsky proposes that Reconstruction be thought of as (for example) extracting *who* in (79) out of *whose mother* and putting the rest of the phrase "back":

(79) Who_1 [he_1 likes [$t's_1$ mother]]

This process is reasonably well motivated, independent of the phenomenon of strong crossover. For example, the semantics of (80a) can be read directly from (80b), as in (80c):

(80) a. $[Whose_1 \text{ mother}]_2$ does Mary like t_2
   b. Who_1 [Mary likes [$t's_1$ mother]$_2$]
   c. For which *x*, Mary likes *x*'s mother

Once we apply Reconstruction to (78b), creating (79), we can apply Condition C to the reconstructed structure and then reject it. But now consider (78c), which Higginbotham (1980a) argues cannot be dealt with by Condition C. Reconstruction as in (80) would give us an apparently uninterpretable LF representation in this case. The problem is that we have two operators, both of which must stay in $\overline{\text{A}}$-positions if they are to have scope. But if they must stay in $\bar{\text{A}}$-positions, we will not get a suitable trace back inside the sentence to be A-bound by *he*. Thus, we need something else to account for this case of strong crossover; Higginbotham argues that Condition C will not suffice. I cannot imagine an answer to that argument, unless someone finds a plausible LF representation to assign to (78c), whereby the crucial phrase is back inside the S. But I do not know what that could be.

I will not go into Higginbotham's exact proposal for cases like (78c). I will merely note that (a) it is essentially descriptive; (b) it works; (c) it generalizes to all of the cases in (78). But if something is needed to account for (78c) and it automatically accounts for the other cases, the motivation for treating a *wh*-trace as an R-expression is substantially lessened.

- *Uriagereka:* If Condition C does not apply to *wh*-traces, is (81) a problem?

(81) *Who$_1$ [t_1 seems [t_1 [t_1 loves Mary]]]

Lasnik: It might well be. (81) is an example of what May (1979) called "improper movement," and it could be dealt with by assuming that Condition C applied to the *wh*-trace in the embedded subject position. That trace would be A-bound by the matrix subject. As an alternative, Aoun has proposed in several of his works that S' breaks a chain. The subject of *seem* needs a θ-role, and it can only receive one by being part of a chain that includes the lower subject. The intervening S' would then not allow a chain to be formed in (81). That might be the answer, but it does seem rather stipulative.

5.2.6 A Constraint on Antecedence

Consider some of the representations for (82):

(82) John thinks he likes him

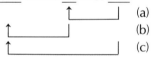

(I will not link *John* to anything else, because we saw that such a linking always violates something.) (82a) violates (58) (the analogue of Condition B). (82b) and (82c) have to be well formed, since the examples in (83) are perfectly grammatical on the relevant readings:

(83) a. John thinks he likes Fred
     b. John thinks Fred likes him

That is, the subject and object of the complement can independently be linked to the matrix subject. Yet (82) cannot have an interpretation where *John* is the antecedent of both *he* and *him* simultaneously. This has the flavor of Wasow's example discussed earlier as (71).

Plausibly, we could take one of two different approaches to rule out the representation in question. We could say that something cannot be the antecedent of more than one thing. That cannot be right, though, because of examples like (84):

(84) John thinks he likes himself

Here, by definition (59), *John* is the antecedent of both *he* and *himself.* Higginbotham's proposal is as follows:

(85) If X and Y share an antecedent, and Y c-commands X, then Y
    must be an antecedent of X.

Notice that (85) is stated as a filter. There is another version of this same basic idea. Montalbetti (1984) formulates (85) as a "relinking rule." In configurations falling under (85), the bad representation is not filtered out; rather, the links must be redone. Thus, if a sentence had both links (b) and (c) of (82), (85) would require replacing (c) by (a), which would violate (58). (Notice that in an indexing theory, no special stipulation like (85) is needed. If *John* and *he* are coindexed, and so are *John* and *him*, then *he* and *him* will be coindexed in violation of Condition B.)

5.2.7   *Further Arguments for Linking*

Apart from analyses of split antecedence, there are two independent arguments for Linking Theory, as opposed to some version of Binding Theory, that we should now consider. One is due to Higginbotham (1985), following work of Finer. Consider (86):

(86) The men told each other that they should leave

By (53), *each other* clearly must be linked to *the men.* Higginbotham claims that (86) is four ways ambiguous, depending on the interpretation of *they. They* could be some other people entirely; that is obvious. *They* could also be interpreted as a group reading about the men. Neither of those readings is particularly interesting. But the other two could be important:

(87) a. A told B that B should leave, and B told A that A should leave
    b. A told B that A should leave, and B told A that B should leave

(87a) is the meaning of (88):[13]

(88) The men told each other PRO to leave

We know how to capture that:

(89) The men told each other that they should leave

The really interesting reading is (87b). (89) apparently does not represent that reading, since there the person being told is the person who is to do the leaving. The meaning we want is that the person doing the telling is the one who leaves. (90) rather nicely represents that meaning:

(90) The men told each other that they should leave

(90) is interesting for the following two reasons. First, it violates (85).[14] (In fact, for essentially this reason, Higginbotham has now given up (85).) Second, there is evidently no way to distinguish (87b) from (87a) with Binding Theory, since if the NPs are pairwise coindexed, then all of them will be coindexed. This phenomenon is therefore a real argument for Linking Theory, since the analysis relies on a central difference between the two devices: linking is not transitive, whereas coindexing is. Crucially, the *linking* relation is carrying the weight of the semantic analysis rather than the *antecedence* relation, since *the men* is an antecedent of *they* on either representation (see (59)). There is a cost associated with the Linking Theory analysis, however. Once (85) is eliminated, we have no way of ruling out (82) on the relevant reading.[15]

Montalbetti offers another genuine argument for Linking Theory. Interestingly, it crucially relies on (85), whereas Higginbotham's argument crucially relies on the denial of (85). Consider the following S-Structure forms (on the bound reading):

(91) a. Juan piensa   que él es inteligente
         John thinks   that he is clever
         'John thinks he is clever'
     b. *Todo chico piensa   que él es inteligente
         every boy   thinks   that he is clever
         'Every boy thinks he is clever'
     c. *Quién piensa que él es inteligente
         who   thinks that he is clever
         'Who thinks he is clever'

These are all good in English. In Spanish, though, only (91a) is good. As far as I know, the analogous property holds generally of pro-drop languages of both the Spanish type (null subjects only) and the Korean type (null arguments). One way of describing the facts in such languages might be as in (92) (see Hong 1985):

(92) An overt pronoun cannot be $\bar{A}$-bound at LF.

Montalbetti instead proposes a linking constraint for these languages. (93) is a first approximation:

(93) At LF an overt pronoun cannot be linked to a variable [that is, to the trace of movement of an operator to an $\bar{A}$-position].

(93) does the same work that (92) does with respect to (91).

However, as Montalbetti shows, the facts are more complicated than this. Consider (94):

(94) a. Juan piensa que María lo   ama
         John thinks that Mary him loves
         'John thinks Mary loves him'

b. Quién piensa que María lo   ama
 who thinks that Mary him loves
 'Who thinks Mary loves him'
c. Cada hombre piensa que María lo   ama
 each man   thinks that Mary him loves
 'Each man thinks Mary loves him'

In Spanish all the examples in (94) are good—yet the last two violate the initial formulation of the LF constraint we are concerned with. Both contain an overt pronoun that is $\overline{\text{A}}$-bound; furthermore, even (93) does not distinguish (94b, c) from (91b, c). Montalbetti observes that there is a kind of complementarity here. In (91), when the pronoun was bad, pro would have been good. In (94) the pronoun is good and pro would be bad. That suggests a modification of (92). The generalization seems to be that for an NP in an $\overline{\text{A}}$-bound position, if pro is possible, then pro is necessary. If pro is not possible, then an overt pronoun is. Here is a rough version of the generalization:

(95) An overt pronoun cannot be $\overline{\text{A}}$-bound if a null pronoun in that position is possible.

In general, pro is possible only as a subject of a finite clause in Spanish-type languages.

In terms of Linking Theory, this can be stated as in (96), which is roughly Montalbetti's proposal:

(96) At LF an overt pronoun cannot be linked to a variable if a null pronoun in that position is possible.

Consider the LF representation in (97) (for (91b)):

(97) *Todo chico _t_ piensa que _él_ es inteligente

 'Every boy thinks he is intelligent'

(96) rules out (97), because it has a pronoun that is linked to the trace of QR (that is, a variable). Furthermore, pro is possible in Spanish in the position of the pronoun. LF representation (98) will be allowed even though the pronoun is linked to a variable, since pro is not possible in that position:

(98) Todo chico _t_ piensa que el rey _lo_ conocerá algún día

 'Every boy thinks that the king will meet him some day'

So far Binding Theory and Linking Theory cover the same phenomena. However, Montalbetti argues that evidence can be adduced in all of this that supports Linking Theory as opposed to Binding Theory. He claims an example can be constructed in Spanish (though not necessarily in the other languages where the central phenomena in question obtain) that differentiates the two theories. Consider (99):

(99) a. Juan dijo que (pro) piensa que él es inteligente
John said that (pro) thinks that he is clever
'John said that he thinks that he is clever'

b. Quién *t* dijo que (pro) piensa que él es inteligente
who *t* said that (pro) thinks that he is clever
'Who said that he thinks that he is clever'

According to Montalbetti, both examples in (99) are grammatical in Spanish. The problem is, of course, that (99b) has an overt pronoun that is Ā-bound. (95) will incorrectly rule it out, whereas (96) will let it in. Montalbetti's precise proposal uses the notion *formal variable*, which, for our purposes, is simply the trace of movement from an A-position to an Ā-position. Thus, QR leaves behind a trace that is a formal variable; so does *Wh*-Movement. (100) states the constraint in these terms:

(100) An overt pronoun cannot be linked to a formal variable if a null pronoun in that position is possible.

Consider (99b), with the linking in (101):

(101) Quién *t* dijo que (pro) piensa que él es inteligente

The overt pronoun in (99), *he*, has a formal variable as one of its antecedents, but it is not *linked* to a formal variable; instead, it is linked to pro, which is not a formal variable. Notice that pro is linked to a formal variable, but that is all right, because (100) is only a constraint on the distribution of *overt* pronouns. So our account rules in (99), and it still rejects the bad cases. Consider again (91c), repeated here as (102):

(102) *Quien *t* piensa que él es inteligente

who think that he is clever
'Who thinks he is clever'

(102) is ruled out (in Spanish) because *he* is linked to a formal variable. The same would hold for (91b), as long as (100) operates at LF.

- *Epstein:* Suppose that *he* is not linked to the formal variable in (102). How do we prevent the representation in (103)?

(103) *Quién *t* piensa que él es inteligente

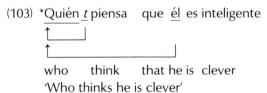

who think that he is clever
'Who thinks he is clever'

Lasnik: Just the right question. The linking rules allow free linking. I mentioned in passing that Montalbetti proposes an operation very similar to Higginbotham's filter (85), to rule out that possibility:

(104) If X and Y share an antecedent and Y c-commands X, then Y is an antecedent of X.

This is an obligatory relinking rule that requires a representation such as (103) to be replaced with (102), which does violate (100). Thus, as I mentioned earlier, the analysis crucially relies on Montalbetti's version of Higginbotham's filter.

Now consider (94b), repeated here as (105):

(105) Quién _t_ piensa que María lo   ama

    ⌐   ⌐

    who   _t_ thinks that Mary him loves
    'Who thinks that Mary loves him'

Here the overt pronoun is linked to a formal variable, but pro is not possible; hence, the constraint correctly does not rule the sentence out. •

Montalbetti claims that what we have just seen is an argument for Linking Theory because these facts are easy to describe in this theory. He argue that they could not be stated at all under Binding Theory. In fact, that is true, but just barely. If we replace "cannot be Ā-bound" in (95) by "cannot be locally bound by a formal variable," we get almost all of Montalbetti's results. The notion "local binding," which has wide application in syntactic theory, is that of Koopman and Sportiche (1982) and Chomsky (1981b, 1982). Essentially, A locally binds B if A binds B and there is no intervening binder. Although *él* in (99b) is bound by the variable *t*, it is not locally bound by that variable, since its nearest binder is pro. There is only one class of facts not amenable to this description, illustrated in (106):

(106) Nadie   pensó   que las fotos   que él tomó probarían
    nobody thought that the photos that he took would-prove
    que (pro) estuvo ahí
    that (pro) was   there
    'Nobody thought that the photos he took would prove that
    he was there'

Montalbetti reports that this example is acceptable on the relevant reading, even though *él* is locally bound by the LF trace of *nadie*. This follows immediately in his account, since *él* need not be linked to that trace but rather may be linked to pro, which in turn is linked to the trace. Thus, linking receives some empirical support.[16]

It should be kept in mind, however, that although Higginbotham and Montalbetti have each offered one argument for Linking Theory, we cannot add them together to get two arguments for Linking Theory. This is because the arguments rely on (virtually) contradictory positions concerning (85).

Chapter 6   Some Open Questions: Topics for Further Research

Throughout this course I have put aside a number of important questions so that we could proceed in an orderly fashion (or at least in a not entirely chaotic fashion). All of those questions are worthy of detailed investigation. I will conclude with an assortment of intriguing open questions and unresolved difficulties. Some of these have come up already in one form or another; others I will present for the first time. The fact that there are so many (and more could easily be added) should not be taken as cause for alarm. Rather, it should be taken as a sign of progress in the field that such deep questions can now be raised. As we look at some of the problems, the general outline that the solution will have to take will come into focus. I encourage you to treat this material not as an indictment of the version of syntactic theory we have been exploring, but rather as an opportunity for further research.

6.1   The Case Filter

In section 1.4 we considered some of the central phenomena motivating the Case Filter (1):

(1) *$\begin{bmatrix} \text{NP} \\ \text{lexical} \\ -\text{Case} \end{bmatrix}$

(1) has a certain plausibility as a morphological well-formedness condition, and it directly accounts for a large number of contrasts. For example, in (2) an NP-trace is possible in a position where a lexical NP is not:

(2) a. John is likely [$_S$ t to be clever]
     b. *It is likely [$_S$ John to be clever]

And in (3) PRO is possible in a position where a lexical NP is not:

(3) a. Mary tried [$_{S'}$[$_S$ PRO to win the race]]
     b. *Mary tried [$_{S'}$[$_S$ Bill to win the race]]

Thus, as discussed earlier, (1) has substantial support. However, as also noted (section 1.8), there is one major difficulty confronting (1). Apparently, *wh*-trace, which is not lexical (not morphologically realized), requires Case:

(4) *Who is it likely [t to be clever]

In the first detailed discussion of (1), Chomsky (1980) did in fact account for examples such as (4). He proposed that *who*, rather than the trace, is the lexical NP that lacks Case.[1]

As also pointed out earlier, however, even where there is no lexical *wh*-phrase, an example with the abstract configuration of (4) is still excluded:

(5) a. *The man (that) it is likely [*t* to be clever] ...
    b. The man (that) it is likely [*t* is clever] ...

Lasnik and Freidin (1981) concluded that along with lexical NPs, the trace of *Wh*-Movement must also be Case-marked. Although this correctly describes the facts, it strips the Case Filter of its intuitive morphological plausibility.

Chomsky (1981b), basing his suggestion on a proposal of Aoun (1979), offers an alternative view of the Case Filter that overcomes this difficulty.[2] On this alternative, lexical realization is not the crucial property; rather, it is argumenthood. To be "visible" for θ-marking at LF, an argument must have Case. A Caseless argument will not be assigned a θ-role at LF and will thus be in violation of the θ-Criterion, a condition regarded by Chomsky as being "virtually a condition of adequacy at the level of LF" (Chomsky 1981b:336).[3] This proposal handles both lexical arguments and *wh*-traces, since the latter are arguments. Two new problems are created, however. The first we have already seen. PRO surely does not require Case (in fact, it probably never receives Case at all, since by the interaction of Conditions A and B it must be ungoverned). Yet PRO clearly can receive a θ-role. If this were not so, (3a) would unequivocally violate the θ-Criterion.

The second problem is that expletives, like lexical arguments, require Case:

(6) a. *It is likely [it to rain]
    b. *It is likely [there to be a man here]
    c. *I tried [it to seem that Bill was intelligent]
    d. *It is likely [it to seem that Bill is intelligent]

Under the morphological interpretation of the Case Filter, these are all correctly predicted to be ungrammatical, since the expletive subject of the complement in each case is morphologically realized. But on the "visibility" interpretation, the situation is less clear. For (6a), Chomsky has suggested that subjects of weather predicates are argument-like in certain respects; he calls them "quasi arguments." One bit of evidence for this is that weather *it* can apparently control PRO, an ability generally thought to be reserved for arguments:

(7) It often rains without PRO snowing

For (6b), it is at least plausible that there is a chain-like relation between *there* and the associated argument. If we suppose that *a man* is not Case-marked, it could become visible via association with Case-marked *there*. As for (6c,d), recall from the discussion of Accessible SUBJECTs that Chomsky argued that an "extraposed" clause receives its θ-role by association with a coindexed expletive. The visibility account could provide a way to instantiate this. Since the expletive subject of the embedded clause is not Case-marked, it will render the chain (it,S') invisible for θ-marking. (6c,d) will then violate the θ-Criterion. Though this account is appealing, it is not without difficulty. First, as noted in section 2.3, the motivation for the θ-transmission hypothesis is weakened by, for example, (8):

(8) John is likely [t to be intelligent]

Presumably, a complement S needs a θ-role just as much as a complement S' does. Yet in (8) there is no expletive in subject position that could be coindexed with the clause.

Second, this account relies on the claim that an S' argument, like an NP argument, must be Case-marked (either directly or by association with a Case-marked argument). However, contrasts such as the one in (9) cast serious doubt on that:

(9) a. *I am proud John
     (compare *I am proud of John*)
   b. I am proud that John won the race

In (9) the S' complement of *proud* evidently is not Case-marked, yet the sentence is completely well formed. Given this, it is not at all clear that we can deduce the Case requirement on expletives in the way Chomsky suggested.

Thus, neither version of the Case Filter—morphological or θ-theoretic—is entirely satisfactory. Detailed investigation of the particular phenomena causing problems for each is crucial at this stage of our understanding.

6.2 *Tough*-Movement

Example (10) illustrates a phenomenon that has been under investigation for at least two decades and has represented a major challenge to the theory since Chomsky 1973:[4]

(10) a. John is tough to please
     b. It is tough to please John

In both (10a) and (10b) the subject of *to please* is an empty category with roughly the interpretation of *one*—so-called arbitrary PRO. In (10b) *please* straightfowardly assigns its object θ-role to *John*. In (10a), on the other hand, although the θ-relations seem essentially the same as those in (10b), and although *please* must discharge its object θ-role, *John* is not in the position to which that θ-role should be assigned. Of course, abstractly, that is a familiar sort of situation, quite reminiscent of (11) (see section 1.6):

(11) John is likely to win the race

Here, *to win the race* has a subject θ-role to assign, and *John* is interpreted as bearing that θ-role, arguing for a D-Structure representation like (12):

(12) *e* is likely [John to win the race]

The analogous derivation is not, however, available for (10b). Consider the hypothetical D-Structure representation (13):

(13) *e* is tough [PRO to please John]

The difficulty is that we have solid evidence that the trace of NP-Movement obeys Condition A (see section 2.1.4). Yet the movement necessary to produce (10a) from (13) will violate the SSC. That is, the resulting trace will be free in its GC.[5]

In part to address this problem, Chomsky (1977) proposed an analysis quite similar to the one that he proposed for Topicalization (see section 6.5): movement is involved, but it is not *John* that moves, but rather a (null) *wh*-phrase. *John* is base-generated in matrix subject position:[6]

(14) John is tough [*wh* [PRO to please *t*]]

Chomsky (1981b) adopts essentially the same analysis but notes a problem for the θ-Criterion. *John*, an argument, is in a D-Structure position to which no θ-role is assigned (as evidenced by the grammaticality of (10b)). To solve this, Chomsky suggests that *John* is inserted, not at D-Structure, but somewhere later in the derivation. Thus, the θ-Criterion is not violated. However, Kevin Kearney observed that this raised new problems. He noted that the subject of a *tough*-construction need not be "simple," like *John*, but can contain complex structures, including ones involving θ-relations:

(15) The claim that John saw Mary is hard to understand

The NP *the claim that John saw Mary* involves θ-assignment by *claim*, by *saw*, and by *saw Mary*. If such θ-relations are established at D-Structure, as we have assumed throughout, then that NP must exist at that level.[7]

One final problem raised by (14) concerns Condition C of the Binding Theory. If *John*, the null operator, and *t* are all coindexed, the structure violates this condition, assuming, as we have, that a *wh*-trace is an R-expression. As yet, there is no general account of *tough*-constructions that provides principled answers to all these questions.

6.3   Weak Crossover

The phenomenon of weak crossover, illustrated in (16), has been under intense investigation for a number of years:

(16) ?*Who$_1$ does his$_1$ mother love t_1

A case like (16) shares with strong crossover the fact that one of a pair of coindexed NPs has "crossed over" another. However, weak crossover diverges from strong crossover in that in the former the trace is not c-commanded—hence, not bound—by an NP in an A-position. Given this property, of course, no account in terms of Condition C (such as that for strong crossover discussed in section 2.1.3.2) is even conceivable. As mentioned in chapter 3, Koopman and Sportiche (1982) presented a very interesting account. Recall their definition of variable as a locally $\bar{\text{A}}$-bound category. Given that definition, they proposed (17), the Bijection Principle:

(17) a. Every variable must be bound by exactly one operator.
    b. Every operator must bind exactly one variable.

Consider, in this light, example (16). There *who* locally binds both *his* and *t*. That is, *who* binds both of these elements, and there is no nearer binder of either, since neither *his* nor *t* c-commands the other.

Note that in (16) S-Structure and LF do not differ in any relevant way and hence provide no evidence about the level of representation relevant to the Bijection Principle. (18), which seems to have the same grammatical status as (16), is more informative in this regard:

(18) ?*His$_1$ mother loves everyone$_1$

(19), the LF representation of (18), is identical to (16) in relevant respects:

(19) Everyone$_1$ [his$_1$ mother loves t_1]

Here *everyone*, just like *who* in the earlier example, binds two variables, in violation of (17b), whereas at S-Structure there would be no such violation. Thus, we have evidence that the Bijection Principle constrains LF representations.

Haïk (1983), commenting on an earlier version of Koopman and Sportiche's study, pointed out a problem for this account.[8] Consider (20):

(20) Every man$_1$ likes some symphony he$_1$ heard

Haïk noted that the representation of this example violates the Bijection Principle, but the sentence does not have the status of a weak crossover example. In fact, it is perfect. Consider the LF representation of (20):

(21) Every man$_1$ [some symphony he$_1$ heard]$_2$ [$_S$ t_1 liked t_2]

Every man in (21) locally binds two variables. *Every man* binds *he*; in fact, it is the nearest binder of *he*. Hence, *he* is a variable. In addition, *every man* binds its trace—in fact, it is the nearest binder of the trace—so the trace is also a variable. But the Bijection Principle says that an operator is not allowed to bind two variables.

Koopman and Sportiche (1982) suggested the following answer to this problem: the second quantifier in (20) adjoins not to S but to VP:

(22) Every man$_1$ [$_S$ t_1 [some symphony he$_1$ heard]$_2$ [$_{VP}$ liked t_2]]

In (22) t_1 is a variable, but *he* is not, since it is locally bound by t_1 rather than by the operator. Assuming that the semantics of such a representation as (22) can be worked out, this is a not unreasonable solution. However, if the example is complicated slightly, it becomes clear that adjunction to VP is not a general solution to the sort of problem that Haïk raised. Consider (23):

(23) Every man$_1$ asked some actress$_2$ that he$_1$ met about some play
    that she$_2$ appeared in

Once again, if the object quantifier phrase is adjoined to S by QR, we recreate the problem of representation (21). So let us instead use Koopman and Sportiche's proposal and adjoin *some actress that he met* to VP, as in the LF representation in (24):

(24) [$_S$ Every man$_1$ [$_S$ t_1 [$_{VP}$[some actress that he$_1$ met]$_2$ [$_{VP}$[some play
    that she$_2$ appeared in]$_3$ [$_{VP}$ asked t_2 about t_3]$_{VP}$]$_{VP}$]$_S$]$_S$

Notice that the quantificational expression *some play that she appeared in* could not go all the way up to S-adjunction; if it did, *she* would not be in the scope of *some actress*. Hence, this expression, along with the direct object QP, must adjoin to VP. *Every man* in (24) thus binds one variable, just as required by the Bijection Principle. But now look at *some actress that he met*. It binds *she* and now is its nearest binder. But it also binds t_2 and is its nearest binder. This is so because *she* and t_2 do not c-command one another. Thus, the operator *some actress that he met* violates the Bijection Principle. Haïk's problem reappears, even though we have adjoined to VP.

- *Hong:* Why can the quantificational phrase not adjoin to PP in (24), instead of VP?
  Lasnik: That is a possibility well worth considering, but I think there are two problems with it. First, it is not at all obvious that a QP adjoined to PP will be correctly assigned sentential scope. Recall that a substantial part of the motivation for QR is that it puts the QP into its appropriate scope position. (This is also a potential problem even with the VP adjunction case; but one could perhaps argue that a VP adjunct is "high enough" to have sentential scope.) Second, a slight alteration in the example makes it clear that even PP adjunction will not suffice. Consider an example like (24), but involving a double object construction:

(25) Someone$_1$ gave [every actress that he$_1$ met]$_2$
    [a book that she$_2$ appreciated]

In (25) there is no PP to adjoin to. Since neither S adjunction nor VP adjunction avoids the problem, as discussed, it appears there is no way to keep from violating the Bijection Principle.   •

Since (25), like (23), is perfect, the Bijection Principle account of weak crossover is called into question.

Higginbotham points out another type of case that creates a similar difficulty:

(26) Which man$_1$ [t_1 liked [which symphony he$_1$ heard]]

(26) is basically identical to (20). But if we adopt the standard assumption that *wh*-phrases all end up in Comp at LF, then Koopman and Sportiche's account of (20)—namely, VP adjunction—is unavailable. (26), like the other examples we have been considering, is incorrectly treated as a case of weak crossover.

6.4 Illicit NP-Movement

Consider the following ungrammatical sentence that ought to violate Condition A but does not:

(27) *John$_1$ seems that he$_1$ likes t_1

If *he* were not coindexed with *John*, the trace of *John* would be an anaphor free in its GC, but with *he* and *John* coindexed, the trace is bound in its GC. True, the binding is unusual in that the binder of the trace is not the element it is a trace of. But Condition A does not specify that an NP-trace be bound by such an element, but simply that it must be bound in its GC.[9]

There is a potential approach to (27) in terms of Linking Theory due to Finer (1984). Remember that linking is obligatory under movement. Furthermore, an anaphor must be linked to something in its GC that c-commands it. Now suppose that there is a principle like (28) (see section 5.2, ex. (57)):

(28) An anaphor cannot be multiply linked.

In that case (27) should be ruled out. This is a principle that often turns up in expositions of Linking Theory. Thus, it looks as though Linking Theory provides a genuine explanation for (27). The problem is that, contrary to appearance, there is no independent justification for this principle. It might seem that (28) is needed to rule out (29) (an analysis discussed in section 5.2.2):

(29) *John asked Mary about themselves

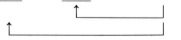

It is clear that (28) would, in fact, rule out (29). But before we conclude that (28) is needed for (29), let us briefly look at one example that we have considered before (section 2.1.5):

(30) *We like myself

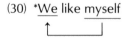

Clearly we need some principle to exclude (30). It will not work to say that if one element is linked with another, the two are coreferential. That is not a general principle, as split antecedents showed. Apparently, then, we need a principle that works only for anaphors, along the lines of (31):

(31) If α is an anaphor and is linked to β, then α and β are coreferential.

And that seems irreducible. But once we have (31), it does not seem that (28) does any work for (29). (31) clearly should exclude (29) because *themselves* cannot be coreferential with either *John* or *Mary*. (28) is thus not a deep explanation for (27), since it is now apparently motivated only by (27) itself.

Returning now to the problem of (27), I would like to consider still other accounts. For example, it has been widely proposed that a chain cannot have two Case-marked positions—which is what in fact happens in (27). Both *John* and its trace are Case-marked. Notice, by the way, that there must be a chain in (27); otherwise, it would violate the θ-Criterion. The S-Structure position of the argument *John* is not a θ-position. Although it is possible that this sort of Case condition on chains is needed, it is suspicious that it overlaps to such a great extent with other conditions. For example, consider (32):

(32) *John$_1$ seems t_1 is crazy

(32) would now violate *three* conditions: (a) the Case condition we are discussing; (b) Condition A; and (c) the ECP. I do not know whether (32) is three times as bad as a similar case that violates only one condition; but I doubt it.

Suppose that the Case condition is stated as in (33):[10]

(33) A chain cannot contain two Case-marked members.

Now consider (34):

(34) **John tried [[Bill$_1$ to seem [that [he likes t_1]]]]

The chain (Bill,t) in (34) has only one Case-marked position—namely, the position occupied by the trace—yet the sentence is wildly ungrammatical. Thus, a further Case condition is needed:

(35) The head of an A-chain must be in a Case-marked position.

However, it is not so obvious that the head of a chain must be in a Case-marked position. Consider (36):

(36) John tried [PRO$_1$ to be arrested t_1]

The chain (PRO,t) is headed by PRO, which, being necessarily ungoverned, is not Case-marked. Thus, (36) must be weakened to (37):

(37) The head of an A-chain must be in a Case-marked position
or be PRO.

Then for an example like (34) with PRO in place of *Bill*, we will need to strengthen (33) to (38):

(38) An NP-trace cannot be Case-marked.

Now let us see whether it is possible to construct an example that contains the head of an A-chain in a Case-marked position and a trace in a non-Case-marked position and that nonetheless exhibits "illicit NP-Movement" as in (27). As a first step in this direction, consider a structure like (39):

(39) Mary is proud of Bill

Plausibly, *Bill* is the complement of *proud*. Notice that there are gaps in the paradigm of complements. There are NP complements to verbs and prepositions, but in English there are no NP complements to adjectives or nouns. Rather, in cases where we would expect such complements to nouns or adjectives we find a sort of zero preposition: a Case assigner (see section 2.2.3.2). Suppose we assume, then, that in all these instances we do have an NP complement, even though we need *of* just in order to satisfy the Case Filter, since nouns and adjectives do not assign Case in English. As a result, the insertion of *of* should be optional: a stipulation of obligatoriness would be redundant with respect to the Case Filter (as discussed in section 2.2.3.2). In this light, consider (40):

(40) *$John_1$ seems that he_1 is proud t_1

John and *t* must be a chain, since *t* is in a θ-position and *John* is not. The chain contains only one Case-marked element, and that element is the head of the chain. Crucially, the trace does not have Case because, in line with the above remarks, I have elected not to do *Of Insertion*. Furthermore, as with (27), Condition A is satisfied. Thus, even the strong Case requirements we have considered do not suffice to fill the Condition A loophole we have discovered.

A recent suggestion of Chomsky's concerning Case assignment can potentially handle the problem of (40). Chomsky proposes that there is no such rule as *Of Insertion*. Rather, adjectives or nouns assign Case in English, but the Case they assign is a version of genitive Case whose realization is *of*. Within this approach, and if we stipulate that Case assignment is obligatory, then (40) will violate the same principle as the other examples: it will have a Case-marked NP-trace.

Surprisingly, we can still construct an example like (40), but one in which the trace is in a position that could not conceivably be Case-marked, even under the proposal just mentioned. To see this, we must first consider some properties of nominals. A well-known problem first discussed by Chomsky (1970) is that, even though (41a) can be salvaged by changing it to (41b), it is impossible to salvage something like (41c) (compare (41d)):

(41) a. *The destruction Rome
      b.   The destruction of Rome
      c. *The belief John to be clever
      d. *The belief of John to be clever
      e.   The belief that John is clever

This is very worrisome. We can claim that (41c) is ruled out by the Case Filter—but why can't we salvage it by inserting *of*? In the terms we were considering a moment ago, the question should be, why can *belief* not Case-mark *John*? Notice that this *is* a configuration of S'-Deletion. If it were not, PRO should be able to appear there, in the complement subject position, but it cannot, as (42) shows (see section 2.2.3):

(42) *John's belief [PRO to be clever]
    (compare *John's belief* [*that he is clever*])

So it is a strange kind of construction: neither PRO nor a lexical NP can occur in the relevant site. I do not pretend to have a solution to this problem. But I will use the fact that this construction does not permit *of* (that is, does not permit Case assignment by the noun) to construct an example to get around the attempted answer to (40):

(43) **John$_1$ seems [that [[his$_1$ belief [t_1 to be clever]] is ill-founded]]

The chain in question here is (John,t). Note that *John* is Case-marked, and t is not (even under the extended version of Case assignment). Further, Condition A is satisfied, with *his* binding t in its GC, the NP. Finally, t is antecedent-governed by *his*, satisfying the ECP. Although the example violates Subjacency, it is drastically worse than a mere island violation.

Interestingly, Chomsky (1981b) has a stipulation in his definition of chain that would precisely have the effect of excluding the illicit NP-Movement under discussion. The stipulation actually does no work in the book, but it is there. What Chomsky proposes is a *local binding* condition on chains:

(44) $C = (\alpha_1, \ldots, \alpha_n)$ is a *chain* only if α_i locally A-binds $\alpha_i + 1$.

The consequence of such a condition is that if *John* and its trace are supposed to be successive links of a chain, then nothing can intervene that is also a binder of the trace. So it is the nearest binder that can be a link in the chain, and in the cases in question there is always an intervening binder that is not a link in the chain. (This intervening binder is precisely what allows the construction to satisfy Condition A.) Perhaps Chomsky inadvertently solved our problem, though it remains for further research to determine whether (44) follows from deeper principles.[11]

6.5 Topicalization

Chomsky (1977) examined, among other things, "Topicalization" constructions such as (45):

(45) John, I like

Prior to Chomsky's investigation, the traditional analysis of this construction was that it involved the movement of *John* from object position frontward. Chomsky argued that this was not the right analysis and that instead *Wh*-Movement should account for this phenomenon. In fact, it patterns with *Wh*-Movement in a number of respects. First, it seems to cause strong crossover violations:

(46) a. John$_1$, Mary$_2$ thinks I like e_1
     b. *John$_1$, he$_1$ thinks I like e_1

The contrasts in (46) seem like the others we have seen for strong crossover (see section 2.1.3.2). Second, the movement in question is "unbounded." In (46a) the topic phrase is in the next clause up, and it can be even higher:

(47) John$_1$, Mary thinks that John said that Susan believes I like e_1

Third, this movement obeys island constraints, ultimately the Subjacency Condition:

(48) a. ?**Syntactic Structures*, I wonder who read *t*
     b. ?**Syntactic Structures*, I met the man who wrote *t*

Finally, we can add to the paradigm the *that*-trace effect:

(49) John$_1$ I think (*that) t_1 won the race

   Here are the details of Chomsky's (1977) analysis. He compared (45) with (50):

(50) John, I like him

Following Ross (1967), he called the phenomenon illustrated in (45) *Topicalization* and the one in (50) *Left Dislocation*. As Ross and Chomsky observed, although they are similar in many ways, they differ in major respects. For example, Left Dislocation structures do not exhibit island effects:

(51) a. *Syntactic Structures*, I wonder who read it
     b. *Syntactic Structures*, I met the man who wrote it

But that is exactly what we should expect: in (51) there is no gap; if there is no gap, there has been no movement; and if there has been no movement, there are no island effects (which follow from the fact that Subjacency is a constraint on movement). When there is a gap, presumably movement is involved (since the empty category cannot be anything other than a trace), and we should expect island phenomena. Now what is the configuration in each case? Chomsky argued that they are as follows:

(52) a. [$_{S''}$[$_{Top}$ John] [$_{S'}$[$_{S}$ I like him]]]
     b. [$_{S''}$[$_{Top}$ John] [$_{S'}$[$_{S}$ I like *t*]]]

We need only one new rule to produce these configurations:

(53) S" → Top S'

With (53), we can explain both how we get (52a) and why this configuration does not obey movement constraints: it is base-generated.[12] What about (52b)? Chomsky's argument is that we need the configuration in (52a) independently for Left Dislocation structures, so it is available for Topicalization structures as in (52b). Suppose, then, that *John* is base-generated in Top in both constructions, but that in (52b) something has moved. Suppose in particular that some sort of *wh*-item has moved, a null *wh*-item that ends up in Comp and leaves behind a trace. Then we account for the desired similarities and differences between Left Dislocation and Topicalization.

As we have seen, this analysis makes some nice predictions with respect to island effects and the ECP. But it makes another that is problematic—namely, that wherever Topicalization is possible, Left Dislocation should be possible as well, since pronouns do not seem to have any specific constraints in the contexts in question, such constraints as Subjacency and the ECP being relevant only to movement. But as Baltin (1982) has pointed out, this prediction is not correct:

(54) a. (?)He is a man to whom liberty, we could never grant *t*
     b. *He is a man to whom liberty, we would never grant it

Consider also the following examples:

(55) a. That *LSLT* you should read *t*, is obvious
     b. *That *LSLT* you should read it, is obvious

All these contrasts are unexpected in the light of Chomsky's analysis.

The generalization for English appears to be this: in the matrix sentence both Topicalization and Left Dislocation are possible. But in embedded sentences only Topicalization is possible, not Left Dislocation. Chomsky's initial rule in the grammar was (53), but then he provided for recursion through S' and S" as in (56):

(56) S' → Comp S"

This permitted S" to be generated in embedded sentences, to allow embedded Topicalization structures. We now have reason to believe that this is not correct, because if S" can be generated in embedded sentences, there is no way to rule out (54b) and (55b). But if S" cannot be generated in embedded sentences, then, according to Chomsky's analysis, Topicalization structures should also be ill formed in embedded sentences. Apparently we need some mechanism for generating topicalized sentences that is independent of the existence of a base-generated Top configuration. Of course, such an analysis is available: the old traditional analysis, that all we are doing is moving an NP to the front of the sentence.[13] We might, then, say that Topicalization involves (or can involve) the adjunction of an NP to S. (Notice, by the way, that this does not exclude Chomsky's analysis for matrix sentences; in this case (45) might be structurally ambiguous. It could arise from a Top configuration and movement of a null operator, or it could arise through adjunction of *John* to S.) The arguments we have seen for a *Wh*-Movement analysis, especially island effects and ECP effects, can now be reconsidered as simply arguments for movement, period, if we continue to assume that Subjacency constrains all movement and the ECP constrains all traces. I leave open here the issue of how long-distance Topicalization takes place. One possibility is successive cyclic adjunction, though on that approach it is difficult to account for *wh*-island effects as in (48a). That is, if movement does not take place through Comp, why should it matter whether or not Comp is occupied? This suggests that movement must take place via Comp, even if the ultimate landing site is not Comp but rather S-adjoined position. This raises two issues that I note in passing: (a) Why *must* movement take place via Comp? and (b) Does movement from Comp to a non-Comp position violate any constraints?[14]

Putting aside these questions, let us now look briefly at a rather curious Topicalization paradigm:

(57) a. Who thinks that I like John
b. Who thinks that John I like
c. Who thinks that I like who
d. *Who thinks that who I like

This is somewhat mysterious. (57b) is a further example of something we have seen before: Topicalization in an embedded clause. (57c) is a standard multiple question. Surprisingly, the two processes cannot be combined to give (57d). The descriptive generalization seems to be that a *wh*-phrase cannot undergo Topicalization; but why that should be remains unclear. Another way to describe the fact would be to say that the S-adjoined *wh*-phrase is not available for LF movement. Thus, it will not be able to raise to the matrix [+wh] Comp in order to receive its appropriate scope.

On such a description, this phenomenon might be related to the following one: a quantifier in an embedded clause can, marginally, take matrix scope, as in (58). But if the quantifier has been topicalized, as in (59), its scope is limited to the embedded clause:

(58) Someone thinks that Mary solved every problem

(59) Someone thinks that every problem, Mary solved

In the latter example the S-adjoined operator, like the one in (57d), is apparently unavailable for LF movement. Intuitively, if an operator is in a scope-type position at S-Structure, it is stuck there.[15]

Another phenomenon with the same flavor as the two we've just seen is illustrated in (60):

(60) a. I don't think that Mary solved any problems
b. *I don't think that any problems, Mary solved

One might imagine an account of "negative polarity" items such as *any* that would involve QR. That is, at LF the negative polarity item would have to raise to the item licensing it. On that account, (60b) would fall under the same descriptive generalization as (57d). To be licensed, *any problems* would have to raise. But by virtue of being in S-adjoined position at S-Structure, it would be ineligible to move.

At this point this remains highly speculative. Additionally, it begs the question of why LF movement from an S-adjoined position is barred.

I turn finally to an interesting and very difficult question concerning the status of the trace that is left by Topicalization. (46b), which could be recreated as an embedded structure, indicates that this trace should be treated as a variable, in order to account for the existence of strong crossover effects. However, there is a major problem with this. (61) indicates that the trace is not a variable at all:

(61) Himself$_1$, John$_1$ likes t_1

If the trace in (61) is a variable, and if variables are subject to Condition C, this should be a standard crossover violation.[16] So it looks as though the trace is somehow an anaphor. But if the trace is an anaphor, then why are the long-distance cases acceptable at all? (Why do they not violate Condition A?) Furthermore, if the trace of Topicalization is an anaphor, the following example ought to be grammatical:

(62) *Him$_1$, John$_1$ likes t_1

But (62) is impossible. We have a real mystery on our hands. Now consider (63):

(63) ?Him$_1$, John$_1$ thinks Mary likes t_1

This is slightly odd, perhaps, but much better than (62). The following curious pattern is emerging: if the NP that is topicalized is an anaphor (as in (61)), then the trace behaves like an anaphor; if the NP that is topicalized is a pronoun (as in (62) and (63)), then the trace behaves like a pronoun; and if the NP that is topicalized is an R-expression (as in (46b)), then the trace behaves like an R-expression. We have seen nothing else like that. A direction for a solution to this is in the air: in the case of topic constructions, at LF we put the "topic" back where it came from before we apply the Binding Conditions. That is, a Reconstruction-like process (see section 5.2.5) would be the input to the Binding Conditions.

This still leaves at least one major problem. Recall (from section 1.3.2) that Condition C must be satisfied at S-Structure. (64a) has the status of a Condition C violation, yet at LF (as in (64b)) there is no A-bound R-expression. QR has moved the phrase containing *John* outside the c-command domain of *he*:

(64) a. *He$_1$ likes everyone that John$_1$ knows
     b. [Everyone that John$_1$ knows]$_2$ [he$_1$ likes t_2]

There are a number of possibilities for resolving this apparent contradiction. I will briefly mention two of them but will not consider them in detail. First, we might posit a new level of representation that follows Reconstruction but precedes QR, to which the Binding Conditions would apply. (64b) would correctly be ruled out, then, whereas (61) would correctly be permitted. Second, perhaps Conditions B and C must be satisfied at *both* S-Structure and LF, whereas Condition A only needs to be satisfied at S-Structure *or* LF. Notice that it will not do to demand LF satisfaction of Condition A, as indicated by the grammatical (65a) and its LF representation (65b), derived by QR:

(65) a. John likes every picture of himself

    b. [Every picture of himself$_1$]$_2$ [John$_1$ likes t_2]

In this case we have virtually the opposite of what we saw in (61). Here the S-Structure representation seems to conform to a condition that the LF representation does not conform to, yet once again the example is grammatical.

Under the proposal we are now considering, it is as if Condition B and Condition C are filters applicable to both S-Structure and LF (crucially, not to D-Structure—see section 2.1.3). Condition A, on the other hand, involves assignment of a necessary feature to an anaphor (for example, to make it referentially complete). The feature, call it [+α], can be assigned at any level, but only at LF are anaphors checked to determine whether they have the [+α] specification. On this interpretation, the analogy to γ-assignment and the γ filter of section 4.5 is quite striking.

Notes

Chapter 1

1. In the literature the term *LF* is used with systematic (and often confusing) ambiguity. Sometimes it is used to mean the output of the LF component, namely, a level of representation; and sometimes it is used to mean the entire component.

2. The term was originally *deep-structure*, and (along with its companion *surface structure*) it created all sorts of confusion outside of linguistics. *Deep* was taken to mean "profound" or "important" in anthropology, literary criticism, and other fields, obviously a misunderstanding of the concept, since this level is no more profound or important than any other. The terms used now are less likely to create such confusion.

3. This constraint is a direct descendant of the Functional Uniqueness Principle proposed by Freidin (1978). The θ-roles relevant to (3) include agent, patient, theme, goal, and instrument.

4. Note that by this reasoning we have really only eliminated PS rules characterizing relations between heads and complements, but not *all* PS rules.

5. See section 2.1.1 for detailed discussion of this structural notion.

6. In most dialects *for* is not even allowed to be there. No one, as far as I know, has a principled and descriptively accurate account for this.

7. Not all verbs are Case assigners. (i) presumably should be a Case Filter violation, just as (ii) is:

(i) *It seems [John to be here]
(ii) *It is likely [John to be here]

Thus, *seem* differs from *believe* in its ability to assign Case.

8. If this account is to be maintained, we must assume that it is the underlying *for*, rather than *want*, that is the Case assigner in (32a), repeated here as (i):

(i) I wanted John to leave

If S'-Deletion were available with *want*, then the impossibility of Exceptional Passive would remain unexplained. On this account, (35a), repeated as (ii), is now problematic:

(ii) I want to be clever

If the null subject of *to be clever* is not an appropriate recipient of Case, then we must say either that the underlying *for* that introduces the complement of *want* may be deleted prior to Case assignment or, alternatively, that optionally *for* need not be generated. See Lasnik and Freidin 1981 for discussion of the problems surrounding this issue.

9. There is one open question here. Mysteriously, when a clause is the subject of another clause, it apparently does need Case. Contrast (i) and (ii):

(i) I believe [[that [John loves Mary]] to be surprising]
(ii) *It is likely [[that [John loves Mary]] to be surprising]

In (i) the clause *that John loves Mary* is in a position that can be exceptionally Case-marked by *believe*. In the ungrammatical (ii) the same clause is in a position to which no Case is assigned.

10. Chomsky's original (1964) proposal to account for this fact was that *Wh*-Movement cannot apply twice within a clause.

In (55c) *Wh*-Movement has applied to both *who* and *what* in the embedded sentence.

11. The grammaticality of (56b) indicates that a *that* in Comp, unlike a *wh*-phrase in Comp, does not prevent another *wh*-phrase from escaping through that Comp. See chapter 4 for more detailed discussion of this phenomenon.

12. See chapter 3, note 8, for an argument that it is in fact the trace rather than the *wh*-phrase that causes the violation.

13. This fulfills a promissory note in Chomsky 1970, where the structural similarity between NPs and Ss was emphasized. But that parallelism was not as complete as one would expect. In the case of S it looked as though a maximal projection, VP, was assigning a θ-role to a subject, but in the case of NP it looked as though a one-bar projection was assigning this θ-role. Now the parallelism is stronger: NPs are subjects of Infl' in the same way that NPs are subjects of N'.

Chapter 2

1. Forerunners of c-command were "in construction with" (Klima 1964), "superior to" (Chomsky 1973), "command" (Langacker 1969), and "kommand" (Lasnik 1976).

2. Alternative definitions have been proposed, the most important of which is probably that of Aoun and Sportiche (1983). In their formulation "branching node" is replaced by "maximal projection." For our purposes at this point, the differences between the two formulations are not significant. We will return to this issue in section 2.3.5.

3. Note that for an example such as (i), both constraints, the TSC and the SSC, are operative:

(i) *John$_1$ thinks that Mary likes himself$_1$

Not only is *himself* not bound in its finite clause; there is also an intervening subject. In part to avoid this redundancy in the theory, Chomsky (1980) proposed limiting the effects of the TSC to *nominatives*. Since *himself* in (i) is accusative rather than nominative, this version of the TSC, the *Nominative Island Condition* (NIC), would not be relevant. Then only the SSC would rule out (i).

4. "Coreference" is actually not quite the right notion, since *who* is not a referential expression at all.

5. The first argument was implicit in the analysis of the *wanna* contraction paradigm discussed in section 1.8. Incidentally, we can now construct a third argument based on the grammaticality of (i):

(i) Which man do you think likes himself

The reflexive must be bound in its GC, and the only appropriate NP is the trace of *which man*. (For a similar case, Chomsky (1973) argued that *which man* itself is the binder, but that introduced a severe complication in the theory, which did not even generalize to all relevant cases.)

6. I will put aside here the problematic issue of what such terms as *coreferential* actually mean. Surely, they do not have to do with *actual* reference. *Intended* reference is closer, but still not without difficulty. See Higginbotham 1980b and Heim 1982 discussion.

7. Chomsky (1980) proposed a much more complicated indexing system that made available three possibilities, and, with a principled modification, four. See Lasnik 1981 for details. But in the framework of Chomsky 1981b the system was simplified to these two possibilities: same index or different index. Sportiche (1985) proposes a richer indexing system, in the spirit of Chomsky 1981b, wherein an index is a set of integers rather than a single integer. The phenomenon of overlap in reference

can be accommodated in such a system with only a minor revision of the definition of *free*.

8. But see section 5.2 for an interesting approach that Higginbotham has developed to handle these issues. Also, see the previous note.

9. The ungrammaticality of (i) provided the only argument, with *e* a subject blocking a relationship between *the men* and *each other*, via the SSC.

(i) *The men told Mary [*e* to visit each other]

10. A methodological remark is in order here. There is a possible derivation of the string of words *I believe to be here* that we predict to be ungrammatical, namely, (i):

(i) *I believe [PRO to be here]

PRO in (i) would receive Case—a violation, by hypothesis. If we are trying to account for the grammaticality of a sentence, and we find one well-formed derivation, then we have succeeded. But if we are trying to account for the ungrammaticality of a sentence, we must be sure it is ungrammatical on *every* derivation. It is not sufficient to display one bad derivation.

11. If this is troublesome, here is an analogue: suppose there is a law to the effect that handguns must be registered. There are two ways to comply. The first, of course, is to have guns and register them; the second is to have no guns. It is the second way that is of interest here.

12. Even apart from these considerations, there is reason to believe that at least some properties of Control are independent of the Binding Theory. For example, something must state that in (i) Control is exercised by the object, whereas in (ii), it is exercise by the subject:

(i) I told John to leave
(ii) I promised John to leave

13. Even Chomsky has fallen into this trap. See Chomsky 1982:36.

14. There is actually evidence for this formal claim. (i) is grammatical:

(i) He left

However, if an item c-commanded itself, then *he* would be bound in its GC in violation of Condition B, since coindexation *is* a reflexive relation (something is coindexed with itself). Similar arguments can be constructed for (ii), which would violate Condition C, or (iii), which would be grammatical if c-command were reflexive:

(ii) John left
(iii) *Each other left

15. This begs a number of technical questions that we will return to.

16. α properly contains β if α contains β and α is not equal to β.

17. It is coindexed with a category that contains *each other*—namely, *each other* itself—but not with a category that *properly* contains *each other*.

18. A priori, a question arises here. If extraposition is involved in (107), what does the extraposed sentence adjoin to? I note this issue but will not pursue it further.

19. The phrase "for a governed element" is needed because sentences like (i) are grammatical:

(i) PRO solving linguistics problems is fun

Thus, we do not want the root clause invariably to be a GC for PRO. This stipulation contrasts with the theory as we have been developing it, whereby the distribution of PRO was deduced. Now it is true that we deduce that PRO is ungoverned, but (115) does much of the work, which is unfortunate, since it weakens the explanatory force of the theory.

20. See Bouchard 1985 for an argument to this effect.

Chapter 3

1. The Bijection Principle will be discussed in detail in section 6.3.

2. Chomsky (1982) went further, suggesting that Condition C can now be entirely dispensed with. But this suggestion ignored other phenomena, such as (1').

3. For example, if there is a trace in the lower Comp in (1), the initial trace will be locally $\overline{A}$-bound. Crucially, though, we do not want that initial trace to be a variable, under this approach.

4. Chomsky ignores traces in Comp for the purposes of (4)—he does not assign features to them, nor does he use them to assign features to anything else. It is as if they were not there.

5. Later Chomsky had to modify (4b). At this point in the book (Chomsky 1982) he was assuming that there are only three kinds of empty categories, and (4) defines only three kinds of empty categories. By the end of the book he needed a fourth category, pro, the null subject in pro-drop languages such as Spanish: (4b) precludes the existence of pro, which is $[-a, +p]$. For the moment, since we are looking only at English, we will not need to consider pro. Later we will look at the modification that allows this additional case.

6. For now let us simply assume that this *e* is c-commanded by *John* and is not c-commanded by the object of *arrested*. It is then bound—in fact, locally bound—by *John*.

7. Notice that if we do not ignore the trace in Comp, *e* is locally $\overline{A}$-bound—not by an operator, but still, its nearest binder is an $\overline{A}$-binder. So *e* would be determined as $[-p]$. In any event, Condition A would rule (13) out in either case.

8. No Case requirement is violated if, as argued by Freidin and Lasnik (1981), it is a *wh*-trace (rather than a *wh*-phrase) that must have Case. This follows immediately under an approach where the Case Filter is deduced from the "visibility" requirement for θ-assignment (see Aoun 1979, Chomsky 1981b:337). Under such an approach, an argument is invisible for θ-assignment if it is not Case-marked, thus violating the θ-Criterion. It is presumably a *wh*-trace, and not a *wh*-phrase, that ultimately realizes a θ-role.

9. But Williams (1977) analyzes so-called across-the-board movement in just these terms:

(i) Which report did you read *e* and file *e*

Such movement is apparently limited to coordinate structures, but it would be worth thinking about whether it could be involved in parasitic gaps.

10. See the discussion of (27), where it will be clear that selectional restrictions are of no relevance to the general phenomenon.

11. See Chomsky 1977 for extensive discussion.

12. A resumptive pronoun is a pronoun that appears where one would expect a *wh*-trace. In many languages it is possible to say something like (i):

(i) The man that I like him

In some languages that is the standard relative construction. Interestingly, in English, resumptive pronouns are best in situations where traces would be impossible. So if we construct an example that would violate a strong island constraint, then it is usually not too bad to have a resumptive pronoun instead, perhaps reflecting some sort of functional strategy. For instance:

(ii) a. The man that I wonder whether he won the race
     b. The man that I read his book

The examples in (ii) are reasonably acceptable, though with a trace in place of the pronoun they become completely impossible.

13. [−a] is also an option, by the alternative algorithm presented later in Chomsky 1982. The empty category in question would then be pro and would be ruled out by the general constraints on the distribution of pro.

14. In this regard, (52) differs from all the other parasitic gap examples we have considered.

15. Why they were allowing the double *wh* interpretation, even if only marginally, remains a mystery.

16. Remember that under functional determination, Chomsky argued that Condition C is unnecessary—at least for empty categories. But without functional determination Condition C is clearly necessary. Brody does, in fact, assume Condition C.

17. Because of that, it looks doubtful that the Case Filter is simply a morphological filter (see section 1.4; also see section 6.1 for further discussion).

18. Even if we were dealing with intrinsic features, a similar problem would arise. We would have to say that the empty category with the features [−a, −p] is not in the lexicon (that is, is not available for insertion into a base structure). [+a, +p], in turn, *is* in the lexicon; so is [−a, +p], in certain languages. Apparently, pronominal empty categories are, and nonpronominal empty categories are not, available for lexical insertion.

Chapter 4

1. So far we have considered only NP-trace, but (6) (and our later modification of it) holds of *wh*-trace as well.

2. One way to instantiate this would be to say that Comp has only one position. This is the approach taken by Lasnik and Saito (1984). Or if we wanted to say that Comp has more than one position, then we could rely on some version of the Doubly Filled Comp Filter of Keyser (1975) and Chomsky and Lasnik (1977).

3. See Stowell 1981 for discussion.

4. This question presumably does not even arise if we take an intermediate trace to have no semantic content.

5. See also Pesetsky 1982b for the source of the idea.

6. May (1979) gives an account for the Comp-to-Comp restriction on movement of Chomsky (1973) based on independently needed conditions. May shows that it can be deduced from Condition C that once an NP moves to Comp, it cannot then move to an A-position.

7. The subject position under consideration receives its sole θ-role from the predicate *to leave*. Moreover, it is clear that the trace in subject position does not receive Case from *likely*. In English, adjectives do not assign Case, as (i) shows:

(i) *It is likely John to leave

(Also see section 1.4.2.)

8. That proviso is necessary because we do not want a subject of a finite clause to be lexically governed.

9. It is not clear why (23a) sounds odd. The best answer to (21a) is actually a full sentence including the paired items:

(i) John read *Syntactic Structures* and
Mary (read) *The Sound Pattern
of English*

10. Notice that (21c) is fine as an echo-question, which suggests quite strongly that echo-questions are not regular ques-

tions. So if someone asks me *What will Aloysius read?*, and I have never heard the name *Aloysius*, I might say, *What will who read?* That is perfectly grammatical, but it is not a normal request-for-information sort of question. Echo-questions differ from regular questions in several ways. For instance, a verb like *wonder* needs an embedded question. But an embedded echo-question will not do. So *I wonder you will see who?* is impossible. Something like *you saw who* is translated not as "For which *x*, you saw *x*" but as "I didn't quite hear what name you said, could you repeat it?" It is presumably also significant that an echo *wh* need not be a maximal projection: *I saw a diagonalized matrix.—You saw a what?*

11. There are problems with this. For the classic cases that Chomsky discussed, it works very well. But there also exist what might be called "pure Superiority effects," which do not seem to fall under the ECP. I won't be concerned with them here, but they could be important. One such case is (i) versus (ii):

(i) ?*What did you tell who to read
(ii) Who did you tell to read what

In each case both traces are complements, so the ECP as previously formulated is irrelevant. Yet (i), with its Superiority violation, is substantially worse. See Hendrick and Rochemont 1982 for discussion of similar cases.

12. The technical name given to modifiers like *why* is *adjuncts*, as opposed to *complements*—which, for instance, subcategorize verbs, whereas adjuncts do not.

13. Recall that although we need to find only one licit derivation for a grammatical sentence, it does not suffice to find one illicit derivation for an ungrammatical sentence. *All* derivations must be illicit.

14. Korean and Japanese, which, like Chinese, lack syntactic *Wh*-Movement,

share to a substantial extent the properties I will discuss.

15. Apart from the Subjacency-like effects we are exploring, *why* in situ is perfectly grammatical in Chinese, as (i) shows:

(i) Lisi weisheme likai
    Lisi why   leave
    'Why did Lisi leave'

16. This claim relies on the fact, to be discussed later, that adjuncts are not subject to *that*-trace effects (see section 4.5).

17. The following is certainly a coherent, if complicated, thought:

(i) What is the reason such that Mary wonders who John hit, where the hitting was for that reason

But (i) cannot be expressed using (55).

18. (50b) and (51b) are relevant to this point. A clearer example is (i):

(i) *Why$_1$ [do you wonder [who [said [t_1' [John left t_1]]]]]

t_1 is antecedent-governed, so the "offending" trace must be t_1', the intermediate trace of *why*.

19. Traces in argument positions, on the other hand, are clearly required by the Projection Principle.

20. Some languages of the type that Huang investigated (for example, Japanese) often exhibit an overt complementizer, but no *that*-trace effects arise. Movement in these languages happens at LF. If we can delete complementizers in LF, then this fact will follow quite nicely.

21. This crucially assumes what Lasnik and Saito (1984) argued for in detail: that γ-marking only takes place at levels, never in the middle of a component.

22. Notice that if (65) applies only at LF, one further stipulation is needed to rule out *that*-trace violations. Consider the following derivation:

(i) S-Structure:

Who$_1$ [do you think [that [t_1 left]]]

$_{[-\gamma]}$

LF:

Who$_1$ [do you think [[t_1 left]]]

$_{[-\gamma]}$

e [do you think [who$_1$ [t_1 left]]]

Who$_1$ [do you think [t_1 [t_1 left]]]

$_{[+\gamma]}$ $_{[+\gamma]}$

In this derivation, unlike all the others that we have considered, the γ feature in a trace changes in the course of a derivation. Apparently, this must be prohibited, suggesting the following constraint:

(ii) γ-marking does not apply to γ-marked traces.

Chapter 5

1. As a matter of fact, the trace in (3) might be $\bar{A}$-bound by Agr. But Agr must not be a relevant $\bar{A}$-binder in English, because this theory is designed to explain the *that*-trace effect. If Agr is a suitable binder, such examples would always be allowed, as we will see.

2. Aoun and Sportiche (1983) defined c-command solely in terms of maximal projection and not in terms of branching (see section 2.1.1). It is not entirely clear how that type of definition could make the necessary distinctions between Comps with and without a *that*.

3. For Aoun, that does not follow from the internal structure of the Binding Theory altogether, because his Condition A must not be limited to NPs. There are, of course, classic ECP effects that involve elements other than NPs. If we are going to eliminate the ECP, replacing it by Condition A, then the latter cannot apply only to NPs; it must also apply to the trace of, say, *why*. Thus, we have an asymmetry: Condition C is crucially limited to NPs, whereas Condition A applies to all traces.

4. Notice that to say that (6) is good in Chinese is false. Strictly speaking, (6) does not exist at all in Chinese, because there is no overt *Wh*-Movement in this language. This does not contradict Aoun's claim, but it does not directly support it either.

5. (34) apparently also raises the problem of (10b) once again. It is not clear how both LF traces can be bound in the appropriate way.

6. Japanese and Chinese seem parallel in relevant respects.

7. A similar problem comes up with the Binding Theory (see section 2.1.5). (i) does not violate Condition A but must be excluded nonetheless:

(i) *John$_1$ likes themselves$_1$

The semantics developed in that section handled this problem.

8. "Antecedence," as defined in (59), is the transitive closure of linking. Note that with respect to (45'), the crucial difference between (46) and (58) is the mention of c-command in the latter. In (45') *John* does not c-command *him*, correctly rendering (58) irrelevant.

9. Wasow considered (71) interesting because nothing blocks a coreferential relation between the first and the third NPs in question, as in (i):

(i) The woman who loved *him* told Mary that *John* was nice

Furthermore, nothing blocks a coreferential relation between the second and the first NPs in question, as in (ii):

(ii) The woman who loved *him* told *John* that it was raining

Yet for some reason (71), where all these NPs are coreferential, is illicit. Wasow proposed a special condition to account for this fact. However, as argued in Lasnik 1976, it follows immediately if the core notion is coreference. That is, if the second *him* cannot be anaphorically related to *John*, then the two cannot be coreferential.

10. Notice that (72) also rules out (i), as (52) did:

(i) He likes John
   |_____↑

A Condition B analogue would not rule out (i), since *John* does not c-command *he*. Of course, (ii) is still ruled in,

(ii) [His mother] likes John
    |_____↑

since *his* does not c-command *John*.

11. If (65) is dropped, as discussed earlier, (74a) would be ruled out by (68).

12. Those who do not want to tie any version of the anaphora principles to coreference must find other principles to appeal to. Something like (i) is occasionally proposed:

(i) a. Don't be redundant.
    b. Don't be ambiguous.

(See Reinhart 1983) for discussion of such principles.) (ib) could be relevant for cases like (ii):

(ii) John likes him

Suppose there were no syntactic principle precluding (ii), on the relevant reading. Reinhart suggests that a syntactic principle precluding coreference in (ii) is inappropriate, because a perfectly natural principle of communication is at work. *Him* could be anyone, including *John*. Since it is available, the speaker must use the more specific expression: *himself*. But consider (iii):

(iii) John thinks John is clever

In a sense, (ia) and (ib) are at odds here. We know the effect of (ia) (compare (75a)) —a very weak effect. For (iii), what Reinhart wants to say is that there is some stronger principle of communication that would force the speaker to use a pronoun. The principle should have an effect comparable in strength to (ib). But (ib) itself is exactly the opposite of what is needed for (iii). (iv) is much more ambiguous than (iii):

(iv) John thinks he is clever

The proposed new principle is along the lines of (v):

(v) Use a bound variable, if possible.

For Reinhart, all bound pronouns and anaphors are bound variables. I have difficulty accepting (v) as a principle of communication. (v) does not really have the effect either of reducing ambiguity or of reducing redundancy (both plausible candidates for pragmatic principles). If often seems independent of both of these desiderata.

Notice too that cases like (66) cannot obviously be dealt with at all by this approach. (66) is not redundant. It is certainly not more ambiguous than the sentence in which *he* replaces *the bastard*. Furthermore, there is no possibility of using a bound variable instead, because the bound variable would lose information. It is difficult to see how a conversational maxim would say anything about (66).

13. Interestingly, (88) has only this one reading. Somehow, that should be given by the theory of Control, whatever the details are. The object of *tell* is the controller of PRO. In Linking Theory that will be represented by a link that is obligatory, since (88) is a structure of obligatory control.

14. One potential solution to the conflict between (85) and (90) would be to propose that the complement sentence is extraposed. Then *they* would not be c-commanded by *each other*. This structural proposal would allow (i), however, arguably an incorrect result

(i) I told him that John should leave
   |_____↑

15. If we do away with (85), we can still bring back a version of Condition B:

(i) A pronominal must be disjoint
    in reference from any NP that
    c-commands it in its GC.

I have occasionally argued that Linking Theory would need something like (i) (which Higginbotham (1985) has now pretty much adopted), for a very simple reason. Consider (ii):

(ii) He likes him

We cannot link *he* to *him* or vice versa. But if we do not link anything to anything, what tells us that *he* and *him* necessarily refer to different people? (i) would.

16. There is some question about how general the phenomenon in (106) is. There are Spanish speakers who share Montalbetti's judgments, for the most part, but for whom a non-c-commanding pro cannot "save" the overt pronoun. These speakers reject the crucial examples, those with the structure of (106).

Chapter 6

1. To allow well-formed instances of *Wh*-Movement, as in (i),

(i) Who did you see *t*

Chomsky argued that the process of *wh*-fronting involved first Case-marks the *wh*-phrase, then moves it. The difference between (4) and (i) is that in the former *who* is not in a Case configuration even prior to movement.

2. The proposal we are about to examine is the one alluded to at the end of section 1.4.

3. Although Chomsky explicitly limits this visibility requirement to LF, there is evidence that it should hold of S-Structure as well. Consider (i):

(i) a. *It seems [a man to be here]
   b. *There seems [a man to be here]

If Case visibility is strictly a property of LF, there is no obvious way to exclude (i). This is because the null hypothesis is that raising is possible in LF exactly as it is possible in the syntax. But then the LF representation of (i) could be (ii),

(ii) A man seems [*t* to be here]

which satisfies all requirements. Under the morphological interpretation of the Case Filter, (i) is immediately explained: an S-Structure requirement is violated. The visibility account does not fare as well. However, there is a plausible way to extend the latter so that it will account for the example in question. Recall from chapter 1 that the Projection Principle holds of all syntactic levels: D-Structure, S-Structure, and LF. As suggested there, a reasonable interpretation of this principle is that the θ-Criterion constrains all three levels. But then visibility should be relevant at S-Structure no less than at LF, and (i) will correctly be rejected. Of course, this raises the new question of why D-Structure does not have to obey visibility. If it did, (iii) for example could never be a well-formed representation at S-Structure, since at D-Structure *John* is Caseless:

(iii) John was arrested *t*

Intuitively, the answer is that visibility must be satisfield wherever it could, in principle, be satisfied. Since Case is not assigned until S-Structure, visibility could not be satisfied there. Hence, by the above reasoning, it need not be.

4. A number of other adjectives pattern the same way, including *easy*, *difficult*, *fun*, and *boring*.

5. In the late 1960s, prior to Chomsky's (1973) postulation of the SSC, such a movement analysis did not raise this problem and was, in fact, the standard analysis. Immediately after Chomsky postulated the SSC, Lasnik and Fiengo (1974) tried to get around the problem by claiming that the complement in these cases was not an S, but just a VP. Then the SSC would not be violated, because there would be no subject. That analysis was consistent with all the theoretical principles that existed at the time, but it is not consistent with the θ-Criterion, according to which there must be a subject to receive the θ-role the VP has to assign.

6. Recent evidence for a *Wh*-Movement analysis, as opposed to an A-Movement analysis, is that *tough*-constructions support parasitic gaps, as in (i):

(i) This book is tough to understand without reading carefully

(See section 3.2, ex. (38).)

7. The framework of Chomsky 1955/75 provides a possible solution. There, only simplex sentences were generated by the base rules. The simple structures underlying them could be merged by "generalized transformations" into more complex sentences.

8. Actually, we already saw one potential problem in section 3.2.5. Parasitic gap constructions are incorrectly predicted to be as bad as weak crossover constructions.

9. Interestingly, (27) presents the very rare situation where the theories of Chomsky 1973 and Chomsky 1981b actually make different predictions. The earlier theory would, in fact, rule out (27), since the movement process itself would violate the TSC and the SSC.

10. One troubling aspect of (33) is that to make it work, we must stipulate that Case assignment is obligatory, a requirement that overlaps almost entirely with the Case Filter.

11. See Rizzi 1986 for discussion of another phenomenon neatly describable in terms of the same local binding condition.

12. Notice that it does not even obey the very powerful Coordinate Structure Constraint of Ross 1967:

(i) John, I like Bill and him

Compare (ii):

(ii) *John, I like Bill and

13. Notice that Topicalization licenses parasitic gaps (see section 3.2):

(i) This article, I filed without reading

Apparently, the descriptive generalization that *Wh*-Movement supports parasitic gaps should be extended to $\overline{\text{A}}$-movement more generally (recall that A-movement does not support parasitic gaps).

14. Chomsky (1973) had an explicit prohibition against this movement, but it is not at all clear that such a constraint is needed in the current framework. May (1979) was able to deduce the central effects of the Comp-to-Comp restriction from Condition C (as mentioned in section 5.2.5). But Condition C will not be relevant here, since the ultimate landing site is an $\overline{\text{A}}$-position rather than an A-position.

15. This might be regarded as a special case of a constraint on LF movement proposed by Aoun, Hornstein, and Sportiche (1981). Lasnik and Saito (1984) point out certain facts about Polish *wh*-questions that are incompatible with Aoun, Hornstein, and Sportiche's proposal, as well as with the descriptive generalization we are considering.

16. Furthermore, *t* in (61) is bound in its GC and hence is apparently not subject to Condition B either. Finally, it is not at all clear how *himself* satisfies Condition A.

References

Anderson, M. (1979). Noun phrase structure. Doctoral dissertation, University of Connecticut, Storrs.

Aoun, J. (1979). On government, Case-marking, and clitic placement. Ms., Massachusetts Institute of Technology.

Aoun, J. (1982). The formal nature of anaphoric relations. Doctoral dissertation, Massachusetts Institute of Technology.

Aoun, J. (1986). *Generalized binding*. Dordrecht: Foris.

Aoun, J., N. Hornstein, and D. Sportiche (1981). Some aspects of wide scope quantification. *Journal of Linguistic Research* 1.3.

Aoun, J., and D. Sportiche (1983). On the formal theory of government. *The Linguistic Review* 2.3.

Baltin, M. (1982). A landing site theory of movement rules. *Linguistic Inquiry* 13.1.

Belletti, A., and L. Rizzi (1981). The syntax of "ne": Some theoretical implications. *The Linguistic Review* 1.2.

Bouchard, D. (1985). The binding theory and the notion of accessible SUBJECT. *Linguistic Inquiry* 16.1.

Bresnan, J. (1970). On complementizers: Toward a syntactic theory of complement types. *Foundations of Language* 6.3.

Bresnan, J. (1972). Theory of complementation in English syntax. Doctoral dissertation, Massachusetts Institute of Technology.

Brody, M. (1984). On contextual definitions and the role of chains. *Linguistic Inquiry* 15.3.

Chomsky, N. (1955). *The logical structure of linguistic theory*. Ms. [Segments published by Plenum, New York (1975).]

Chomsky, N. (1964). *Current issues in linguistic theory*. The Hague: Mouton.

Chomsky, N. (1965). *Aspects of the theory of syntax*. Cambridge, MA: MIT Press.

Chomsky, N. (1970). Remarks on nominalization. In R. Jacobs and P. Rosenbaum, eds., *Readings in English transformational grammar*. Waltham, MA: Ginn and Co.

Chomsky, N. (1973). Conditions on transformations. In S. Anderson and P. Kiparsky, eds., *A festschrift for Morris Halle*. New York: Holt, Rinehart and Winston.

Chomsky, N. (1976). Conditions on rules of grammar. *Linguistic Analysis* 2.4.

Chomsky, N. (1977). On *wh*-movement. In P. W. Culicover, T. Wasow, and A. Akmajian, eds., *Formal syntax*. New York: Academic Press.

Chomsky, N. (1980). On binding. *Linguistic Inquiry* 11.1.

Chomsky, N. (1981a). On markedness and core grammar. In A. Belletti, A Brandi, and L. Rizzi, eds., *Theory of markedness in generative grammar*. Pisa: Scuola Normale Superiore.

Chomsky, N. (1981b). *Lectures on government and binding*. Dordrecht: Foris.

Chomsky, N. (1982). *Some concepts and consequences of the theory of government and binding*. Cambridge, MA: MIT Press.

Chomsky, N. (1986a). *Knowledge of language: Its nature, origin, and use*. New York: Praeger.

Chomsky, N. (1986b). *Barriers*. Cambridge, MA: MIT Press.

Chomsky, N., and H. Lasnik (1977). Filters and control. *Linguistic Inquiry* 8.3.

Davis, L. (1984). Arguments and expletives. Doctoral dissertation, University of Connecticut, Storrs.

Emonds, J. (1970). Root and structure preserving transformations. Doctoral dissertation, Massachusetts Institute of Technology.

Emonds, J. (1976). *A transformational approach to syntax*. New York: Academic Press.

Engdahl, E. (1983). Parasitic gaps. *Linguistics and Philosophy* 6.1.

Epstein, S. (1984). A note on functional determination and strong crossover. *The Linguistic Review* 3.3.

Fiengo, R. (1974). Semantic conditions on surface structure. Doctoral dissertation, Massachusetts Institute of Technology.

Finer, D. (1984). Linking and illicit NP movement. Ms., University of Wisconsin.

Freidin, R. (1978). Cyclicity and the theory of grammar. *Linguistic Inquiry* 9.4.

Freidin, R., and H. Lasnik (1981). Disjoint reference and *wh*-trace. *Linguistic Inquiry* 12.1.

Haïk, I. (1983). On weak cross-over. In *MIT working papers in linguistics* 5. Department of Linguistics and Philosophy, Massachusetts Institute of Technology.

Heim, I. (1982). The semantics of definite and indefinite noun phrases. Doctoral dissertation, University of Massachusetts, Amherst.

Hendrick, R., and M. Rochemont (1982). Complementation, multiple *wh*, and echo questions. Ms., University of North Carolina and University of California, Irvine.

Higginbotham, J. (1980a). Pronouns and bound variables. *Linguistic Inquiry* 11.4.

Higginbotham, J. (1980b). Anaphora and GB: Some preliminary remarks. In J. Jensen, ed., *Proceedings of the tenth annual meeting of NELS*. University of Ottawa.

Higginbotham, J. (1983). Logical Form, binding, and nominals. *Linguistic Inquiry* 14.3.

Higginbotham, J. (1985). On semantics. *Linguistic Inquiry* 16.4.

Hong, S. (1985). A- and $\overline{\text{A}}$-binding in Korean and English. Doctoral dissertation, University of Connecticut, Storrs.

Huang, C.-T. J. (1982a). Move *wh* in a language without *wh*-movement. *The Linguistic Review* 1.4.

Huang, C.-T. J. (1982b). Logical relations in Chinese and the theory of grammar. Doctoral dissertation, Massachusetts Institute of Technology.

Jackendoff, R. (1977). Constraints on phrase structure rules. In P. W. Culicover, T. Wasow, and A. Akmajian, eds., *Formal syntax*. New York: Academic Press.

Kayne, R. (1980). Extensions of binding and Case-marking. *Linguistic Inquiry* 11.1.

Keyser, S. J. (1975). A partial history of the relative clause in English. In J. Grimshaw, ed., *Papers in the history and structure of English.* (UMass Papers in Linguistics 1.) Department of Linguistics, University of Massachusetts, Amherst.

Klima, E. (1964). Negation in English, In J. A. Fodor and J. J. Katz, eds., *The structure of language.* Englewood Cliffs, N.J.: Prentice-Hall.

Koopman, H., and D. Sportiche (1982). Variables and the Bijection Principle. *The Linguistic Review* 2.2.

Langacker, R. (1969). On pronominalization and the chain of command. In D. Reibel and S. Schane, eds., *Modern studies in English.* Englewood Cliffs, N.J.: Prentice-Hall.

Lasnik, H. (1976). Remarks on coreference. *Linguistic Analysis* 2.1.

Lasnik, H. (1981). On two recent treatments of disjoint reference. *Journal of Linguistic Research* 1.4.

Lasnik, H. (1985). A note on illicit NP movement. *Linguistic Inquiry* 16.3.

Lasnik, H., and R. Fiengo (1974). Complement object deletion. *Linguistic Inquiry* 5.4.

Lasnik, H., and R. Freidin (1981). Core grammar, Case theory, and markedness. In A. Belletti, A. Brandi, and L. Rizzi, eds., *Theory of markedness in generative grammar.* Pisa: Scuola Normale Superiore.

Lasnik, H., and M. Saito (1984). On the nature of proper government. *Linguistic Inquiry* 15.2.

May, R. (1977). The grammar of quantification. Doctoral dissertation, Massachusetts Institute of Technology.

May, R. (1979). Must Comp-to-Comp movement be stipulated? *Linguistic Inquiry* 10.4.

Montalbetti, M. (1984). After binding: On the interpretation of pronouns. Doctoral dissertation, Massachusetts Institute of Technology.

Perlmutter, D. (1971). *Deep and surface constraints in syntax.* New York: Holt, Rinehart and Winston.

Pesetsky, D. (1982a). Paths and categories. Doctoral dissertation, Massachusetts Institute of Technology.

Pesetsky, D. (1982b). Complementizer-trace phenomena and the Nominative Island Constraint. *The Linguistic Review* 1.3.

Postal, P. (1966). A note on "understood transitively." *International Journal of American Linguistics* 32.1.

Postal, P. (1970). On coreferential complement subject deletion. *Linguistic Inquiry* 1.4.

Postal, P. (1971). *Cross-over phenomena.* New York: Holt, Rinehart and Winston.

Radford, A. (1981). *Transformational syntax.* Cambridge: Cambridge University Press.

Reinhart, T. (1976). The syntactic domain of anaphora. Doctoral dissertation, Massachusetts Institute of Technology.

Reinhart, T. (1983). Coreference and bound anaphora: A restatement of the anaphora questions. *Linguistics and Philosophy* 6.1.

Riemsdijk, H. van, and E. Williams (1986). *Introduction to the theory of grammar.* Cambridge, MA: MIT Press.

Rizzi, L. (1982). *Issues in Italian syntax.* Dordrecht: Foris.

Rizzi, L. (1986). On chain formation. In H. Borer, ed., *Syntax and semantics*. Vol. 19: *The syntax of pronominal clitics*. New York: Academic Press.

Ross, J. R. (1967). Constraints on variables in syntax. Doctoral dissertation, Massachusetts Institute of Technology.

Sportiche, D. (1985). Remarks on crossover. *Linguistic Inquiry* 16.3.

Stowell, T. (1981). Origins of phrase structure. Doctoral dissertation, Massachusetts Institute of Technology.

Taraldsen, T. (1978). On the Nominative Island Condition, vacuous application, and the *That*-Trace Filter. Indiana University Linguistics Club, Bloomington.

Taraldsen, T. (1981). The theoretical interpretation of a class of "marked" extractions. In A. Belletti, L. Brandi, and L. Rizzi, eds., *Theory of markedness in generative grammar*. Pisa: Scuola Normale Superiore.

Wasow, T. (1972). Anaphoric relations in English. Doctoral dissertation, Massachusetts Institute of Technology.

Williams, E. (1977). Across-the-board application of rules. *Linguistic Inquiry* 8.2.

Zubizarreta, M.-L. (1982). On the relationship of the lexicon to syntax. Doctoral dissertation, Massachusetts Institute of Technology.

Index

An italicized page number indicates a definition.